Joseph

Smith's

Response

to

Skepticism

Joseph Smith, Jr., 1805-44

Joseph

Smith's

Response

to
Skepticism

ROBERT N. HULLINGER

Signature Books   Salt Lake City   1992

A version of this book was published in 1980 as *Mormon Answer to Skepticism: Why Joseph Smith Wrote the Book of Mormon* by Clayton Publishing House, St. Louis, Missouri.

Cover design by Connie Disney

∞ The paper used in this publication meets the minimum requirements of American National Standard for Information Sciences—Permanence of Paper Printed for Library Materials, ANSI Z39.48-1984.

Composed and printed in the United States of America.
96   95   94   93   92   6   5   4   3   2   1

LIBRARY OF CONGRESS CATALOGING-IN-PUBLICATION DATA

Hullinger, Robert N.
    Joseph Smith's response to skepticism / Robert N. Hullinger.
        p.   cm.
    ISBN: 0-941214-83-4
    1. Smith, Joseph, 1805-44. 2. Book of Mormon—Evidences,
authority, etc. 3. Authority (Religion)—History of Doctrines—19th
century. 4. Deism—History—19th century. 5. Skepticism—
History—19th century. 6. Revelation—History of doctrines—19th
century. 7. Mormon Church—Doctrines—History—19th century.
I. Title.
BX8695.S6H85   1992
289.3—dc20   89-27211
                                                              CIP

To Charlotte,
my inspiration,
and
to Lisa, Jennie, and Rob,
our on-going revelations
. . . well, most of the time.

Table of Contents

Preface and Acknowledgements ix

Introduction xiii

[Part I. The Defender]

1. The Purpose of the Book of Mormon 1

2. Translator or Author 9

[Part II. A Defense Needed]

3. New England and Western New York 19

4. The Palmyra Region 35

[Part III. Sources for the Defense]

5. The Indians' Lost Book of God 49

6. Ezekiel's Two Books 65

7. Isaiah, Buried and Sealed 73

8. Masonic Ritual and Lore 99

[Part IV. Case for the Defense]

9. A God of Revelation 121

10. Prophecy Proves Revelation 143

11. Records of Revelation 153

[Part V. The Defense Rests]

12. An American Prophet 167

    Epilogue 179

    Appendix 1 183

    Appendix 2 191

    Bibliography 195

    Scriptural Index 209

    Index 219

Preface and Acknowledgements

As a child in Grand Island, Nebraska, I treasured the legend told me by a worldly-wise fifth grader: every time I crossed Koenig and Locust streets I traveled the Mormon Trail. Since this was on my way to school, I walked daily with those pioneers, struggling westward in the face of adversity. It has been a long time since I walked alongside those men and women, but their story I still find fascinating, even though my path to Zion as an ordained Lutheran minister leads in a different direction.

The reader should note that Thomas Paine's *Age of Reason* is used in this study to indicate what kind of climate popular deism fostered in Joseph Smith's world. I do not necessarily imply that the Mormon prophet read Paine's book, though I believe he did.

Even if one believes that Joseph Smith was at best a scoundrel, one still must account for the Book of Mormon. If Smith was trying to sway the world for his own purposes, one still must deal with the way he chose to do it. That means looking at the appeal of the Book of Mormon. I prefer to put the best construction on Joseph Smith, let his expressed motives speak for themselves, then draw conclusions from the evidence. This approach may not always rule out a negative opinion of Joseph Smith, but it allows for a more charitable estimate of his intentions.

Many people helped bring this book to life, first in 1980 and again in this revised edition. George B. Arbaugh provided the initial impetus by encouraging me in my brash suggestion that I help him update his 1932 study, *Revelation and Mormonism.* Neither of us could have foreseen that my conclusions would call into question his central thesis about the Book of Mormon. Pastor Walter E. Kraemer of Oakland, California, lent moral support during my research days in Berkeley. Arthur Carl Piepkorn of Concordia Seminary, St. Louis;

Jan Shipps of Indiana-Purdue University, Indianapolis; H. Michael Marquardt of Sandy, Utah; and Dan Vogel of Columbus, Ohio, all shared with me some of their research. In addition, Mssrs. Marquardt and Vogel critiqued the manuscript at different stages of production. Richard L. Bushman, noted Mormon and early American historian, reviewed the earlier manuscript, except chapter 8. Other Saints of both the LDS and RLDS churches read portions of the manuscript. Of course, none of these scholars necessarily accepts my conclusions. Appreciation is also due archivists of the Church of Jesus Christ of Latter-day Saints in Salt Lake City and of the Reorganized Church of Jesus Christ of Latter Day Saints in Independence, Missouri, for their helpfulness. Gertrude and Clara Moellering of Cincinnati, members of Prince of Peace Lutheran Church which I serve, provided a working translation of Diedrich Willers's 1830 letter.

Special gratitude is due Pastor Wesley P. Walters, recently deceased, who shared a great deal of source material from his files, the conclusions of his pioneering work in Mormon origins, and much time and effort in reading critically and helpfully several drafts of this work. His standard of scholarship and detail set a goal toward which I strained in completing this study.

Finally, the reader will notice that variations of nineteenth-century English usage are reproduced as they occur in the sources. No "sic" calls attention to typographical and other errors. No italics or capitalizations are there except those that occur in the sources. Only an occasional editorial bracket is used to clarify.

Acknowledgement is made to the following for permission to quote from the sources indicated or to reproduce the items cited: Alfred A. Knopf, for *Among the Mormons: Historic Accounts by Contemporary Observers; Brigham Young University Studies,* for "View of the Hebrews: Substitute for Inspiration?"; Church of Jesus Christ of Latter-day Saints, for Joseph Smith's Letter Book, Joseph Smith's "Manuscript History of the Church," and the preliminary manuscript of Lucy Mack Smith's *Biographical Sketches;* Charles Scribner's Sons, for *Religion in America: An Historical Account of the Developments of American Religious Life*; Concordia Publishing House, for *Church, State, and the American Indians* and *Religious Bodies of America; Concordia Theological Monthly,* for "Joseph Smith, Defender of the Faith," where portions of the Introduction, chapters 1, 3, 9, 10, and 11 first appeared; Cornell University Press, for *The Burned-over District: The*

Social and Intellectual History of Enthusiastic Religion in Western New York, 1800-1850; Deseret Book, for *History of the Church of Jesus Christ of Latter-day Saints;* Harper and Row, *The Lively Experiment: The Shaping of Christianity in America* and *The Story of Religions in America;* Harvard University Press, for *Nature's Nation;* Herald Publishing House, for *Restoration Scriptures: A Study of Their Textual Development; Journal of Mormon History,* for "The Prophet Puzzle: Suggestions Leading Toward a More Comparative Interpretation of Joseph Smith"; *Lutheran Quarterly,* for "The Lost Tribes of Israel and the Book of Mormon," where portions of chapter 6 first appeared; Michigan State University Press, for *Quest for Empire: The Political Kingdom of God and the Council of Fifty in Mormon History* (1967); *Religious Bodies of America;* Reorganized Church of Jesus Christ of Latter Day Saints, for photographs of the E MS 2 Nephi excerpt and the Anthon Transcript; and Wesley P. Walters, for photographs of Albert Neely's bill.

Introduction

The man who established a religion in the age of free debate, who was and is to-day accepted by hundreds of thousands as a direct emissary from the Most High—such a rare human being is not to be disposed of by pelting his memory with unsavory epithets. Fanatic, impostor, charlatan, he may have been; but these hard names furnish no solution to the problems he presents to us. . . . [T]he wonderful influence which this founder of a religion exerted and still exerts throws him into relief before us, not as a rogue to be criminated, but as a phenomenon to be explained.

—Josiah Quincy,[1] mayor of Boston

When the Book of Mormon appeared in late March 1830 and a new church was organized early the following month, America saw the beginning of yet another effort to defend Jesus Christ against all adversaries.[2] To lead the way out of perplexity generated by religious strife, denominational polemics, and rationalistic views of Jesus, the Mormon prophet Joseph Smith forged his own theology of revelation.

Many, if not most, of those he hoped to lead responded by attacking his character and person. To discredit him, they recited his money-digging activities and court trials. They dismissed his "Golden Bible" because of its style and language and its preoccupation with contemporary concerns.

As early as 1831 the influence of Sidney Rigdon, an ex-Campbellite minister, was cited to explain the origin of the new scripture.[3] Rigdon was supposed to have purloined the manuscript of a fanciful romance dealing with the origin of the American Indians. Eber D.

xiii

Howe, an anti-Mormon newspaper publisher in Painesville, Ohio, publicized the theory in 1834 in a book that is still influential.[4] A hundred years later this theory found its best presentation in a work by George B. Arbaugh.[5]

At the turn of the twentieth century, psychology was used as a tool to explain Joseph Smith. Once again he was assumed to be author of the Book of Mormon. He was an epileptic, a dissociated personality, and paranoid—but nevertheless capable of producing an elaborate hoax. This explanation is also still being offered today.[6]

Fawn M. Brodie buried the purloined manuscript theory[7] in her 1945 biography of Joseph Smith, *No Man Knows My History*. But Brodie's greatest service was considering how ideas current in the 1820s related to the personal life of the Mormon prophet. This strengthened the case for an environmentally-based understanding of Smith. However, her portrait of Smith suffers from some blurred edges.

For example, Marvin S. Hill, a Mormon scholar, called Brodie to task for explaining Smith solely through his personal charisma and dismissing his religious motivations, thereby neglecting the religious force and appeal of his message.[8] Jan Shipps, a non-Mormon historian, similarly stressed the need to see beyond Smith as saint or fraud in order to reveal a "larger than life *whole* man." To that end she challenged scholars to determine to what extent the scriptures Smith produced can be used as "primary source material" for better understanding him.[9] This study is a partial acceptance of that challenge.

Mario DePillis, a Catholic scholar, emphasized that as with other religious innovators, Joseph Smith's quest was ultimately for religious authority.[10] De Pillis looked to Smith's explanation of his first vision as the springboard for understanding his quest.[11] Smith found that no church was right and determined not to join any until the full gospel became clear to him. DePillis was the first non-Mormon to take seriously Smith's response to early nineteenth-century society.[12] Although De Pillis was aware of the importance of the Book of Mormon as a base for Smith's claim to authority, he looked primarily to developments which followed publication of the Book of Mormon. To overcome skepticism about his new American scripture, Smith created a dual priesthood, settled doctrinal questions, and mediated God's revelations in order to reestablish divine control.[13] My study hopefully complements De Pillis's findings by concentrating on Joseph Smith's basic objective in producing the Book of Mormon.

There has been a growing awareness that deism was an important part of the cultural and intellectual milieu of Joseph Smith's time, along with the revivalism and sectarian strife of New York's "burned-over district." Psychologist I. W. Riley first saw deism as important in the story of Book of Mormon anti-Christ Korihor, but he did not see how deism was also part of a complex which included Freemasonry and Roman Catholicism.[14] American historian David Brion Davis saw Mormonism as a link in the Puritan tradition opposing deism, revivalism, Methodism, and Unitarianism, but he did not develop this insight.[15] Milton Backman and Ivan Barrett, both Mormon writers, saw deism as part of the contemporary context but did not believe that Smith was particularly influenced by it.[16] Richard Bushman, a Mormon historian, suggested ways in which Smith himself responded to skepticism but did not discuss this subject in the context of the Book of Mormon. He found that the first vision story was designed to meet rationalistic demands for evidence.[17]

Religious authority in the 1820s was based on the assumption that the Bible was a special revelation from God rather than a natural revelation deducible from nature. Behind this lay convictions about the nature of deity—that God was personal and in reach of humanity rather than an absentee landlord. I believe that Joseph Smith tried to defend faith in a personal God against denominational strife and popular skepticism. He staked out the principle of continuous, personal revelation as the ground for battle and regarded himself as defender of God. The Book of Mormon was an apologetic for Jesus Christ.[18]

Mormon readers should know at the outset that as a practicing Lutheran I do not share many of their beliefs regarding the Book of Mormon and Joseph Smith. I do not believe that the Book of Mormon is a historical narrative of ancient Americans during the period from 600 B.C. to 400 A.D. Rather, I believe that the book is a product of the early nineteenth century and was written by Joseph Smith. Whatever motives led Joseph Smith to produce the Book of Mormon—whether he was trying to sway the world for his own purposes or was trying to affect the world in a positive way—we must still deal with the way he chose to do it, and that means looking seriously at the obvious appeal of the Book of Mormon which remains just as strong today as it was in 1830. I prefer to put the best construction on Joseph Smith and his intentions; to let his expressed intentions speak for themselves and then to draw conclusions from the evidence, as I understand and interpret it. Such an approach, too often missing in Mormon and non-Mormon discussions of early Mormonism allows for a more charitable—and what I believe is a more accurate—appraisal of Joseph Smith than has been previously achieved.

NOTES

1. *Figures of the Past* (Boston, 1883), in William Mulder and A. Russell Mortensen, eds., *Among the Mormons: Historic Accounts by Contemporary Observers* (New York: Alfred Knopf, 1958), 132.

2. Unless otherwise noted, the Book of Mormon edition I use is that published in 1920 by the Church of Jesus Christ of Latter-day Saints, Salt Lake City, Utah.

3. James Gordon Bennett cited a "Henry Rangdon," "Ringdon," or "Rigdon" as the person. A successful journalist, Bennett interviewed people who knew the first Mormons and wrote a two-part article for the *New York Courier and Enquirer* in 1831. See Leonard J. Arrington, "James Gordon Bennett's 1831 Report on 'The Mormonites,'" *Brigham Young University Studies* 10 (Spring 1970): 355-64.

4. *Mormonism Unvailed* (Painsville, OH, 1834).

5. *Revelation in Mormonism: Its Character and Changing Forms* (Chicago: University of Chicago Press, 1932).

6. Isaac Woodbridge Riley, *The Founder of Mormonism: A Psychological Study of Joseph Smith, Jr.* (New York: Dodd, Mead & Co., 1903); Eduard Meyer, *Ursprung und Geschichte der Mormone mit Exkursen über die Anfänge des Islams und des Christentums* (Halle: Max Niemeyer, 1912); Walter F. Prince, "Psychological Tests for the Authorship of the Book of Mormon," *American Journal of Psychology* 28 (July 1917): 373-89; but compare Theodore Schroeder, "Authorship of the Book of Mormon," *American Journal of Psychology* 30 (Jan. 1919): 1-13; Bernard DeVoto, "The Centennial of Mormonism," *American Mercury* 19 (Jan. 1930): 1-13 (Arbaugh, 227-29, rejects Prince and DeVoto); and Fawn M. Brodie, *No Man Knows My History: The Life of Joseph Smith*, 2d ed. (New York: Knopf, 1971), 418-21.

7. Brodie, appendix B.

8. Marvin S. Hill, "Secular or Sectarian History? A Critique of *No Man Knows My History*," *Church History* 40 (Mar. 1974): 78-96.

9. "The Prophet Puzzle: Suggestions Leading Toward a More Comprehensive Interpretation of Joseph Smith," *Journal of Mormon History* 1 (1974): 6, 19, 20.

10. "The Quest for Religious Authority and the Rise of Mormonism," *Dialogue: A Journal of Mormon Thought* 1 (Spring 1966): 69-88.

11. This has traditionally been dated in 1820.

12. Milton V. Backman, Jr., *American Religions and the Rise of Mormonism* (Salt Lake City: Deseret Book, 1965), does this from a Mormon perspective. Compare also Ivan J. Barrett, *Joseph Smith and the Restoration: A History of the Church to 1846* (Provo, UT: Brigham Young University Press, 1973), 5-13.

13. De Pillis, 82.

14. Riley, 151-59. J. E. Homans [Robert C. Webb, pseud.], *The Real Mormonism: A Candid Analysis of an Interesting but Much Misunderstood Subject in History, Life, and Thought* (New York: Sturgis & Welton, 1916), 429-43, objected to Riley's placing exerpts from Paine in parallel with Korihor's remarks, which he charges tear Paine out of context.

15. David Brion Davis, "The New England Origins of Mormonism," *The New England Quarterly* 37 (June 1953): 158.

16. See Backman and Barrett.

17. Richard L. Bushman, *Joseph Smith and Skepticism* (Provo, UT: Brigham Young University Press, 1974). Bushman found that William Paley's arguments were used—that Smith was a neutral observer of the vision and became committed to it in spite of persecution and personal loss.

18. See my "Joseph Smith, Defender of the Faith," *Concordia Theological Monthly* 42 (Feb. 1971): 72-87.

1.

The Purpose of the Book of Mormon[1]

He said he verily believed that an important epoch had arrived—that a great flood of light was about to burst upon the world . . . that a GOLDEN BIBLE had recently been dug from the earth . . . and that this would . . . settle all religious controversies and speedily bring on the glorious millennium.

—John A. Clark,[2] rector of Palmyra, New York, Episcopal Church, 1826-28

There has been a long history of probing Joseph Smith's probable motives for writing the Book of Mormon. Mario DePillis, a Catholic historian, has argued that Smith wanted to end sectarian fighting.[3] Jan Shipps, a non-Mormon scholar, concluded that Smith found or wanted to find Indian artifacts: "that the discovery or the desire for the discovery inspired the writing of the Book of Mormon."[4]

However, neither view sufficiently considers the many statements Joseph Smith himself made about the purpose of the Book of Mormon. The *History* which he began dictating in 1838 is only moderately helpful, for by that time he had greatly modified his original theology. One must go back to the early period before and during the production of the Book of Mormon and the organization of the new church. Smith states the overall purpose for the new scripture on its title page, and the book's goals are elaborated through its plot and character development. The Book of Mormon

1

offers support for Christian claims for the Bible, for Jesus Christ, and for God. It is intended to inspire faith and encourage faithfulness; to corroborate biblical facts, prophecies and doctrine. The book's sources, the concerns it deals with, and the solutions it proposes all relate to this: to make the remaining descendants of the lost tribes of Israel (the American Indians) aware of their relationship with God and to convince Jews and gentiles that "Jesus is the CHRIST, the ETERNAL GOD, manifesting himself to all nations."

The first ambition of the Book of Mormon was to provide proof: of God, of Jesus Christ, of the Bible, of itself. According to the Book of Mormon, God is unchanging in the way he relates to humanity (D&C 20:12, 17). He created men and women, gave them commandments, and gave his son to save the human race when Adam transgressed (vv. 18-20). It proves that God is merciful (1 Ne. 1:20) and inspires people in all generations to do his will and work (D&C 20:11). Jesus was sinless, suffered crucifixion, died, rose on the third day, ascended into heaven, now rules with God, and has secured salvation for the human race.

Not only is God unchanging but so is his message. The Book of Mormon is a witness for and proof of the truth of the biblical message (D&C 20:11). That message was the same in the pre-Christian era as it is now. People knew of his future mission long before Jesus came as Redeemer. The Book of Mormon prophet Nephi wrote of his foreknowledge of Jesus Christ and, to convince his posterity that this was true (2 Ne. 11:2-6), added the testimony of his brother Jacob as well as that of biblical Isaiah. The Book of Mormon thus witnesses to the reality of God and his message. It also provides for its own defense, its own witness. According to the book, an angel would deliver golden plates to Joseph Smith. Joseph would translate the characters inscribed upon them and thus produce a new record. Three witnesses would see the plates and then would know that their translated contents were true (27:12). Their testimony added to that of the Book of Mormon would stand as proof of God's power and word (Ether 5:2-4). Joseph Smith would be ordained to bring to an unbelieving generation the message of the Book of Mormon; he would bring forth the Church of Christ. The three witnesses' testimony would confirm both the message that Smith would bring and the new scripture he would translate (D&C 5:6-15).

The Book of Mormon would speak to native Americans, to Jews, to gentiles, to the world. It would inform the Indians[5] of God's promises (D&C 3:20) and covenants with their ancestors, that they were members of the House of Israel (ibid.; Morm. 7:1-2). It would convince them of the error of their forbearers' traditions and iniquity (Alma 37:8-9; Mosiah 28:1-2). If Indians were to learn how their Nephite-Lamanite ancestors slaughtered each other until only Lamanites were left, they might believe the gospel that missionaries would bring them (Morm. 5:9, 11, 14). The Book of Mormon would convince them that the message of the Bible is true; and when they believed the biblical message, they also would accept the Book of Mormon (1 Ne. 13:39). When the Indians accepted the new scriptures, they would come to a knowledge of God and the redemption of Jesus Christ.[6] The Book of Mormon would lead them to end their hatred of others, to befriend each other, and to stop their contentions (Alma 26:9). Their faith in Jesus and restored covenant with God would bring peace and thus fulfill God's promises to Israel. In return the Indians would become a "delightsome people" (W of M 8).

The Book of Mormon would also help in bringing Jews to accept Jesus as Messiah. The Book of Mormon is a witness that the man they killed was Christ and God (Morm. 3:21). If they accept this, then God would restore them to their own land; for unbelief had kept them dispersed (5:14; 2 Ne. 15:15-18).[7] The Book of Mormon would come into public view about the time that the Lord began that restoration, and it would hasten the day.

Joseph Smith also wanted gentiles to accept Jesus as Savior. Like Jews, gentiles had to be convinced that the Bible was true (1 Ne. 13:39). If they were to know of God's decree, come to repentance, and be kept from following the dismal example of previous generations, then they had to learn how the unbelieving rebellion of the Indians' forefathers had led to their destruction (Ether 2:11). Once convinced, gentiles would perform a two-fold mission for Jesus. They would use the Nephite reports of Jesus' messages given during his post-resurrection appearances in American to convince Jews that he was their Redeemer (Morm. 5:9, 14-15; D&C 14:10). At the same time they would also convert the Indians.

Clearly Smith had an inclusive vision. In the face of impending judgment (Morm. 3:20-22), the Book of Mormon was intended to save people by leading them to repentance and preparing them to meet God. Smith wanted them to look to the Messiah, obey him, be faithful to him, and choose eternal life instead of eternal death (2

Ne. 2:28-30). Through faith in Jesus Christ, Smith hoped to see people reconciled to the God of Abraham, Isaac, and Jacob (1 Ne. 6:4; 2 Ne. 35:23). The Book of Mormon is saturated with talk of Jesus Christ so that people could know "to what source they might look for a remission of their sins" (v. 26). The Book of Mormon settles doctrinal differences among those who accept the Christ it presents. Mormon's purpose is to make clear the true doctrine and to dissolve doctrinal disputes by explaining the gospel of Christ (D&C 10:46-63). Existing churches would continue their strife because they misunderstood and misinterpreted the Bible (vv. 46-63), but the Book of Mormon would inaugurate the reestablishment of the true church of Christ (11:16; 18:13).[8]

The power of this restored church would be great. The view of the Book of Mormon is that when the church is accepted, the thousand-year reign of Jesus would come. In the millennial view all depended on restoring the lost ten tribes of Israel and the return of the dispersed tribe of Judah to its homeland. The Book of Mormon describes in detail the conditions to prevail at the time of this restoration. No one would mistake the signs (2 Ne. 25:15-20). When Indians, Jews, and gentiles were persuaded that Jesus is the Christ, the Eternal God, then the Lord would bring Israel's lost tribes back from their hiding places (Morm. 5:12). American Indians were a segment broken off from these ten tribes. Through the Book of Mormon's message, the Indians would rejoin their kinsmen. The Lord's promise to the patriarch, Joseph in Egypt, would thus be fulfilled (2 Ne. 25:11).

The right kind of leader was required to carry out this ambitious program, and the career of that leader was sketched in the Book of Mormon. Accordingly, the biblical Joseph was said to have been promised that a "seer" would come named after him, who would be like Moses in the eyes of God (2 Ne. 3:6-7, 15), blessed to teach the Indians of God's covenants. He would be able use the Book of Mormon to convince the Indians of the message he would bring. This seer's father would also be known as Joseph. Joseph Smith, Jr., was then specifically declared to be the one ordained to bring God's word to his generation. God's word would be heard only through Smith: "a seer, a translator, a prophet, an apostle" (D&C 21:1).[9]

During the Book of Mormon translation, Smith heard himself declared as the one ordained to bring God's word to his generation, and that word would be heard only through him (D&C 5:6, 10). His position was spelled out by Book of Mormon prophet Moroni: "everything which inviteth to do good, and to persuade to believe in Christ, is sent forth by the power and gift of Christ. . . . Nothing that is good denieth the Christ, but acknowledgeth that he is" (Moro. 7:16; 10:6). On the other hand, anything that "persuadeth men to do evil, and believe not in Christ, and deny him, and serve not God . . . is of the devil" (7:17). Smith's own desire to promote the message of Jesus, therefore, was assurance that his work was God's work.

Smith knew himself to be a servant of Christ. But those who judged him the devil's servant remembered the Smith family's past activities as money diggers and their hopes for a profit from sales of the Book of Mormon.[10] Smith admitted that he had thought of using the gold plates for personal gain. He was "tempted of the advisary and sought the Plates to obtain riches and kept not the Command-ment that I would have an eye singled to the glory of God," he said in 1832.[11] Having a history of pre-Columbian America might "be interesting to every man" and the possibility seemed to inspire further thoughts of "gain . . . and income from such a valuable history. Surely, thought he, every man will seize with eagerness, this knowledge, and this incalculable income will be mine."[12] An angel rebuffed Smith's initial efforts to get the plates because "they are not deposited here for the sake of accumulating gain and wealth for the glory of this world; they were sealed by the prayer of faith, and because of the knowledge which they contain they are of no worth among the children of men, only for their knowledge."[13]

Perhaps Smith never fully conquered the impulse to use his book for personal advantage, but his intention to defend God is equally—perhaps more—a factor in this early period. The stories and theology in the Book of Mormon constitute a defense of Jesus. The circum-stances leading to this particular defense, as well as to the form it took, are found in Smith's own time and place in American history.

NOTES

1. Nearly every statement in this chapter, with the exception of conclusions or transitions, is in the Book of Mormon and Smith's early revelations through April 1830. The references cited all include words, phrases, and clauses expressing purpose or result. A Mormon account of the goals for the Book of Mormon is B. H. Roberts's *New Witness for God*, 3 vols. (Salt Lake City: Deseret Book, 1926), 2:61-68.

2. *Gleanings by the Way* (Philadelphia: W. J. & J. K. Simon, 1842), 223-24.

3. DePillis, "The Quest for Religious Authority and the Rise of Mormonism," *Dialogue: A Journal of Mormon Thought* 1 (Spring 1966): 88.

4. Shipps, "The Prophet Puzzle: Suggestions Leading Toward a More Comprehensive Interpretation of Joseph Smith," *Journal of Mormon History* 1 (1974): 11.

5. The term "Indian" does not occur in the Book of Mormon, but it is synonymous with "Lamanite." Lamanites were descended from Laman, the older brother of Nephi. Laman scorned his father's reliance upon the gifts of the spirit and was passed over in favor of Nephi when their father, Lehi, consecrated a successor to the priesthood. The resulting enmity between Lamanites and Nephites led to the total destruction of the Nephites. The surviving Lamanites were cursed with a dark skin because of their unbelief and became ancestors of native Americans.

6. Smith thought that the Book of Mormon would benefit native Americans (Jarom 2, Enos 14:15, Morm. 8:14-16, Moro. 1:4, D&C 3:20). He was certain they would believe the Book of Mormon (Morm. 7:9) when they first were convinced of the truth of the Bible (1 Ne. 13:39). Smith felt that current missionary efforts among the Indians were ineffective. He had Enos say of Nephite attempts to evangelize the Lamanites: "at the present our strugglings were vain in restoring them to the true faith" (vss. 14-15). W. W. Phelps, editor of the first Mormon newspaper, explained that neither Jews nor Indians could be converted "by ministers, though the Gentiles are," but they would be willing to convert when the Messiah returned (*The Evening and the Morning Star*, Aug. 1832, 5).

7. As today, pre-millennial systems at Smith's time depended on the conversion of Jews before the millennial events could proceed.

8. 2 Nephi 3 shows that Smith began the Book of Mormon the second time, after losing the first 116 manuscript pages of the translation, intent on forming a church. Smith is predicted as the one promised to bring back the descendants of his biblical predecessor, Joseph of Egypt, to the Lord. Like Moses, Smith would lead a nation (2 Ne. 3:7-11). The two books of Nephi replaced the lost 116-page manuscript. Evidence from these portions of the Book of Mormon make it clear that Smith meant to found a church, and this intention is even more certain when the revelations given during the translation period (March-June 1829) are considered.

9. The Doctrine and Covenants (D&C) is a compilation of revelations given to Joseph Smith. First published in Kirtland, Ohio, in 1835, the D&C was a revision and enlargement of the Book of Commandments (Independence, MO: W. W. Phelps & Co., 1833). Unless otherwise noted, the citations will be from the 1921 edition published by the Church of Jesus Christ of Latter-day Saints. David Whitmer, one of the three witnesses, agreed that Smith was the "man who is not learned" of Isaiah 29 but not that he was the choice seer. The seer was to be a descendant of Lehi through

the youngest son, Joseph (2 Ne. 3), from whom the Indians descended, and the choice seer was to come from the Indians. *An Address to All Believers in Christ* (Richmond, MO, 1887), 26-27.

10. David Marks, a Free-will Baptist evangelist, stayed at the home of Peter Whitmer, Sr., on 29 March 1830 in Fayette, New York, just a week before the organization of the church. Marks saw two or three of Whitmer's sons and others who told him about seeing the golden plates and spoke of the just-published Book of Mormon. Recalled Marks, "Five thousand copies were published—and they said the angel told Smith to sell the book at a price which was one dollar and eight cents per copy more than the cost, that they might have the temporal profit, as well as the spiritual." See *The Life of David Marks to the 26th Year of His Age* (Limerick, ME: Office of the *Morning Star*, 1831), 341.

11. Smith dictated this in 1832 as a beginning of his history. See Dean C. Jessee, "The Early Accounts of Joseph Smith's First Vision," *Brigham Young University Studies* 9 (Spring 1969): 275-94.

12. Oliver Cowdery to W. W. Phelps, *Messenger and Advocate*, July 1835, 157. This is part of a series of letters presenting a brief history of the church, written with Smith's cooperation. David Marks, *The Life of David Marks to the 26th Year of His Age* (Limerick, ME: Office of the Morning Star, 1831), demonstrated that the impression created by the Book of Mormon on those who had heard it seemed to offer insights into Indian antiquities. "When I was in Ohio, I had quite a curiosity to know the origin of the numerous mounds and remains of ancient fortifications that abound in that section of the country; but could not find that any thing satisfactory was known on the subject. Having been told, that the '*Book of Mormon*' gave a history of them, and of their authors, some desire was created in my mind to see the book, that I might learn the above particulars" (341).

13. Ibid., Oct. 1835, 198.

2.

Translator or Author

The Mormon Bible was communicated to him direct from heaven. If there was such a thing on earth as the author of it, then [Smith] was the author; but the idea that he wished to impress was that he had penned it as dictated by God.

—Matthew L. Davis,[1] Washington, D.C., political correspondent

On a wintry 5 February 1840 political correspondent Matthew L. Davis crossed to Washington, D.C., to hear Joseph Smith expound his new faith and speak about the Book of Mormon. The report he wrote to his wife, quoted above, echoes the assumptions most modern investigators of Mormon origins bring to their task. Mormons suppose that God was involved somehow in the production of the book, even if historical understanding requires that some aspects of Mormon origins be explained differently or laid aside. They believe that the Book of Mormon defends God but add that Smith could not have written it without divine aid.

The earliest participants with Smith in the origins of Mormonism describe that divine aid as coming through a "peepstone" or "seerstone," which Smith had used to translate most of the Book of Mormon. This was the same stone which Smith used to locate buried treasure.[2] Early Mormons Martin Harris and David Whitmer told how Smith put the stone in a hat in which he then buried his face to

9

read the translation of the plates superimposed on the stone.[3] The "Reformed Egyptian" hieroglyphics appeared on the stone with the English translation beneath each character. Smith read the translation to his scribe, who then verbally repeated it to check for accuracy. If the scribe had incorrectly transcribed Smith's dictation, the sentence image remained on the stone until the correction was made.[4] Smith's wife Emma supported Harris's and Whitmer's versions of the story in recalling that her husband buried his face in his hat while she was serving as his scribe.[5] "Translating" for these early witnesses meant "reading."

This is the sense of the translation process which Harris conveyed to Father John A. Clark of Palmyra's Episcopal church. Clark wrote that Smith had found the "GOLDEN BIBLE . . . and two transparent stones, through which as a sort of spectacles, he could read the Bible." Smith looked "through his spectacles . . . and would then write down or repeat what he saw, which, when repeated aloud, was written down by Harris." The spectacles enabled Smith "to read the golden letters on the plates in the box. . . . [B]y means of them he could read all the book contained."[6]

However, Clark mentioned two stones rather than the single stone of the other accounts. Soon after he spoke with Clark, Harris also told Professor Charles Anthon about the "spectacles." According to Anthon, these eye glasses were so large that Smith could look only through *one* of the lenses.[7] There is thus some confusion about whether Smith used spectacles or a stone to translate. Smith was the ultimate source of this confusion and included both versions in the Book of Mormon.[8]

If Smith simply read the translation, he might be expected to repeat a section word for word. Exactly that expectation paralysed Smith when Harris lost 116 manuscript pages in 1828; he chose not to retranslate the pages. In section 10 of the Doctrine and Covenants and in the foreword to the 1830 edition of the Book of Mormon, Smith explained why he did not retranslate the lost material.[9] God knew that evil men who had gained possession of the lost manuscript planned to alter the words to conflict with the forthcoming translation. How they might do this was not explained, but in any case God had provided different plates with the same basic information.

After the loss of the early translation, Smith talked about the power of the eye glasses in a different way. At first they had assured an errorless translation by providing a translation to read. That was necessary to fulfill Isaiah 29:11-12; reference to one "not learned," assumed to be himself, meant that Smith would be equipped to "read" what the "learned" could not. When Harris pled to be allowed to show others the translation, the glasses became the medium of revelation. Smith prayed through the spectacles and received the Lord's answer to Harris's request.[10] Following the loss of the translation, an angel took the glasses but returned them in July 1828 so that Smith could receive section 3 and possibly 10 of the Doctrine and Covenants. Then the angel removed both the glasses and gold plates until 22 September 1828, when he returned them to Smith.[11]

When Oliver Cowdery took over scribal duties in April 1829, he told Smith that he wanted to try his hand at translating the plates. He tried and faltered, thereby forcing yet another shift in the role of the glasses. Cowdery had the idea that translating was merely a matter of reading. Smith answered Cowdery's failure with a revelation. Cowdery should have studied his proposed translation "out in his mind" (D&C 8:1-3) and his bosom would "burn" within him when he felt "that it is right." Thus Cowdery was held responsible for his failure. Earlier Smith had told him that Christ would "tell" him in his "mind" and "heart" the knowledge concerning the engravings of old records. Now it was explained that the translation really took place within a person and not in the lenses of the glasses or in the seer stone.

It was Smith who eventually emphasized the mind and heart of the translator as the medium of translation and deemphasized the inherent power of the spectacles.[12] A contemporary, Diedrich Willers, described this view of translation. He said that Smith wore the glasses and that "the Holy Ghost would by inspiration give him the translation in the English language."[13] In this same vein, Smith told E. B. Grandin that the translation was accomplished by inspiration.

Further, Smith did not need to have the plates present or the leaves open to translate. Martin Harris told John Clark that when Smith first put on the glasses the plates were in the box or chest, but he could read the plates even though the chest was closed.[14] Joseph Smith, Sr., said that after the Lord removed the plates, "Joseph put on the spectacles, and saw where the Lord had hid them, among the rocks, in the mountains. Though not allowed to get them, he could by the help of the spectacles, read them where they were, as well as if they were before him."[15]

Development of the Translation Process Story

Date	Joseph Smith's Activity	Function of Medium Used	Results
1827-June 1828	Reads and translates characters.	Stone and spectacles mediums of translation.	Open plates, stone, and spectacles needed.
July 1828-April 1829	Reads and translates characters; receives revelations.	Spectacles medium or receiving translation and revelation.	Stone and plates not always used, but spectacles used.
April 1829	Explains why Cowdery cannot translate.	Mind and heart medium of translation.	Spectacles not needed, but used.
July 1829-June 1830	Gives plates and spectacles to angel; still receives revelations; corrects manuscript for printer.	Mind and heart medium of translation, revision, and revelation.	Spectacles and plates gone; not needed, not used.
June 1830 on	Writes Book of Moses; revises Bible; corrects and revises Book of Mormon.	Mind and heart medium of translation, revision and revelation.	Spectacles gone, not needed.

After completing the manuscript of the Book of Mormon in 1829, Smith handed the plates and glasses back to the angel.[16] From that time the revelations he received came from his "heart" and "mind." To produce the 1837 edition of the Book of Mormon, 3,000 changes were made to the 1830 edition[17] from revelation and intuition, without the aid of eyeglasses, as did the parenthetical phrase which Smith added to 1 Nephi 20:1 in the 1840 edition.[18] Smith began to write his revision of the Bible, the Book of Moses, in June 1830 and received it by means of a vision, not through glasses.[19] All the work of revising the Bible, the founding revelations, and the making of an alphabet for Egyptian hieroglyphics was done without the glasses, solely by revelation. Smith was no longer merely a "reader."

For both believer and non-believer, the question of Smith as a translator, whatever his method, or simply as author of the Book of Mormon often turns on the issue of his ability and education. The fact that he was "unlearned" and yet could "read" what the "learned" could not was for Martin Harris a sign that Smith's calling was authentic. For unbelievers who also considered Smith uneducated, an alternative theory was needed to explain the book: namely, that Sidney Rigdon, a trained and educated preacher, had guided the creation of the Book of Mormon which was based on a romance of the American Indians written at the turn of the nineteenth century by a man named Solomon Spaulding.

However, not all contemporaries found Smith too "unlearned" to have written the book. Orsamus Turner knew Smith in Palmyra, New York, and opposed the faith he headed. According to Turner, Smith was a "passable" Methodist "exhorter" after catching "a spark of religion." He credited the Smith family with the production of the Book of Mormon and specifically dismissed the Spaulding theory.[20] John Greenleaf Whittier and Josiah Quincy also gave Smith high marks as a person with ability and intelligence.[21]

Certainly Smith was literate. He lamented his inexperience with the written word but knew he had an impressive speaking style.[22] His mother told how he held the family spellbound with Indian stories. Smith himself did some other writing during the translation process. Martin Harris told John Clark that "Smith was to prepare for the conversion of the world . . . by transcribing the characters from the plates."[23] Harris also told Charles Anthon that Smith "deciphered the characters in the book" and "communicated their contents in writing."[24] Mormons today credit Smith with knowing the Bible and being conversant in contemporary affairs—unlike early Mormon apologist Orson Pratt, who denied him even a rudimentary knowledge of the Bible at the time he began to produce new scripture.

Smith needed support from those around him while working on the book. Diedrich Willer reported that the Peter Whitmer home, where Smith spent the final weeks of translating, was the eleventh place he had stayed during the translation process. Willer also reported that inhabitants in each of the places Smith translated had seen visions or angels. Whenever Smith was at odds with his wife Emma, he was unable to continue dictating. He would go into the woods for an hour of prayer, return, and ask her forgiveness. Then he could resume his task.[25] At other times he would go out and pray, and when he became sufficiently humble before God, he could then proceed with the translation.[26] Or he would take time out to skip stones on the Susquehannah River to rejuvenate himself.[27] Smith had dry spells like anyone working on a major, ongoing project.

Many are convinced that no twenty-four-year-old-man could produce the quantity of material in the brief time it took Smith to produce the Book of Mormon; they argue for the necessity of divine help. Smith turned out 8,800 words in eight days with Emma serving as scribe, and 266,200 words in seventy-five days with Oliver Cowdery as scribe. The average jumped from 1,100 to 3,550 words per day. Twenty-five thousand of these words are Old Testament quotations which Smith read from the Bible. The expression "it came to pass" accounts for over 6,000 words. And the task was not accomplished without preparation. For over a year before Smith began his first try at getting the Book of Mormon on paper with Martin Harris in 1828, he was talking about the themes of the book. He had lived with those concerns for two years—possibly more—when he began dictating to Cowdery in 1829.

Still the final value judgment about Smith—as translator or author—will always remain personal. He had the ability, the motive, and the opportunity to write a brief in defense of God. In his time and place, a defense seemed needed when the book came off the press in March 1830.

NOTES

1. Ben E. Rich, *Scrap Book of Mormon Literature* (Chicago: Henry C. Etten & Co., n.d.), 2:404.

2. Compare Wesley P. Walters, "Joseph Smith's Bainbridge, N.Y. Court Trials," *Westminster Theological Journal* 36 (Winter 1974): 123-55, and Jerald and Sandra Tanner, *Joseph Smith's 1826 Trial* (Salt Lake City: Modern Microfilm Co., 1971), for discussions of this aspect of Smith's career.

3. David Whitmer, *An Address to All Believers in Christ* (Richmond, MO, 1887), 12; Martin Harris, in *Latter-day Saints' Millennial Star*, 6 Feb. 1882.

4. B. H. Roberts conceded that the two witnesses heard this version from Smith but the "mere mechanical process" they described was incorrect. Only after Smith had worked out the interpretation in his mind was the translation then "reflected in the sacred instrument, there to remain until correctly written by the scribe." *New Witness for God*, 3 vols. (Salt Lake City: Deseret Book, 1926), 2:137-38. In *Restoration Scriptures: A Study of Their*

Textual Development (Independence, MO: Herald Publishing House, 1969), 40, Richard Howard concludes that the Whitmer-Harris version is untenable. In contrast to Roberts, Howard dismissed the idea that Smith saw the translation of the characters "as if through some kind of visually projected medium." Both agree that Smith used the stone. Although both hold to Smith's working out the translation in his mind, Howard points to the text which Smith and Cowdery improved in the 1837 edition of the Book of Mormon and notes that such improvement would have been unnecessary if the Whitmer-Harris version were correct.

5. She stated this in a personal interview with a committee from the Reorganized Church of Jesus Christ of Latter Day Saints in 1879, shortly before her death. Joseph Smith III, "Last Testimony of Sister Emma," *Saint's Herald*, 1 Oct. 1879, 220.

6. John Clark, *Gleanings by the Way* (Philadelphia: W. J. & J. K. Simon, 1842), 224, 230, 228.

7. Charles Anthon to Eber D. Howe, 17 Feb. 1834. Howe, *Mormonism Unvailed* (Painesville, OH, 1834), 270-72. Hereafter cited as Anthon's 1834 letter. Charles Anthon to T. W. Coit, 3 Apr. 1841, in *The Church Record*, 24 Apr. 1841, 231-32. It appears in Clark, *Gleanings*, 233-38. Cited hereafter as Anthon 1841 letter.

8. The confusion is compounded by the many statements of those who were with Smith during the translation period. Emma Smith and David Whitmer both said that after the spectacles, called Urim and Thummim, were removed from Joseph's possession in June 1828, they were never returned, but that Smith then translated with only one stone. Many witnesses claim that Smith used one stone only in 1829. An excellent discussion of the various stories is James E. Lancaster, "'By the Gift and Power of God': The Method of Translation of the Book of Mormon," *Saints' Herald*, 15 Nov. 1962, 798-806, 817. The term "Urim and Thummim" was used for the single stone *and* the two-stone spectacles, he concludes.

The spectacles appear in the Book of Mormon in Mos. 8:13, 19; 21:27-28; 28:11-19; Om. 20-22; Al. 10:2; 37:21-26; Eth. 3:23, 28; 4:5. Note the confusion that results from Al. 37:23-24. Verse 23 reads: "And the Lord said: I will prepare unto my servant Gazelem, a stone . . . that I may discover unto my people who serve me . . . the works of their brethren"; but verse 24 speaks of "interpreters" used for the same purpose. In Smith's 1830 Bainbridge trial Oliver Cowdery described the spectacles as "two transparent stones, resembling glass, set in silver bows." Reported in the *Evangelical Magazine and Advocate*, 9 Apr. 1831, 120. In the 1830 edition of the Book of Mormon, p. 328, line 8, "directors" is used instead of "interpreters" (Al. 37:31). The 1920 LDS edition was the first to change the word. Cf. Howard, *Restoration Scriptures*, 59.

9. This foreword was not printed in subsequent editions of the Book

of Mormon.

10. Joseph Smith et al., *History of the Church of Jesus Christ of Latter-day Saints,* 7 vols. (Salt Lake City: Deseret Book Co., 1927), 1:21; hereafter HC.

11. Lucy Mack Smith, *Biographical Sketches of Joseph Smith, the Prophet, and His Progenitors for Many Generations* (Liverpool: S. W. Richards, 1853), 125-26. Smith's mother quotes him as having said this. However, his wife Emma wrote in 1876 that Joseph had used the spectacles, the Urim and Thummim, during the 1828 session with Martin Harris but after that a small stone. Emma Bidamon to Sister Pilgrim, 27 Mar. 1876, archives, Reorganized Church of Jesus Christ of Latter Day Saints, Independence, Missouri. David Whitmer also says the same thing. See Lancaster, "Gift and Power," 799-800.

12. Howard, *Restoration Scriptures,* 159, summarized the progression of thought:

Section 6:

1. The "translator" must have righteous desires for heavenly treasure.

2. "Translation" ability is a gift from God.

Section 8:

1. Faith is the key to using the gift of "translation."

2. Faith must be exercised with honesty of heart.

3. Only then will truth be perceived. Such perception is registered in the mind and heart of the "translator" by the power of the Holy Ghost.

Section 9:

1. "Translation" is not an automatic process.

3. The "translator" will know that what he is considering in his mid is either valid or invalid by the God-given impressions and intuitions and feelings born of such a studious, faithful approach.

13. Willers to L. Mayer and D. Young, 18 June 1830. In D. Michael Quinn, "The First Months of Mormonism: A Contemporary View by Rev. Dierich Willers," *New York History* 54 (July 1973): 317-31.

14. Clark, *Gleanings,* 228.

15. Fayette Lapham, "The Mormons," *Historical Magazine* (New Series), 7 (May 1870): 308. This would have to have happened after the angel returned the spectacles to Smith so that he could receive D&C 3, since the spectacles were first taken with the plates.

16. HC 1:19.

17. Howard, *Restoration Scriptures,* 41, states that over 2,000 changes were made in the emended manuscript, which Oliver Cowdery prepared for the printer from the dictated manuscript, in preparation for the 1837 edition, and that an additional 1,000 changes are found in the second edition.

18. 1 Nephi 20:1 and the parenthetical phrase read: "Hearken and hear this, O house of Jacob, who are called out of the waters of Judah, (or out of the waters of baptism), who swear by the name of the Lord. . . ." Hugh Nibley, *Since Cumorah* (Salt Lake City: Deseret Book, 1967), 151, explains that the addition is needed for the modern mind, which would not get the meaning of "waters of Judah," although the original audiences would have understood. The translator, therefore, gave his own rendition of what he perceived to be in the mind of the author.

19. Compare the Book of Moses 1, in the Pearl of Great Price.

20. Orsamus Turner, *History of the Pioneer Settlement of Phelps and Gorham's Purchase* (Rochester, 1851), 214.

21. A twentieth-century, non-Mormon scholar agrees with Whittier and Quincy. According to Jan Shipps, in "Prophet Puzzle" (p. 1), the prophet was an "extraordinarily talented individual—a genius beyond question."

22. Smith referred to his "lack of fluency" in a letter to Moses C. Nickerson, 29 Nov. 1833 (HC 1:441-42). At a church conference on 1 November 1831, Christ notes his servant's weakness in this regard (D&C 1:24). In a letter to W. W. Phelps, Nov. 1832, Smith wrote of language as a "narrow prison" (HC 1:299).

23. Clark, *Gleanings*, 228.

24. Anthon's 1834 and 1841 letters.

25. David Whitmer, *An Address*, 12.

26. In William E. Berrett and Alma P. Burton, *Readings in LDS History from Original Manuscripts*, 3 vols. (Salt Lake City: Deseret Book, 1953), 1:51.

27. Whitmer, *An Address*.

3.

New England and Western New York

Revelation means something communicated immediately
from God to man. . . . [Man's] account of it to another is not
revelation; and whoever puts faith in that account, puts it in
the man from whom the account comes. . . . My disbelief of
the Bible is founded on a pure and religious belief in God.

—Thomas Paine,[1] American deist and political philosopher

When Joseph Smith on the title page of the Book of Mormon
announced his intention to convince "Jew and Gentile that JESUS
is the CHRIST, the ETERNAL GOD, manifesting himself to all
nations," he tried to check forces set in motion by deism and
rationalism.[2] Deism attacked revealed religion in order to defend
what was considered natural religion, a creed holding: (1) There is
a God (2) whom one must revere (3) through moral living. (4) One
should abandon sin because it works to humanity's disadvantage (5)
and also because there is divine recompense here and hereafter.

Natural religion needed no special revelation such as the Bible.
Its ethics and religious principles were arrived at through reason.
Some deists held that the contents of the Bible might be above
reason but not contrary to it. But most denied the Bible any special
status at all: its narratives were neither reliable nor unique, the two
testaments were unrelated, the miracles and prophecies were absurd
if interpreted literally and fraudulent if not, and the mysterious

19

elements were corruptions of later times. Since the very means which won acceptance for the Bible were now negated, Thomas Paine demanded its rejection. Christianity had become a corrupt variation of natural religion. The church had obscured religion with unreasonable and immoral concepts, including the doctrines of the trinity, predestination, arbitrary judgment, and the innocent suffering for the guilty. Worse, it had aggrandized itself at the expense of those it purportedly served.

Rationalism in America was an outgrowth of New England's Puritan heritage. Rationalists repudiated revivalism and accepted special revelation only as long as it was reasonable.[3] Jesus was not co-equal with God the Father but subordinate to him. Jesus' death was seen as a way to alert sinners to God's authority, to the dignity of his government and law, not as a way to appease God. Original sin and Calvinistic predestination were judged contrary to reason. Such notions would make God immoral, but God is benevolent and brings happiness to humanity. Above all, God is a unity; he is one, not three in one.

Boston's Charles Chauncy and Jonathan Mayhew expounded rationalism in the mid-eighteenth century. Gradually it infiltrated the established Congregational Church and led to the formation of the Unitarian Church. Unitarians stressed the unity of God and creation.[4] A simultaneous development was the formation of the Universalists, who shared Unitarian accents but stressed the benevolence of God, who saves all. Universalists began from the ministry of John Murray, an English emigrant. The Universalists first convened in Oxford, Massachusetts, in 1785. They were uneducated and tended to draw their themes from the Bible, whereas Unitarians had educated clergy and often drew inspiration from non-biblical sources. Universalists tended to locate in rural areas, Unitarians in the cities. Writers often confused the Universalists and Unitarians because of their shared teachings.

Rationalists constituted a bridge between deists and pietists.[5] Pietists were conservative Christians who subordinated reason to biblical revelation, held orthodox views on the nature of Christ and God, but were disestablished. Political realities forged a marriage of convenience between rationalists and pietists from the French and Indian War through the Revolutionary War, during which they united against the established churches.[6] Rationalists considered their theological disagreements with pietists of minor importance since both groups believed in God, immortality, and a virtuous life. Pietists ignored differences because both groups rejected the established churches' rituals, creeds, and theologies, and felt that religion was personal. Both opposed the clerical authoritarianism of the conservative, established churches.[7]

The marriage dissolved when the Second Great Awakening brought into the open the division between pietistic and rationalistic Christianity. The anti-clerical and atheistic tendencies of the French Revolution led pietists to see a cause and effect relationship between Jacobin infidelity and barbarity. Alarmed at the demise of the French monarchy, the Prussian and Austrian kings, supported by British diplomacy, declared war on revolutionary France. France went to war with Britain and overran much of Europe in the name of liberty.[8]

France and its revolution were seen as signs of a larger conspiracy, supervised by an Infidel International, to overthrow all religion and government. Sympathy with France became a matter of suspicion. Thomas Jefferson was suspect because of his French ambassadorship from 1785 to 1789. Federalists painted him and by implication members of his party as atheists, Jacobins, foes of private property and civic order. When Paine's *Age of Reason* appeared in 1794, it reinforced the anti-Jeffersonian, anti-Republican excitement because Paine too had been in France and was friends with Jefferson. Federalists pushed into law the Alien and Sedition Acts of 1798 to keep their power and to attack the ideas of the French Revolution.

New England was the center of the storm. Congregational churches were established churches and their clergy members were federalists.[9] Ethan Allen's 1784 publication of *Reason the Only Oracles of Man*, Elihu Palmer's attempted anti-church crusade, Paine's book, the formation of deistic societies, and publication of deistic papers upset the region. Deism and French barbarity were coming to the common people, and New England Christendom was alarmed.

Paine's *Age of Reason*[10] distilled and simplified deistic thinking in order to defend God against established religion. Paine's belief in God required him to reject the Bible, "for in my opinion," he wrote to a friend, "the Bible is a gross libel against the justice and goodness of God, in almost every part of it."[11] Paine articulated a variety of objections to the Bible. The Bible limited God, forcing him to "act like a passionate man, that killed his son, when he could not revenge himself any other way" (p. 65). Christian theology's use of the devil in connection with Jesus' death and the necessity of the

Atonement made Satan's power greater than God's (pp. 29-30). Paine scorned the Bible for attributing to God obscenity, debauchery, vindictiveness, and cruel executions. The innocent were made to suffer for the guilty (p. 24). Genocidal wars were waged by Moses and Joshua because of God's express command (p. 90). Rather than being the word of God, Paine said, the Bible would better be recognized as the word of a demon (p. 34).

Prophecy had long been used as an argument for the divine authorship of the Bible, but Paine ridiculed this notion. Paine traced the development in the Bible from poetry to prediction and maintained that the function of the "seer," who predicted the outcome of impending battles or other immediate interests, was gradually broadened into "prophecy" (p. 141) . Ultimately the prophet was made the historian of the future, and posterity credited him with accurate prediction if he came within a thousand years of the mark (p. 81). Then, Paine stormed, the Bible found a way to exonerate God when prophecy failed. If he blessed people and they kept on sinning, then God changed his mind and destroyed them. If God led a man to prophesy destruction upon an evil nation and it repented, then God spared it. "What a fool do fabulous systems make of man!" (p. 134).

If a prophesied event occurs, Paine said, no one can truly know if it was accidental or foreknown. He refused to grant that God would describe an event important enough for people to know beforehand in terms "so equivocal as to fit almost any circumstances that might happen afterwards" (p. 82). The Bible damaged its own case for predictive prophecy, Paine said, by showing the prophets to have been "impostors and liars." Jeremiah lied for Zedekiah because it served his own purpose (pp. 138-39).

Neither would Paine accept miracles as an argument or evidence for special revelation. The Bible appealed to miracles to produce belief, but that belief depended on those who reported the miracle, not upon the miracle itself. If the miracle were true, it "would have no better chance of being believed than if it were a lie" (p. 139). Further, one cannot truly judge something miraculous unless one knows that it truly occurred beyond natural law. Additional knowledge might reveal a miracle to have been natural after all, and that would remove its belief-producing effect (p. 79).

Paine set his own definition of revelation against the Bible's claim to be special revelation: "Revelation is a communication of something, which the person to whom that thing is revealed, did not know before. . . . Revelation, therefore, cannot be applied to anything done upon earth of which man himself is the actor or the witness; and consequently all the historical and anecdotal part of the Bible . . . is not within the meaning and compass of the word revelation, and, therefore, is not the word of God" (p. 77).

Revelation is "something communicated immediately from God to man" (p. 33). Another person's account of revelation is only hearsay. Language is ruled out as a medium of God's word. Instruments of human communication cannot convey God's word because there is no universal language, translations are subject to error, and copyists and printers make mistakes or purposely alter words (p. 183). Revelation must disclaim any contradiction, for that shows the story is false. Agreement does not make a story true, since the whole may be false, but disagreement absolutely disproves it (p. 38).

Given these terms, Paine denied the Old Testament any status as revelation. Books of testimony, for example, depend upon the certain identity of their authors (p. 153). Mosaic authorship of the Pentateuch was most unlikely because Genesis depends on Chronicles for a time reference. Exodus, Leviticus, and Deuteronomy were written in the third person about Moses at a later time (pp. 91-92). Paine argued for a time lapse between the life of Joshua and the writing of the biblical book by that name because of the many instances of the phrase "unto this day" and because of a comparison dependent upon a time lapse to make its point (pp. 94-95, 118-19). The writer's use of the word "beforetimes" also showed that the books of Samuel came after Samuel's time (pp. 105-109).

There were also contradictions in the Old Testament. Paine found two different numberings of the Ten Commandments, two reasons for celebrating the Sabbath (p. 111), two accounts of Saul's first meeting with David (p. 96), and two accounts of Jeremiah's imprisonment (p. 137). Deuteronomy describes Moses' burial place, although no man was supposed to have known its location (p. 136).

The New Testament fared no better under Paine. The anecdotal character of the four Gospels, their disagreements, and their failures to substantiate each other's details were problems for him (pp. 98-99). Differences in the resurrection stories showed that the writers were neither eyewitnesses nor apostles and that they wrote independently of one another (pp. 41-42, 158-62). If God is wise, Paine asked, how can anyone suppose that he would commit himself and his will to precarious language and manuscripts that are edited, altered, and changed (p. 170)? How can anyone place faith in a book not canonized until 300 years after Christ—and then by a committee vote (p. 170)?

Paine's demolition of the Bible freed him to urge the deistic view. No one should despair of finding revelation or the word of God: "There is a Word of God; there is a revelation. THE WORD OF GOD IS THE CREATION WE BEHOLD: And it is in *this* word, which no human invention can counterfeit or alter, that God speaketh universally to man" (p. 45). "Nature reveals mathematical laws, and man discovers how to apply them to the earth and heavenly bodies. To study nature is to study true theology and discover the existence of God. It was incomprehensible that anyone might want to know more" (p. 53; cf. p. 48).

In addition to the testimony of nature, Paine also allowed the testimony of a conscience. Reason falls infinitely short in discovering God's attributes, but men know judgment as a probability: "If we knew it as a fact, we should be the mere slaves of terror; our belief would have no merit, and our best actions no virtue" (p. 188). The sum total of revelation is the knowledge that God exists and that judgment is probable—the testimony of nature and conscience. Corruption looms ahead for those who want more, for it has "been produced by admitting of what man calls *revealed religion*" (p. 61). The Christian church cannot be reconciled with reason and scientific inquiry. It is maintained by the clergy only because of self-interest (pp. 58-60). For the honor of God, therefore, Paine repudiated all revealed religions and priests and called for a return to the God revealed by nature and reason.

Paine spurred the formation of organized deism in America. *Age of Reason* was widely read and often reprinted. The Deistical Society of New York published *The Temple of Reason* from 1800 to 1803. Revived as the *Prospect*, or *View of the Moral World*, it finally was discontinued in March 1805.[12] Sixty miles north of New York on the Hudson River, the Druidical Society of Newburgh reprinted and circulated the works of Hume, Voltaire, and Paine in taverns, shops, and homes. But it disbanded in 1804.[13]

Jedediah Morse, pastor in Charlestown, Massachusetts, scorned Paine's book as a product of the Infidel International and as a symbol of its power base in America. Yale's president Timothy Dwight offered a reasoned defense, marshalled hatred against deism, and popularized the anti-deistic argument.[14] Nathaniel Emmons of Franklin, Massachusetts, warned that Thomas Jefferson's person, party, and principles endangered patriotism and conservative piety. This comment typified clergy reaction.

Three factors brought efforts to spread deism to an end about 1805. First, the U.S. presidential election of 1800 caused a split between republican-political and deistical-religious sentiment. It was now possible to be one without being the other. Second, political republicanism was rapidly taken over by the revivalists and their supporters. Third, the prophets of deism died: Elihu Palmer in 1805, John Foster in 1806, and Thomas Paine in 1809. The demise of Napoleon brought the struggling, dying Federalist Party to a close.[15] Only then did the cry against French infidelity subside in the churches. In its heyday from 1784 to 1805, deistic influence had been felt from the Atlantic to the Mississippi.

Paine transmitted the results of 150 years of philosophical and biblical inquiry through his book. The rhetoric about proper credentials for biblical authors, copyists' errors, contradictions, the nature of God, and communication with humankind—all reflected contemporary concern about the concept of revelation. Thomas Hobbes and John Locke had left their mark on deistic studies of the Bible. Hobbes (1588-1679) held that all knowledge came from the senses and reason, that the Bible might be above reason but not contrary to it. Locke (1632-1704) held that Christianity is not a product of reason but is not contrary to it. It is a revelation. Revelation teaches matters which reason may not have discovered but which reason can comprehend. Revelation, therefore, communicates knowledge.

Long after deism died as a vital force, this concept of revelation lived on in rationalistic and pietistic churches alike. Rationalists wished to purge Christianity of the doctrines which forced thinking people to choose infidelity, but few were willing to adopt Paine's full repudiation.[16] Between 1750 and 1825 rationalism could be seen operating within the movements of Universalism and Unitarianism. But both groups were reacting against deism. Both groups believed in the unipersonal nature of God and the salvation of all humanity. But they were divided by class, education, and style.

Unitarians were mainly a New England phenomenon centering in the cities of eastern Massachusetts. Universalism developed in western Massachusetts and in Vermont, the hill country of New England. There were Unitarians in western New York, but it was the

Universalists who mixed with the people in the small towns and rural areas where the revivalistic fires burned.

Universalism in its early phase was shaped by men who held differing views of Christianity. John Murray was a Calvinist and a trinitarian. He held that Jesus was Savior but in contrast to Calvinism he taught that all people were the Elect of God. Elhanan Winchester taught that all souls would be saved, but those who were not pure enough would have to suffer a purgatorial existence for as much as 50,000 years to satisfy the justice of God. Hosea Ballou cut Universalism's ties with Calvinism and established it on the basis of reason in *A Treatise on Atonement.*[17] He rejected the trinity. Hell was suffered in this life as a result of sin, and it was from this suffering Jesus came to free us. Ballou rejected the picture of the Old Testament God in favor of a God who wants to make everyone happy. Such a God could not allow men and women to choose misery for themselves, even if free will had to be denied to present this image of God.

Issues raised during the 1790s were to have a long life. Between 1790 and 1820 thousands left the western sections of Connecticut, Massachusetts, and Vermont for western New York and brought with them the deistic-rationalistic-pietistic debate.[18] Their leaving left foreboding in the east that they would "revert to 'barbarism' and thus subvert the moral order of society."[19] Pioneer missionary James Hotchkin described western New York of the 1790s as a "wasteland of infidelity." Not only at Scottsville but also at Wheatland and Rochester, deistic societies had their circulating libraries. Diverse backgrounds and poor transportation kept religious observances from advancing as rapidly as land settlement. The price of land attracted easterners looking for economic improvement. The greater part of the population was irreligious, Hotchkin said. They used the sabbath for business, pleasure, drinking, and carousing.[20]

Eastern churches worried about this dark cloud on the western horizon. In 1798 the Presbyterian General Assembly declared that it perceived a loss of religious observances and respect for institutional religion in the west, plus "an abounding infidelity, which in many cases tends to atheism itself."[21] In response the churches launched the Second Great Awakening to convert the west. Presbyterians and Congregationalists united to supply enough doctrinally sound clergy to serve the scattered settlements. In western New York Presbyterians were the stronger. Through them came the benevolence agencies with their tracts,[22] Bibles,[23] Sunday schools, and the

pietistic rationale. Presbyterians, Congregationalists, and Methodists held regular conferences, sessions, and revival meetings. Their
religious journals informed readers of revival meetings and cam-
paigns, provided theological comment, appealed to a wide reader-
ship, and provided a bond to populations on the move.[24]

The Great Revival of 1799-1800 paved the way for the churches
to organize and settle into western New York. Hotchkin saw the
revival as a means which God used to build up Zion: "The tide of
infidelity which was settling in with so strong a current, was rolled
back and Western New York was delivered from the moral desola-
tion which threatened it."[25] The awakening made its greatest impact
upon that large segment of the population which had resisted deism
during the Revolutionary War.[26] In fact, between 1800 and 1835
revivalism would increase church attendance three-fold.

After 1815 Universalists spread their rationalistic gospel in
western New York and established nearly 90 congregations in the
lower Black River Valley, the Finger Lakes region, and the country
of the Genesee River. Their favorite tactic was to engage pietists in
public debate and refute their opponents' views with popularized
deistic and rationalistic arguments.[27] For example, Mr. Evarts, presiding Methodist elder of the Black River Conference, debated Mr.
Morse of the Universalists in Ellisburg in May 1821 for nearly a week.
Evarts presented the traditional arguments to support "the doctrine
of endless misery." Each side left the debate convinced that it had
won.[28]

Charles Finney took to task much of the preaching against
Universalists. Clergymen fought with arguments from out-of-date
books. "They suppose Universalists hold the doctrine that God is all
mercy." Not so, said Finney, "They reject the idea of *mercy* in the
salvation of man, for they hold that every man is punished in full
according to his just deserts. . . . [T]hey hold to the justice of God
alone as the ground of salvation." The result was that "people either
laugh at them, or say it is all lies, for they know Universalists do not
hold such sentiments."[29] But the appeal to God's justice rather than
his mercy as the basis for human salvation was a deistic argument,
which Universalists had made their own.

During this era another general change was occurring in Protestant ways of thinking. G. A. Koch has observed that the 1790s
seemed the time when American independence would sweep the
globe, but the idea of a social and political millennium faded away

with deism after 1800. Human salvation was seen no longer as coming through revision of social institutions but through an end-of-the-world millennium.[30] Protestants united in their hope of inaugurating the Millennium in the immediate future. New systems of education such as the Oneida Institute, missions to convert the Jews, numerous new sects—all were founded in the belief that such activity would hasten the thousand-year reign of Christ. This was a form of American optimism which was especially strong in the Burned-over District.[31]

Itinerant missionaries and evangelists were motivated by this optimism about the immediate future. Charles Finney, dean of them all, believed that the right kind of ministers at the head of the revivals could bring in the Millennium. If the clergy could rise above doctrinal pettiness and denominational competition in a joint effort and could agree "as to what ought to be done for the salvation of the world," then the Millennium would "come at once." Finney therefore criticized the clergy for the sectarian spirit which went with the joint revivals, since it precluded such possibilities. Clerical cries of "Heresy" and "New Measures" and their "controversial *spirit* and *manner*" in discussing disputed doctrinal issues only confused the churches. Proselyting those at revivals always proved the most divisive practice.[32] Converts were usually "mighty zealous for the traditions of the elders, and very little concerned for the salvation of souls." In Finney's view then, the challenge with any revival was to maintain the spirit of unity. Finney pleaded with colleagues to emphasize only the fundamentals of salvation and to exclude sectarian differences.

Hostilities attendant upon revivalistic and benevolent activities, according to historian Whitney Cross, "made up a sectarian hierarchy. All Protestant churches united in condemning Catholics. All evangelical sects united, too, against Universalists and Unitarians. Methodists, Baptists, and Presbyterians could share their hatred of Christians. Baptist and Presbyterians co-operated in damning Methodists and Free-will Baptists. Presbyterians all too often proved disagreeably intolerant of Baptists. To cap the climax, both Baptists and Presbyterians, particularly the latter, maintained a constant and bitter strife between the enthusiasts and the conservatives in their own ranks."[33] Local newspapers followed the Protestant-Catholic struggle and carried many notices and articles about the threat of Catholicism.

Alongside this religious enthusaism, freethought also experienced a resurgence in the 1820s. From 1824 to 1829 Robert Owen's utopia in New Harmony, Indiana, was meant to be an infidel community. In 1828 the Free Enquirers of New York organized and regularly sponsored lectures for themselves and the public. Within a few months the National Tract Society afforded skeptics a propaganda medium and outlet in the state of New York.[34]

The new wave of infidelity was recognized only by a few as different from the deism of Paine and others. Tracts written years before against Paine and his followers were reissued to combat the new wave. Conservative Christians in particular warned Americans in 1824 that French infidelity and the Reign of Terrors were not associated in the public mind by accident. Paine was castigated— again—in 1826, and the faithful were assured that God's wrath would strike down the infidels. The fitting example was William Carver, a deistic pauper, whose condition in life was living proof of freethought's consequences. "Dying infidel" stories, whose subjects contritely confess lives of shame on their deathbeds, were popular weapons in faith's arsenal.[35]

Protestant antagonism showed itself also in political action. Dissenters were refused the right of testifying in court in 1828 because they were thought to be incapable of swearing an oath. When Finney used the name Universalist as a synonym for "ungodliness," "infidelity," and "terror," he struck a sympathetic chord in the burned-over district.[36] The religious press applied the name to criminals.

The churches found another cause in common when William Morgan published an exposé of Freemasonry and then mysteriously disappeared.[37] Attention focused upon an institution which served many as a church and which formerly had been linked with the Infidel International. Public concern about Masonic secrecy, titles, and ritual centered upon an alleged connection with deism, terrorism, and anti-Americanism.

Congregationalists in New York retained many of their federalist sympathies, sentiments which included a bias against the Masonic lodge. Now they were joined in their outrage by large numbers of pietistically and rationalistically inclined churches and individuals. Since lodge membership carried with it the social and political privilege of the large towns—the urban versus the rural, the professionals against the laborers—the anti-Masonic movement was headed more by lay direction than by clerical. Whitney Cross has explained that Presbyterians and others tried to use such released energies more as "a means to develop universal revivalism and reform than [as] an end in itself. Anti-Masonry thus became another gun in the benevolent system's artillery to convert the world and introduce the millennium."[38]

Church action was largely responsible, Finney believed, for the lodges' almost complete shutdown in western New York. They disbanded and relinquished their charters. By 1830 "the greatest revival the world had then ever seen commenced in the center of the anti-masonic region, and spread over the whole field where the church action had been taken until its converts numbered 100,000 souls."[39]

Early nineteenth-century America fostered many religious responses to these cultural and social problems. Two deserve special notice. Both tried to obviate sectarian abuses: the one by abandoning denominational divisions, the other by starting anew. They both shared the millennial hopes and anti-deistic concerns of Protestantism but were scandalized by rampant sectarianism. As an alternative they offered—themselves.

Shakers attributed Europe's religious wars and America's religious discord to the belief that the Bible is God's word for all future ages. Religious strife demonstrated the Bible's insufficiency. "Instead of the knowledge of the true and quickening Spirit of revelation," they taught, the orthodox position left people with only human precepts for comfort, left them ignorant of the spiritual life. The dogmatic confinement of spiritual revelations to a book written for former ages is attended by dead formalism in Christendom and a rapid increase in infidelity—proof positive of apostasy: "The idea . . . that all inspired revelation ceased with the canon of Scripture is inconsistent with both reason and *Scripture*." Shakers declared the situation desperate. There was a true church in apostolic times, but it had been displaced. According to them, the great apostasy had begun as early as 457 A.D. the anti-Christ took over during the reign of Leo the Great.[40]

Joseph Meachem was a former Free-will Baptist preacher who formed the Shaker movement into a communal society in preparation for the impending Millennium. Before his death, communities were set up in New York, New Hampshire, Connecticut, Massachusetts, and Maine. By 1825 there were at least twenty communities scattered from New England to the western borders of Indiana and Kentucky. In 1827 a Shaker community was formed at Sodus Bay on Lake Ontario just thirty miles from Palmyra, New York.[41] According to the Shakers, evidence abounded that the spiritual manifestations of the time fulfilled ancient prophecy that the last days had come. A new work of God was imminent: "The work which God purposed to do in the latter days, was not to be according to the systems of human intervention known and understood among men; but was to be *a strange work*; and the act which he intended to bring to pass, was to be *a strange act*, even A MARVELOUS WORK AND A WONDER."[42]

The second movement was the restoration sought by the Christian Connection (or Christians) and the Campbellites (or Disciples), both part of what would become America's largest indigenous religious movement.[43] Multiplying church schisms led them to a pole opposite the Shakers. They tried to heal the divisions by scrapping all creeds, confessions, and theological terminology which came after the New Testament. Abandon denominational peculiarities. Bring in the Millennium by restoring a faithful observance of New Testament revelation, they urged, not by seeking new revelation. Return the church to the state prescribed by Jesus.[44]

The Christians were formed from Methodist, Baptist, and Presbyterian secessions from parent bodies in 1793, 1800, and 1801. The Christians held to the divinity of Jesus, but many were anti-trinitarian. Their only creed was the Bible and their only name Christian.

The Disciples regarded the laity as spiritually competent and independent, held to an Arminian theology, and defined faith as an intellectual test given to Jesus' moral principles.[45] They saw faith's essence as obedience to Christ, sympathized with anti-trinitarian sentiments, taught an anthropology which gave people the rational and moral ability to understand and fulfill New Testament demands, and were repulsed by the ordinary revival because of its emotional appeal.

Mario De Pillis has described this struggle among the churches as a "quest for authority." Christians and Disciples located that authority "in the ability of a congregation to find truth in the scriptures."[46] Shakers found their authority in the restoration of the true church and relied on continuing, present-day revelation to direct its life. By contrast, other Protestants relied upon a body of doctrine which they believed agreed with the Bible and taught its principles.

Like Disciples and Christians, Joseph Smith would locate authority in the correct interpretation of the Bible by the church. Like Shakers, he would restore the church and be led to the correct interpretation by new and constant revelation. Like other Protestants, he would see correct doctrine as a mark of the true church. But Smith added something else: a new scripture and a dual priesthood based not on apostolic succession, as in the case of the Roman Catholic claim to authority, but on prophetic succession.[47] In response to the turbulence about him, Smith would seek to heal the wounds of sectarianism and defend God against deism, rationalism, and sectarianism, not by revivals but by the experience of personalized revelation.

NOTES

1. Thomas Paine, *Age of Reason: Being An Investigation of True and Fabulous Theology*, Moncure Daniel Conway, ed. (New York: G. P. Putnam's Sons, 1898), 23, 183, 199. Part I of Paine's *Age of Reason* was first published in 1794, part II in 1796.

2. The following works are invaluable in tracing American deism: G. Adolph Koch, *Religion of the American Enlightenment* (New York: Thomas Y. Crowell Co., 1968); Herbert N. Morais, *Deism in Eighteenth Century America* (New York: Russell & Russell, 1934); Albert Post, *Popular Freethought in America, 1825-1850* (New York: Columbia University Press, 1943); Martin E. Marty, *The Infidel: Freethought and American Religion* (Cleveland: The World Publishing Co., 1961).

3. Compare comments on Charles Chauncy and Jonathan Mayhew in Robert T. Handy, Lefferts A. Loetscher, and H. Shelton Smith, *American Christianity: An Historical Interpretation with Representative Documents* (New York: Charles Scribner's Sons, 1960), 1:382.

4. Unitarianism shifted grounds many times since then. The older Unitarians taught what was called "modal trinitarianism," known usually as Sabellianism: God appeared first in the mode of Father, then as Son, then as Holy Spirit. These were three consecutive appearances rather than simultaneous being—as the orthodox doctrine teaches.

5. The use of "pietist" follows Sidney E. Mead, *The Lively Experiment: The Shaping of Christianity in America* (New York: Harper & Row, 1963).

6. "Established" means that a church body was supported by the state. The established church in Massachusetts was the Congregational Church. This was the kind of support against which the constitutional amendment

was directed. By 1820 the last state to comply with the amendment finally disestablished its favored church.

7. Mead, 39-42.

8. Charles A., Mary R., and William Beard, *New Basic History of the United States* (Garden City, NY: Doubleday & Co., 1960), 162.

9. Mead, 57.

10. The book was written in France while Paine was imprisoned by the Jacobin regime. Paine wanted to show that belief in God did not require acceptance of doctrines and churches which drove people to infidelity and to the excesses of the Jacobins. Page references from the 1898 reprint of Paine's book will appear in the text.

11. "Letter to a Friend," 27 May 1797; in Paine, *Age of Reason*, 199.

12. Morais, 137-39.

13. Koch, 114-29. An "infidel" club was formed about 1794 on the Genesee River on the site of what would later be Scottsville. It had a circulating library "composed of the works of Voltaire, Volney, Hume, Payne [sic], and others of a similar character. No church of the Presbyterian or Congregational order existed in this place till March 1822." James H. Hotchkin, *A History of the Purchase and Settlement of Western New York, and the Rise, Progress, and Present State of the Presbyterian Church in That Region* (New York: M. W. Dodd, 1848), 90. This was west of the Smiths' home at Palmyra.

14. Koch, 239-84; cf. Morais, 159-78.

15. Koch, 281-84.

16. For example, they still retained belief in the Bible as special revelation. Compare Koch, chap. 8, and Marty, *The Infidel*, chap. 6.

17. Hosea Ballou, *A Treatise on Atonement* (Randoph, VT: Serano Wright, 1805). This book was available in Palmyra bookstores.

18. Whitney R. Cross, *The Burned-over District: The Social and Intellectual History of Enthusiastic Religion in Western New York, 1800-1850* (Ithaca, NY: Cornell University Press, 1950), 6.

19. Winthrop S. Hudson, *Religion in America: An Historical Account of the Development of American Religious Life* (New York: Charles Scribner's Sons, 1965), 133.

20. Hotchkin, 24-29.

21. Quoted by William Warren Sweet, *The Story of Religions in America* (New York: Harper and Brothers, 1930), 324.

22. From 1825 to 1827 the American Tract Society, in its first two years of existence, printed 44 million pages and kept 43 million east of the Allegheny Mountains. By 1835 it had printed almost 30 million tracts. Three- fourths of this output stayed in New York. Cross, 25.

23. *Palmyra Register*, 18 Aug. 1818.

24. *The Methodist Magazine* (New York) regularly printed reports of the

Bible societies. Cf. vol. 4 (1821), 312.

25. Hotchkin, 74, 79-118.

26. Cross, 7.

27. Cross, 17-18, 44. David Marks, a young Free-will Baptist evangelist, preached twice in West Bloomfield one Sunday in 1823 "and was much opposed by a Universalist." In April 1827, he "attended a debate, that was appointed to be held between a Calvinistic Baptist and a Universalist." Marks, *The Life of David Marks to the 26th Year of His Life* (Limerick, ME: Office of the Morning Star, 1831), 161, 233.

28. Ernest Cassara, *Universalism in America: A Documentary History* (Boston: Beacon Press, 1971), 128.

29. Charles G. Finney, *Lectures on Revivals of Religion* (Oberlin, OH: E. J. Goodrich, 1868), 171.

30. Koch, 292.

31. Cross, 79.

32. Finney, 211, 312, 192-93, 381, 153, 267, 189.

33. Cross 43.

34. Post, 24, 80, 122.

35. Ibid., 210, 203, n. 17, 76, 221-22, 204-205.

36. Finney, 119, 196.

37. *Freemasonry Exposed and Explained* (New York: William Brisbane, 1826).

38. Cross, 123.

39. Finney, 284.

40. *Testimony of Christ's Second Appearing, Exemplified by the Principles and Practice of the True Church of Christ*, 4th ed. (Albany: The United Society [Shakers], 1856), 592, iii, 460-62. First ed., 1808; second, 1810; third, 1823.

41. Ibid., xi.

42. Hudson, 183-85.

43. Hudson, 122-24; F. E. Mayer, *The Religious Bodies of America* (St. Louis: Concordia Publishing House, 1961), 371-86.

44. Mayer, 383.

45. Note the influence of John Locke at work here.

46. Mario DePillis, "The Quest for Religious Authority and the Rise of Mormonism," *Dialogue: A Journal of Mormon Thought* 1 (Spring 1966): 74.

47. Ibid., 77.

4.

The Palmyra Region

Some of us natives of Manchester have always been ashamed
that Manchester gave Mormonism to the world.

—An old Manchester, New York, resident[1]

The family of Joseph Smith, Jr., shared in the controversy which
kept religious interest alive in western New England in the first third
of the nineteenth century.[2] Contrary to reports picturing them as
an irreligious family, the Smiths showed a steady interest in religion.

Asael Smith, grandfather of the Mormon prophet, was a Congregationalist in Topsfield, Massachusetts. In 1797 when he moved
his family to Tunbridge, Vermont, he left the Congregational church
and became a Universalist. John Murray had been establishing his
brand of Universalism in the region since before the Revolutionary
War. By the time Asael Smith moved to Vermont, he had already
found Congregationalist teachings irreconcilable with reason and
scripture.

In a letter to his children, Asael demonstrated his rationalistic
sympathies; he would not recommend a particular religious denomination to his children. Whatever church they might ultimately join,
he wanted them to test whether it was both scriptural and reasonable.[3] When he heard that his son, Joseph Sr., was attending Methodist meetings in Tunbridge, Asael threw Thomas Paine's *Age of
Reason* at him and told him to read it. Following this, Joseph Sr. had

a vision which convinced him that no denomination "knew any more concerning the kingdom of God, than those of the world, or such as made no profession of religion whatever."[4] Joseph Sr. finally joined the Universalist church in Tunbridge along with his father and Jesse, his brother.[5]

The Mormon prophet's maternal side was Scotch Dissenter stock. Solomon Mack, his maternal grandfather, came from a long line of clergymen. He saw visions in his old age and published his memoirs when he was seventy-eight. Jason, one of his sons, became a Seeker and established a semi-communistic community in New Brunswick with himself as economic and spiritual director.[6] Before her marriage to Joseph Smith, Sr., Lucy Mack was pious but unable to choose one church above another. She tried a Presbyterian church after she married but was disappointed. Finally she was baptized, but only by a minister who did not insist upon her joining a particular denomination.[7]

As a family the Smiths demonstrated the dissatisfaction with the standard churches which was so common among the pietistic, socially displaced population.[8] Critical of church division and the failures of the clergy to meet certain standards of piety, they satisfied their religious impulses apart from existing churches at times, at times uneasily within them.

Joseph Jr., along with his family, moved to Palmyra, New York. Palmyra was then a town of almost 4,000 people, prospering because of the construction of the Erie Canal.[9] Later they moved to a 100-acre farm about two miles south of the village of Palmyra and five miles northwest of Manchester. Manchester had a 600-volume library and a private circulating library.[10] Eight miles south of Manchester was Canandaigua, the county seat. Through the years Palmyra boasted several book stores.[11] Palmyra was just above the Finger Lake area, in the heart of the region where the Universalists had planted ninety congregations. Their Unitarian argument generated so much concern that Abner Chase, the presiding Methodist elder, spoke of Unitarian efforts in the Ontario District as almost successful enough to overthrow the entire "work of God in some Circuits on this District."[12] That was in 1820.

Joseph Jr. knew the Universalist argument from his father, and between his father and mother he must have heard most arguments both pro and con for rationalism and traditional Protestant orthodoxy. Such arguments were also available from other sources. The

Universalist was advertised in the *Wayne Sentinel* in the spring of 1825.[13] Young Joseph spent some of his time during 1825-26 in the Colesville, New York/Harmony, Pennsylvania area. There Smith stayed with Newel Knight and his family, who were Universalists.

The charges tying Universalists to public discord seemed far fetched to many local inhabitants except when applied to Robert Owen's colony at New Harmony, Indiana. The *Wayne Sentinel* printed Owen's "Declaration of Mental Independence" speech, which denounced private property, organized religion (Christianity), and marriage.[14] Some were aware that this represented a new generation of free thought, but the average person in the burned-over district took it as a resurgence of deism.

Some have argued that Joseph Smith was greatly influenced by Campbellite theology through his association with Sidney Rigdon, a Campbellite minister.[15] John Locke's theology was also thought to have found its way into Smith's thinking by way of Rigdon. However, Smith picked up Locke's themes before he knew Rigdon through his familiarity with the arguments of deism, Universalism, and perhaps Locke himself.[16] Just as important was Smith's probable exposure to the Christian Connection.

Nearly one-third of Christian Connection ministers were in New York in 1823. Twenty-five miles from Palmyra in West Bloomfield, the next township west, David Millard pastored a Connection church and edited the *Gospel Luminary*, whose greatest circulation was in the Finger Lakes area. By 1833 over 100 congregations were in New York.[17] Another congregation was located in Williamson, Wayne County, fifteen miles from Palmyra. Oliver True was the minister at Winchester in 1826.[18] The *Gospel Luminary* also listed churches at Canandaigua, West Bloomfield, Mendon, Phelps, and Rochester—all within a twenty-five-mile radius of Palmyra.[19] Mendon, just ten miles from Palmyra, may have been a missionary base.

Because a Presbyterian minister named Luckey attacked his views on the trinity in 1818, David Millard, Connection pastor at West Bloomfield, responded with a thirty-eight-page tract which he expanded five years later into a book.[20] Millard held that Jesus Christ was a being separate from the Father but bore the nature of the One who begot him. This "proper Son of God" existed and came into being before creation and at the incarnation was made flesh. Therefore, he has only one nature, not both human and divine. Although the argument sounded similar to the Universalist or Unitarian view, it was in fact a rejection of the Unitarian position.[21]

The Christian Connection influence disturbed David Marks, the Free-will Baptist itinerant evangelist, who had a recurring dread of the arguments for a uni-personal God. He visited the Connection church at Mendon and heard a well-reasoned Unitarian argument which left him in despair: "I knew not what to believe of Jesus Christ. For the Unitarian arguments had so influenced my belief, and so formed the connection of my thoughts, that I supposed the doctrine that Jesus Christ is the true God, could not be proved from the scriptures." Commenting on this experience, Marks wrote, "My trials originated solely from my *Unitarian views of the character of Christ.*"[22] Marks survived and returned to the orthodox position, but his experience illustrates the upsetting confusion which flourished in the region of Palmyra.

Such concerns and disagreements suggest an important context for Smith's early pronouncements on the character of Jesus. David Millard attacked and denied precisely the position which the Book of Mormon on its title page claims as its purpose: to convince Jew and Gentile "that JESUS is the CHRIST, the ETERNAL GOD."

Marks's story about the threat of "infidel"[23] doctrine was not an isolated concern in the burned-over district. The ghost of Tom Paine kept turning up. Each sighting of the ghost, as in the teachings of the Unitarians and Universalists, recalled the dreaded barbarity of the French Jacobins. Newspaper editors in Palmyra and church journal editors passed them along.

The grim results of deism were spelled out in the "dying infidel" stories. One young man, beyond comfort because he had "rejected the Gospel," cried out on his deathbed: "Some years since, I unhappily read Paine's Age of Reason; it suited my corrupt understanding; I imbibed its principles; after this, wherever I went, I did all that lay in my power to hold up the Scriptures to contempt. . . . Paine's Age of Reason has ruined my soul."[24] This story appeared in the Palmyra newspaper in 1820. A year later a story with a happier outcome appeared in the same newspaper. Paine's "profane pages" had "infused too successfully the poison of infidelity into the minds of many Americans." A New Jersey deistical society was cited as an example. The local society president persecuted Christians, but his wife began to attend revival meetings. In 1808 he went with her: "The infidel was reclaimed,—his society was broken up, and all around were obliged to confess this was the finger of God."[25]

Paine appeared again in the Palmyra paper after a five-year lapse. The *Wayne Sentinel* published an item about an unpublished manuscript of Paine's, *The Religion of the Sun*, which had turned up in the papers of Thomas Jefferson. The newspaper also ran Benjamin Franklin's letter to "Thomas Payne" in which Franklin urged Paine not to publish *Age of Reason* because the country needed religion to keep it going.[26] These items were published in the same issues which covered the rising controversy over the disappearance of William Morgan, who had just published an exposé of the Masonic Lodge.

Deism also came under attack from the tract societies. During the 1820s auxiliary societies in western New York gave $14,732 for tracts from the American Tract Society. A contemporary described the results: "In the cities and large villages, and in many country towns, a systematic monthly distribution of tracts has been carried on, and the results have been highly gratifying to the benevolent heart. . . . [T]he system of *colportage* has to considerable extent been adopted in Western New York."[27] Palmyra had had an Auxiliary Missionary Society active at least since 1818.[28] Publishers of the Palmyra newspaper sold such tracts in their bookstore; tracts were printed for individual distribution and also bound into annual volumes.

In July 1824 the managers of the New York Tract Society (Methodist) issued a report in which they described four new tracts published since the previous year. Tract No. 46 was entitled "Three queries to deists."[29] The first asked deist readers how they happened to renounce Christianity. It suggested that deists were living immoral lives and had adopted deistic thinking to justify themselves.[30] They bolstered themselves and their position by winning others over to their way of thinking. But could these deists actually promise peace of mind to those friends they might win to their side?

The second question had to do with consistency. Almost all deistic writers, it was asserted, wrote favorably about Christianity. "*Paine*, perhaps, has said as little in this way as any of your writers, yet he has professed respect for the character of Jesus Christ. 'He was,' says he, 'a virtuous and an amiable man. The morality that he preached and practised was of the most benevolent kind.'" Christian writers, the tract concluded, are not plagued by "these fits of inconsistency."

The third query: why do deistic principles fail in the hour of death? Many infidels, Voltaire, for example, died tormented that they might be facing judgment. But no Christian "at the approach of death, was troubled or terrified in his conscience for having been a Christian."[31]

Shortly after its organization in 1825, the American Tract Society published twelve tracts dealing with deism. Tract No. 123, "Leslie's Method with the Deists," and Tract No. 374, "Short Method with A Skeptic," were based on Charles Leslie's 1805 *A Short and Easy Method with Deists*. This work emphasized the use of miracles as an offensive weapon in the debate.[32]

In 1824 a revival surged through Palmyra, eventually involving the Palmyra Presbyterian church and its pastor, Benjamin Stockton. On 16 December 1824, a meeting was held at the church to organize a tract society.[33] *The Methodist Magazine*, begun in New York in 1818 and named after a counterpart in London, covered the revivals around the state and kept track of the fortunes of deism. The publishers of the Palmyra papers printed excerpts from the journal and may have had it in their circulating library.

From 1817 on revivals were a common feature of life in Palmyra.[34] During the 1820s the Palmyra newspapers printed reports of revivals throughout the state and elsewhere. Camp meeting notices, especially those of the Palmyra Methodist church, were another indication of revival activity. In 1829 Methodist evangelist Lorenzo Dow preached to 3,000 people in the field next to the Methodist church, and in 1831 Charles Finney himself visited the community.[35]

The Methodists sponsored a revival in June 1826 a mile from Palmyra. People came from as far as 100 miles away, so many that more than 100 tents were needed. Between 8:00 a.m. and nightfall, five sermons were preached. The service at 5:00 p.m. featured a sermon that "contemplated the whole process of personal salvation, from its incipiency to its consummation in the world of light." The address electrified the crowd. Afterwards, according to one account, "the Rev. Goodwin Stoddard exhorted, and invited seekers within the circle of prayer in front of the stand. Hundreds came forward; some said nearly every unconverted person on the ground."[36]

Exhortation was a part of every revival. The exhorter's role was to help those who had been touched by the preaching make a commitment while they still were open to the message. Orsamus Turner, one of the publishers of the Palmyra newspaper who had known the young Joseph Smith when he was in his mid-teens, wrote that Smith caught a "spark of Methodism in the camp meeting, away down in the woods, on the Vienna Road," and that "he was a very passable exhorter in evening meetings." Earlier, Turner wrote, Smith had been a member of Palmyra's "juvenile debating club," helping to solve "some portentuous questions of moral or political ethics."[37]

On 15 September 1824 a notice appeared in the *Wayne Sentinel* telling of a revival in progress: "A reformation is going on in this town to a great extent. The love of God has been shed abroad in the hearts of many, and the outpouring of the Spirit seems to have taken a strong hold. About twenty-five have recently obtained a hope in the Lord, and joined the Methodist church, and many more are desirous of becoming members." The Reverend George Lane, one of the leaders, wrote a report of this revival. It began in the spring of 1824 and broke out "afresh" on 25-26 September, the time of the Methodist quarterly meeting. A young woman named Lucy Stoddard was converted and gave convincing testimony to many, but she died of typhus soon after. Many were with her at her death. She testified of her faith, sang a hymn, and died. Lane wrote: "The effect produced by this death was the happiest. While it confounded the infidel, it greatly strengthened believers, especially young converts."[38]

By October the Presbyterian church was beginning to benefit from the revival. At that time the church was part of the Presbytery of Geneva, which filed this report in February 1825: "In the congregation of Palmyra . . . More than a hundred have been hopefully brought into the kingdom of the Redeemer. . . . Sabbath Schools, Bible classes, Missionary & Tract Societies are receiving unusual attention, & their salutary influence is apparent."[39] During this revival the Palmyra Prebyterian Church formed a branch of the American Tract Society.

By September 1825, the Palmyra revival had brought approximately 208 members to the Methodist church, 99 to the Presbyterian, and 94 to the Baptist. Only five years earlier Methodist elder Abner Chase had written that Unitarian (Universalist) efforts were about to swamp the entire "work of God" in the Palmyra vicinity. The Palmyra revival was another sign that infidelity could be defeated.

But Charles Finney's concern that revivals too often encouraged sectarian bickering rather than promoting unity seems confirmed by what happened to the Smith family in response to the Palmyra revivals. Joseph Smith found himself perplexed about conflicting claims to truth.[40] He was influenced by George Lane, but his mother, brothers Hyrum and Samuel, and sister Sophronia joined the Presbyterian church. His father remained unaffiliated. According to his mother, the elder Smith had earlier sought "for the ancient order, as established by our Lord and Saviour Jesus Christ, and his Apostles."[41]

Rather than choose the Methodist way, which would have offended the Presbyterian members of his family, Joseph Jr., like his father, remained apart. "Do not ask me to join them," he told his mother. "I can take my Bible, and go into the woods, and learn more in two hours, than you can learn at meetings in two years, if you should go all the time."[42]

Nor could his father forget that when his eldest son Alvin died in November 1823, the Presbyterian minister who conducted the funeral—probably Benjamin Stockton—intimated that Alvin had gone to hell.[43] On 25 September, the very day that George Lane reported the revival "appeared to break out afresh," Joseph Sr. and some friends exhumed the body of Alvin—dead some ten months. Smith had heard rumors that Alvin's body had been "removed from the place of his interment and dissected." After proving to his satisfaction that the rumors were false he ran an ad to stop them.[44] Such an occurrence could only have reopened the wounds made by the insinuation that Alvin had gone to hell. The concern about Alvin helps to explain why father and son did not join the Presbyterians with the others.[45] The future prophet would attend many churches, but he always shied away from committed membership.[46]

This antagonism to the Presbyterians also may help suggest why Joseph Jr. reported his mind was "awakened" by Methodist George Lane. Revival sermons recounted testimonies of sinners who were led to faith; stories of Christians who died in hope of eternal life and infidels dying in fear without hope; admonitions to forsake the evils of the day (including liquor drinking, sabbath breaking, gambling, spiritual sloth, levity, and free thought); and stories showing the dangers of unbelief. George Lane's preaching, according to Oliver Cowdery in his brief history of Smith, "was calculated to awaken the intellect." Anti-deistic polemic would have been part of the sermon material. Lane had shown himself interested in confounding "the infidel." The little town of Palmyra was not deaf to the voices of the times, for newspapers, church journals, sermons, tracts, and daily conversation were filled with items of current interest, not the least of which was the perceived menace of infidelity in its many forms.

NOTES

1. In Mitchell Bronk, "The Baptist Church at Manchester," *The Chronicle: A Baptist Historical Quarterly* 11 (Jan. 1948): 24.

2. Thomas F. O'Dea, *The Mormons* (Chicago: University of Chicago Press, 1957), 7. This section is not meant to be a complete coverage of the Smiths' fortunes while they were living in the Palmyra area but rather a tracing of the ways by which Joseph Smith would have become familiar with the influence of skepticism. For complete coverage, see Fawn M. Brodie, *No Man Knows My History: The Life of Joseph Smith*, 2d ed. (New York: Alfred Knopf, 1971); and Lawrence C. Porter, "A Study of the Origins of the Church of Jesus Christ of Latter-day Saints in the States of New York and Pennsylvania, 1816-1831," Ph.D. diss., Brigham Young University, 1971.

3. Marvin S. Hill, "Secular or Sectarian History? A Critique of *No Man Knows My History*," *Church History* 42 (Mar. 1974): 89-90. The reading "Trumbull" in this article should be Tunbridge.

4. Lucy Mack Smith, *Biographical Sketches of Joseph Smith, the Prophet, and His Progenitors for Many Generations* (Liverpool: S. W. Richards, 1853), 57-58.

5. Porter, 13, reproduced the articles of incorporation of the Tunbridge Universalist church, which included the signatures of Asael, Joseph Sr., and his brother Jesse. The document was attested 6 Dec. 1797. Asael was moderator of the congregation.

6. Lucy Mack Smith, 37.

7. Ibid.

8. Mario De Pillis makes this argument in "The Quest for Religious Authority and the Rise of Mormonism," *Dialogue: A Journal of Mormon Thought* 1 (Spring 1966): 68-88; and in "The Social Sources of Mormonism," *Church History* 337 (Mar. 1968): 50-79.

9. See the description of Palmyra in the *Palmyra Herald*, 19 June 1822; also Brodie, 3.

10. Brodie, 10. The remains of the old Manchester Rental Library and its membership record book are today housed in the basement of the Ontario County Historical Society in Canandaigua. The record book includes the date and book number of each book checked out to each member from 1826 into the 1840s. Each book has a number written on the library book plate. Thus one can discover who checked out what book and on what date. Some of the book titles are: William Wilberforce, *A Practical View of the Prevailing Religious System . . . Contrasted with Real Christianity*, 1799 edition, first published in England in 1797. It was in this book that

the English evangelical dubbed Unitarianism a "half-way house" to "absolute infidelity." Another book in the library was Andrew Fuller's *The Gospel Is Its Own Witness . . . Christian Religion Contrasted with the Absurdity of Deism,* Boston, 1803. This book was written by a noted Baptist theologian and pastor of the church at Kettering, England. See Robert Paul, "Joseph Smith and the Manchester (New York) Library, *Brigham Young University Studies* 22 (Summer 1982): 333-56.

11. The T. C. Strong bookstore was operating in 1818 and ran a two-column ad listing its books (*Palmyra Register,* 15 Sept. 1818). Leonard Westcott opened a store in 1821 and offered to take rags in payment for books (*Western Farmer,* 11 Apr. 1821). E. F. Marshall opened a new store in December 1822 (*Palmyra Herald,* 4 Dec. 1822). Ads for bookstores in Canandaigua and Rochester also appeared. J. D. Evernghim operated a bookstore from 1 October 1823 to May 1824 (*Wayne Sentinel,* 1 Oct. 1823 and May 1824). All publishers of the Palmyra paper, including Timothy C. Strong, Pomeroy Tucker, John H. Gilbert, Egbert G. Grandin, also operated a bookstore along with the printing business and ran a circulating library.

12. "Revival of Religion on Ontario District," *Methodist Magazine* 7 (Nov. 1824): 435.

13. *Wayne Sentinel,* 13 April 1825.

14. Ibid., 25 Aug. 1826.

15. For example, George B. Arbaugh, *Revelation in Mormonism: Its Character and Changing Forms* (Chicago: University of Chicago Press, 1932).

16. Locke's works, particularly his *Essay on Human Understanding* which sets forth his view on revelation, were on sale in Palmyra bookstores. The work was also in the Manchester Rental Library and is recorded in the Record Book as one of its holdings. On 31 January 1844, Joseph Smith donated many books to the Nauvoo Library and Literary Institute. Among them were the essay by Locke and Parker's *Lectures on Universalism.* Compare Kenneth W. Godfrey, "A Note on the Nauvoo Library and Literary Institute," *Brigham Young University Studies* 14 (Spring 1974): 389.

17. R. Whitney Cross, *The Burned-over District: The Social and Intellectual History of Enthusiastic Religion in Western New York, 1800-1850* (Ithaca, NY: Cornell University Press, 1950), 263.

18. *Wayne Sentinel,* 8 Oct. 1823, carried a notice that True performed a marriage in Williamson.

19. *Gospel Luminary,* Aug. 1826.

20. *The True Messiah* (Canandaigua, 1823).

21. Millard also demonstrated the Christian Connection notion that the Church of Christ was the only correct name for the church.

22. Marks, *Life of David Marks,* 217, 219.

23. Martin E. Marty analyzed the usefulness of the "infidel" concept to the churches in chapter 2 of *The Infidel: Freethought and American Religion*

(Cleveland: The World Publishing Co., 1961).

24. *Palmyra Register*, 12 July 1820. Compare also *Palmyra Herald*, 17 July 1822, for the miserable death of a profane man.

25. *Palmyra Register*, 7 Feb. 1821.

26. *Wayne Sentinel*, 25 Aug. and 4 Aug. 1826.

27. James H. Hotchkin, *A History of the Purchase and Settlement of Western New York, and of the Rise, Progress, and Present State of the Presbyterian Church in That Section* (New York: M. W. Dodd, 1848) 261-62.

28. *Palmyra Register*, 19 Aug. 1818.

29. *Methodist Magazine* 7 (1824): 437.

30. This tract was reprinted under the title "Three Queries to the Rejecters of Christianity" and published as Tract #258 in *The Publications of the American Tract Society* 8 (1833?).

31. *Wayne Sentinel*, 24 Mar. 1826. Tucker and Gilbert advertised tracts from the New York Tract Society. *Christian Almanacks* for 1824 reprinted from the Boston edition and published by the American Tract Society were on sale at the J. D. Evernghim & Company book store, 48 pages for ten cents. This makes it likely that the store carried tracts from the same firm. *Wayne Sentinel*, 8 Oct. 1823.

32. Charles Leslie, *A Short and Easy Method with Deists, wherein the Certainty of the Christian Religion is Demonstrated by Infallible Proofs from Four Rules, in a Letter to a Friend*, New American Edition (Cambridge, 1805).

33. *Wayne Sentinel*, 15 Dec. 1824, 15 Dec. 1826.

34. Hotchkin, 378, records revivals for the Palmyra Presbyterian church for 1817, 1824, and 1829. There were others in neighboring towns in others years. Wesley P. Walters has thoroughly discussed the revivals during this period and in this region in "New Light on Mormon Origins from the Palmyra Revival," *Dialogue: A Journal of Mormon Thought* 4 (Spring 1969): 60-81. Another important study, though less well researched, is Milton V. Backman's "Awakenings in the Burned-over District: New Light on the Historical Setting of the First Vision," *Brigham Young University Studies* 10 (Spring 1969): 301-20.

35. *Wayne Sentinel*, 28 Aug. 1829; *Palmyra Reflector*, 1 Feb. 1831.

36. Z. Paddock, ed., *Memoir of Rev. Benjamin G. Paddock* (New York: Nelson & Phillips, 1875), 181; compare pp. 177-81. In 1819 a camp meeting was held in Carpenter's Notch: "Among the effective efforts from the stand of this meeting was a sermon from M. Pearce and an exhortation from G. Lane. The sermon was well argued, and closed under a high degree of excitement which electrified the whole encampment. The exhortation was a melting and overwhelming appeal to the unconverted. Many hardened sinners yielded to the call and were converted." George Peck, *Early Methodism within the Bounds of the Old Genesee Conference from 1788 to 1828* (New York: Carlton & Porter, 1860), 314-15. Compare also *Methodist*

Magazine 5 (1822): 474-75 for the account of camp meetings where the sequence is preaching followed by exhortation and prayer.

37. O[rsamus], Turner, *History of the Pioneer Settlement of Phelps and Gorham's Purchase* (Rochester, NY: Wm. Alling, 1851), 214. In "An Account of a Camp-Meeting Held in Telfair County, Geo.," *Methodist Magazine* 7 (1824): 436, another note in the role of the exhorter was struck: "It was common for these young converts, as soon as they felt the pardoning love of God, to rise and declare what God had done for their souls, and conclude be exhorting sinners to seek salvation. Among others, there were several children from twelve to fourteen years of age, earnestly engaged in exhorting their friends to fly to Jesus."

38. *Methodist Magazine* 8 (1825): 158-61.

39. Geneva Presbytery, "Records," 5 Oct. 1824 and 1 Feb. 1825, Book D, 16, 27. Cited in Walters, "New Light on Mormon Origins," 64-65, 76n25, 29.

40. He wrote that when the revival was over and "the converts began to file off, some to one party and some to another, it was seen that the seemingly good feelings of both the priests and the converts were more pretended than real; for a scene of great confusion and bad feelings ensued—priest contending against priest, and convert against convert . . . in a strife of words and contest about opinion" (Joseph Smith et al., *History of the Church of Jesus Christ of Latter-day Saints*, 7 vols. [Salt Lake City: Deseret Book Co., 1927], 1:3; hereafter HC).

Joseph's mother wrote that it was this conflict which caused her son to reflect seriously upon divided Christendom: "While these things were going forward, Joseph's mind became considerably troubled with regard to religion" (*Biographical Sketches*, 74). However, the preliminary manuscript differs from the published version on this point. The published version places Joseph's anxiety over religion after mention of a revival and following the seventh vision of Joseph Smith, Sr. In the preliminary manuscript, instead of a revival introducing her son's anxiety, the setting is a family discussion on the diversity of churches, followed by the vision of the angel Moroni. In the 1853 edition, Joseph's anxiety is followed by the first vision, which is taken from the prophet's own 1838 *History*.

The story Joseph Smith, Jr., told about his anxiety over sectarian rivalry during a revival and his subsequent prayer of faith followed by the first vision has traditionally been dated in 1820. However, Walters contends that no such revival took place in 1820 but that one did occur in 1824.

41. *Biographical Sketches*, 56-57.

42. Ibid., 90.

43. In an interview with E. C. Briggs (*Deseret News*, 20 Jan. 1894), the prophet's younger brother William said it was Stockton. The manuscript version of Joseph Smith's *History of the Church* carries a dedication at the

beginning: "In Memory of Alvin Smith Died the 19th Day of November In the 25th year of his age year 1823." Compare "Manuscript History of the Church," Book A-1, in archives, Church of Jesus Christ of Latter-day Saints, Salt Lake City, Utah. This statement and one that Alvin had been saved (HC 2:380) indicate that Stockton's charge still bothered Joseph Smith even in his later years.

44. *Wayne Sentinel*, 29 Sept. 1824.

45. Another factor may have been the way people in the burned-over district perceived Universalists. Presbyterians regarded the views of Joseph Sr. as heretical. Still another aspect of the situation may be spelled out in a romantic novel based on the diaries of a woman who lived in Palmyra during this period. Her grandson used the diaries to write a novel in which the Palmyra Presbyterian church is pictured as the church attended by the town leaders, who controlled the economic destiny of the community. See Samuel Hopkins Adams, *Canal Town* (Toronto: Random House, 1944).

46. An old resident of Manchester told Mitchell Bronk (p. 24) that "Joe occasionally attended the stone church; especially the revivals, sitting with the crowd—the sinners—up in the gallery. Not a little of Mormon theology accords with the preaching of Elder Shay." Note that this could well have happened during the Palmyra revival of 1824-25. The Reverend Anson Shay was a charter member of the Manchester Rental Library and likely read Andrew Fuller's *The Gospel Is Its Own Witness* and his "Three queries to deists." Fuller was a prominent Baptist theologian, and Smith could have absorbed such anti-deistic messages through sermons.

5.

The Indians' Lost Book of God

They [the American Indians] have two flat sticks about one foot long, tied together, on which are several characters, which they say, the Great Father gave to their prophet, and mean as much as a large book.

—W. W. Phelps,[1] an early Mormon apologist

In 1805, twenty-five years before the founding of the Mormon church, an anglo missionary asked permission of the Six Nations to work among the native Americans in the region. The chiefs meeting in council asked Seneca Chief Red Jacket to speak for them. "You have got our country, but are not satisfied; you want to force your religion upon us," he told the missionary. "We understand that your religion is written in a book. If it was intended for us, as well as you, why has not the Great Spirit given to us . . . and to our forefathers the knowledge of that Book, with the means of understanding it rightly? If there is but one religion, why do you white people differ so much about it?"[2]

Thomas Paine had asked similar questions in his critique of Christianity. The Book of Mormon offered answers to such questions in trying to convince the Indians that "Jesus is the CHRIST, the ETERNAL GOD." Why does Mormon scripture cast the ancestors of the Indians in the principal roles? How could they be used to defend God against popular deism? Why were they used to project a new theology?

The growth of America has always involved the fate of the original inhabitants, making the Indians of international importance. They wiped out a white force of 1,400 men at a battle on the Wabash River in the Northwest Territory in 1791, exposing the Canadian border. In 1811 the Indian leader Tecumseh led his forces to defeat at the Battle of Tippecanoe. When Tecumseh sought refuge with the British in Canada, many American politicians blamed the British for the uprising. This became one of the factors leading to war with Britain in 1812.

Once a region became U.S. territory, a period of upheaval and relocation set in. Land agents bought land from Indian tribes. Reservations were established for those Indians who wished to remain within U.S. boundaries. White settlements sprang up around the Indians, and cultural contact brought pressure on the Indian way of life. Eventually, if not as soon as the transition began, the majority of tribes moved west of the U.S. borders.

In western New York in the 1820s the process of relocation had almost been completed. Immediately after the Revolutionary War the Phelps and Gorham Purchase carved out the future home of the Joseph Smith, Sr., family.[3] The land abounded in relics. This was the country of the Six Nation Federation of the Iroquois tribes: Mohawks, Oneidas, Onondagas, Cayugas, Senecas, and the Tuscaroras further south. Centuries before, following a series of battles which failed to determine supremacy, the tribes united to end an almost constant state of warfare. They left in their wake palisaded forts—one chain extended to Pennsylvania fifty miles away.

The Palmyra region also had Indian mounds. Throughout the 1820s such Indian sites were featured in Palmyra newspapers. For example, the papers described the excavation of burial mounds near Cuyahoga River in Ohio, another in Virginia, and still others in Fredonia, New York, and Worthington, Ohio; rock inscriptions found in or near Dighton, Massachusetts, Pompey, New York, and Washington County, Missouri; a tomb in Tennessee and an excavation near Schenectady, New York. Such discoveries provided both concrete knowledge of Indians and room for speculation.[4]

From the mounds came skeletal remains of a man judged to be seven feet, four inches tall, an embalmed corpse with auburn hair and facial contours which were neither Indian nor Spanish, as well as artifacts which were both Indian and European. Rock inscriptions revealed a public edict of Pope Leo X dated in 1520 inscribed in Latin with strange symbols, hieroglyphics, and art work in Missouri which little resembled "the rude sketches made by the Indians of the present day."[5]

In 1810 a Mr. Miller opened the mound at Worthington, Ohio. Indians living nearby told Miller that the mounds had been there longer than anyone could remember. The writer of the newspaper article conjectured that the human remains "found in these mounds must have been . . . of human beings inhabiting the country, of whom the Indians had no knowledge."[6]

The reporter who wrote of Pope Leo's edict speculated about the first settlers of North America. They were probably Asiatics, descendants of Shem, Noah's son, who crossed the Pacific to settle in North America. The descendants of Japeth, Shem's brother, settled in Europe and then crossed the Atlantic, driving the Shemites into South America. He supported this theory with the observation that the language, manners, and customs of the South American Indians resembled those of Europeans: "What wonderful catastrophe destroyed at once the first inhabitants, with the species of the mammoth, is beyond the researches of the best scholar and greatest antiquarian."[7]

Another reporter concluded from the Latin inscription and other discoveries "that this country was once inhabited by a race of people, at least, partially civilized, & that this race has been exterminated by the forefathers of the present and late tribes of Indians in this country."[8] Dr. Edmund James of the U.S. Army, who reported the inscribed rocks in Missouri, wrote of the "departure of that forgotten race of men who left their emblematic inscriptions to commemorate some event in their history; perhaps, 'Their own heroic deeds, and hapless fall,' and the commencement of the flight to the west before the barbarians who have exterminated their arts and remembrance."[9] The life of current tribes did not match what the mounds, tombs, and inscriptions seemed to reveal.

Timothy Dwight's description of the Iroquois in his four-volume *Travels in New England and New York* was congruent with this view. According to the information he gleaned, the Mohicans considered themselves the original inhabitants and the Iroquois interlopers. The Iroquois admitted as much, "asserting that they had fought their way to their present possessions, and acquired their county by conquering all who had resisted them."[10] According to Dwight, their savage spirit was enough for them to conquer any tribe. This fall to the Iroquois was celebrated by James Fenimore Cooper's 1826 *The Last of the Mohicans*, which was available in the *Wayne Sentinel* bookstore in Palmyra.[11]

As they watched the remnants of once powerful tribes limp westward to relocation areas, the anglo immigrants in western New York compared their pitiful condition to what they assumed the status of the former inhabitants had once been. The *Wayne Sentinel* reprinted an article from the *Batavia Peoples' Press* which summed up the speculation. It seemed that the former civilization was nearly as developed as that of the colonists. It was pictured as a powerful, civilized, politically advanced nation which God or disease had decimated for some heinous, national sins. But who really knew? "There appears to be a gap in the history of the world, as far as relates to them, which can never be closed up," opined the paper.[12]

Thomas Jefferson conjectured that the corpse from the Tennessee tomb was "a relic of a civilized people who formerly inhabited this country—but who, ages since ceased to be. Who they were—from whence they sprung—and what was their destiny—remains locked up in the womb of the past, one of those inscrutable events which defy human ken or human examination; which loom up on the far-off ocean of by-gone years, with enough of reality about them to convince us that they are no fiction, but yet clothed with an indistinctiveness which defies investigation. The origin, the history, the destiny of that people, together with the cause of their extinction," was, Jefferson believed, "'consigned to the receptacle of things forever lost upon earth.'"[13]

Civilized Indians had been destroyed by barbarians who remained, and Indians-as-hostile-savages was a familiar motif in the Palmyra press during the period: Indians massacring anglos (*Palmyra Register*, 3 May 1820); white women falling captive to Indian savages (*Wayne Sentinel*, 17 Aug. 1824); children captured and raised by Indians (*Palmyra Register*, 3 July 1822); Indians fighting with each other (*Palmyra Register*, 19 July 1820). Even the Cherokees, who had long been regarded as one of the most Christianized Indian nations, threatened to kill their own delegates to a peace conference upon their return from Washington because the tribe did not like the treaty the delegates had signed (*Wayne Sentinel*, 15 Aug. 1828).

Colonial attitudes toward Indians survived into the nineteenth century. There was the desire to get their lands, to kill or drive them away. But there coexisted a guilty awareness that this was wrong and with this guilt a sense of obligation: convert and civilize them, or at least civilize them.[14]

In the early nineteenth century the government tried first to civilize Indians through Christian missions. In 1820 John C. Calhoun, Secretary of War, held up to Congress the Cherokees, Choctaws, Wyandots, Senecas, and Shawnees as prime examples of what civilization could do. In 1820-21 Congress granted over $16,000 to establish mission schools in several states and carried that policy through the twenties. By 1824 twenty-one schools were supported in this manner and by 1826 there were thirty-eight.[15]

The readers of the Palmyra papers could follow the progress of the civilizing process. In 1821 a report from the Brainard mission among the Cherokees concluded: "It no longer remains a doubt whether the Indians of America can be civilized—the Cherokees have gone too far in the pleasant path of civilization to return to the rough and unbeaten track of savage life."[16] Another report from the same tribe urged Christians to "pursue the labour of love which we have commended, . . . and the Indian will become temperate and industrious."[17] As proof of the gospel's power to civilize, an article reported that the Oneidas had formed an agricultural society.[18] A notice that copies of the Bible were being printed in an Indian language and that they were bringing Indians to Christianity was therefore printed with a note of approval.[19]

The missionary effort was on one level a reparation for the way colonists had mistreated the Indians.[20] Another motive prominent in the nineteenth century was that Jesus Christ had ushered in the "millennial morn": "Why are kings become nursing fathers and queens nursing mothers,—why are the nations flinging away their gods and asking for the True God and the Bible, and why are all civilized nations aroused to relieve the miseries of the heathen, if the set time to favour Zion is not come?"[21]

Success was at best mixed. Red Jacket opposed missionaries among his people, but others invited them in. He wrote his assessment of the results in a letter in 1821. The introduction of preachers "has created great confusion among us, and is making us a quarrelsome and divided people." Whenever the Black Coats secured consent to come in, he wrote, "confusion and disorder are sure to follow; & the encroachments of the whites upon our lands, are the invariable consequences." The preachers "were the forerunners of their dispersion." Indians quarreling, whites plundering, Indian population decreasing—all this happened in "proportion to the number of preachers that came among them." Red Jacket feared "that these preachers, by, and by, will become poor, and force us to pay them for living among us, and disturbing us."[22]

Contact with Indian tribes and antiquities led some to conclude that no one would ever discover the origin of the Indians and the lost race. In fact, many were using the mystery of Indian origins to demonstrate the incompleteness of the Bible. For example, Jedidiah Morse, one of the leading ministers of New England, wrote of the controversy in 1793: "Those who call in question the authority of the sacred writings say, the American [Indians] are not descendants from Adam, that he was the father of the Asiatics only, and that God created other men to be the patriarchs of the Europeans, Africans and Americans. But this is one among the many weak hypotheses of unbelievers, and is wholly unsupported by history."[23]

The discovery of Indians in the New World raised a serious theological issue: If the Flood had left only Noah and his family in the Old World, where did the Indians come from? Unbelievers argued that the Indians were racially unrelated to Old World peoples and could not possibly have migrated to the New World thousands of years before nagivation.

Against these theological attacks, believers began proposing theories connecting Indians with the Old World. Some identified the Indians with the legend of the lost ten tribes.[24] Catholic priests had made this connection in the sixteenth century, partly as a response to pre-Adamite theories of Indian origins. Rabbi Manasseh ben Israel in the mid-seventeenth century published a book-length treatise on the subject in London.[25] James Adair's 1775 *History of the American Indians*, which was specifically designed to combat the pre-Adamite theory and defend the Bible, brought ben Israel's theory to English-speaking readers.[26] The Indian-Israelite connection was accepted by some Puritans and prominent American clergy, set forth in a series of books in the early 1800s,[27] and debated by members of the New York Historical Society.[28]

In September 1825 Mordecai M. Noah, prominent in publishing and political circles in New York, dedicated the City of Ararat as a refuge for world Jewry. He issued a proclamation to that effect and delivered a speech setting forth the rationale of his enterprise. He had an explanation for the origin of the Indians and their predecessors. Given their manners, customs, and "admitted Asiatic origin," he proclaimed that the Indians were "in all probability the descendants of the lost tribes of Israel." He added, "Measures will be adopted to make them sensible of their origin, to cultivate their minds, soften their condition and finally re-unite them with their brethren the chosen people."[29] His speech was printed in the two following issues of the *Wayne Sentinel* along with further comment: "The discovery of the lost tribes of Israel, has never ceased to be a subject of deep interest to the Jews. That divine protection which has been bestowed upon the chosen people . . . has, without doubt, been equally extended to the missing tribes, and if, as I have reason to believe, our lost brethren were the ancestors of the Indians of the American Continent, the inscrutable decrees of the Almighty have been fulfilled in spreading unity and omnipotence in every quarter of the globe. . . . It is . . . probable that from the previous sufferings of the tribes in Egyptian bondage, that they bent their course in a northwest direction, which brought them within a few leagues of the American continent, and which they finally reached. Those who are most conversant with the public and private economy of the Indians, are strongly of opinion that they are the lineal descendants of the Israelites, and my own researches go far to confirm me in the same belief."

Noah listed similarities between Indians and Jews which he felt supported the identification. He concluded: "Should we be right in our conjecture, what new scenes are opened to the nation—the first of people in the old world, and the rightful inheritors of the new? Spread from the confines of the northwest coast of Cape Horn, and from the Atlantic to the Pacific. If the tribes could be brought together, could be made sensible of their origin, could be civilized, and restored to their long lost brethren, what joy to our people, what glory to our God, how clearly have the prophecies been fulfilled, how certain our dispersion, how miraculous our preservation, how providential our deliverance."[30]

The Indian-Israelite connection was almost always tied to some aspect of belief in the Millennium. Ethan Smith's ministerial career from the late 1700s to the early 1800s was engaged in the struggle against Thomas Paine's brand of popular deism. *View of the Hebrews*,[31] his major contribution to the defense of biblical revelation, appeared first in 1823 and then, revised and enlarged, in two printings in 1825. It was widely available in New England and New

York. The book presented the millennial hope that the conversion of the Indians would help usher in the thousand year reign of Jesus. A literalistic approach to the restoration passages of the Old Testament, particularly those of Isaiah and Jeremiah, led Smith to look for their fulfillment just before the impending Millennium. Ethan Smith thought he had discovered the fate of Israel's lost tribes, where they were, and what had befallen them. By distinguishing between the Jews as *dispersed* and the ten tribes as *outcast*, God "surely must have provided a place for their safe keeping as a distinct people, in some part of the world, during that long period."[32]

But where were they? Smith found many clues as to their present location in the Old Testament and Apocrypha. Jeremiah 30-31 speaks of Ephraim (the ten tribes) as scattered to the "coasts of the earth" in the "north country." Ephraim was in the "isles afar off," which signifies any land over "great waters." 2 Esdras 13 declares that the ten tribes went north from Palestine past Armenia, bound for a land where no one had dwelt since the Flood. Amos 8:11-12 speaks of the tribes' wandering from the north to the east, from sea to sea.[33] These sounded like descriptions of America.

Smith concluded that the more civilized Israelite tribes separated from those who depended on hunting. Hunters gradually forgot about their common ancestry and waged frightful wars upon the others. After many centuries, civilized tribes were finally overcome and destroyed. This destruction explained the forts, mounds, and vast enclosures which pre-dated Columbus's discovery—ruins which had no connection with the current Indian population. In this way Smith accounted for abandoned Indian cities along the Ohio to the Mississippi, estimated by Caleb Atwater to be almost 5,000 in number. The ruins and artifacts were eloquent witnesses to the accomplishments of these early inhabitants. "And nothing appears more probable," Smith wrote, "than that they were the better part of the Israelites who came to the continent . . . while the greater part of their brethren became savage and wild. No other hypothesis occurs to mind, which appears by any means so probable."[34]

Convinced then of the literal expulsion of the lost tribes, Ethan Smith also argued for their literal restoration. Zechariah 8:7 speaks of the Lord saving his people from the east country and west country. Since no one from a west country was restored to the land of Israel during the return from Babylon, Smith deduced that the west country referred to must be America. In other words, the return from Babylon was not the only one referred to by scriptures. Smith awaited a restoration for the lost tribes of Israel—the Indians—which was both "distinct from and future of that event."[35]

One of the most important traditions used to prove this theory was that of a lost book. According to Smith, the Indians told of "a book which God gave, was once theirs; and then things went well with them. But other people got it from them, and then they fell under the displeasure of the Great Spirit; but that they shall at some time regain it."[36] He quoted Elias Boudinot, who supposedly followed Indian authority in explaining "that the book which the white people have was once theirs."[37]

According to Smith, Indian tradition held that once they lived "away in another country, had the old divine speech, the book of God; they shall at some time have it again, and shall then be happy." He passed along the report of a conversation between a missionary and the elderly wife of a Cherokee chief, who told him "that when she was a small child, the old people used to say that good people would come to instruct the Cherokees at some future period; and that perhaps she and others of her age would live to see the day. And now she thought that, perhaps, we and the other missionaries had come to give them that instruction."[38]

The Pittsfield parchment story was the most important evidence Ethan Smith produced to support the stories of the Indians' lost book.[39] Joseph Merrick of Pittsfield, Massachusetts, owned land on "Indian Hill," where he allegedly discovered a black leather strap, sewn with sinews and containing dark yellow leaves of an old parchment. In 1815 he brought them to the Rev. Mr. Sylvester Larned of Pittsfield.[40] Larned discovered the standard texts of a Jewish phylactery on the leaves. He wrote Merrick a letter with his translation of the Hebrew script and then took the leaves to Cambridge for further examination.[41] There he left them with a Dr. Eliot, who died soon after. Smith later tried unsuccessfully to locate the parchment leaves, although he continued to believe in their existence.

A second report of a lost book surfaced soon after the Pittsfield parchment story. An old Indian told the Rev. Mr. Stockbridge "that his fathers in this country had not long since had a book which they had *for a long time preserved*. But having lost the knowledge of reading it . . . they buried it with an Indian chief."[42]

Smith combined the two accounts of the Pittsfield parchment

and the Stockbridge book buried with the chief. He concluded that this was the kind of evidence one might expect to connect the Indians with Israel. The parchment leaves seemed obviously Indian, for Jews buried their old or illegible phylacteries and Bible pages in a sheet of paper. They would never have used animal sinews for thread. The whole episode, concluded Smith, "might have been thus safely brought down to a period near to the time when the natives last occupied *Indian Hill*, in Pittsfield; perhaps in the early part of the last century."[43]

The possibility of Israelite identity for American Indians offered America a profound opportunity. According to Ethan Smith's view of Isaiah 18, Isaiah was appealing to the future European Christian stock in America to restore the gospel to the outcast Israelite-Indian tribes.[44] After such restoration, which included the return of the Bible to the Indians, American Christians would be able to christianize them. Smith had God say through Isaiah: "[W]ere not your fathers sent into that far distant world, not only to be (in their posterity) built up a great protecting nation; but also to be the instruments of gathering, or recovering the miserable remnant of my *outcasts* there, in the last days?"[45] By converting the Indians, Christians could help inaugurate the Millennium.

Smith spelled out the theory's value in the on-going debate with skeptics: "New evidence is hence furnished of the divinity of our holy scriptures . . . striking characteristics are found of the truth of ancient revelations."[46] Smith had met the infidel on what he considered fair ground and challenged him to explain the phenomena: "Whence their ideas that their ancestors once had the book of God; and then were happy; but that they lost it; and then became miserable; but that they will have this book again at some time?"[47]

The restoration of the ten tribes would confound infidelity, wrote Ethan Smith. Indian traditions were beginning to exhibit the new evidence, "a powerful evidence of the truth of revelation." The preservation of the Jews was a "kind of standing miracle in support of the truth of revelation. . . . But the arguments furnished from the *preservation and traditions* of the tribes, in the wilds of America from a much longer period, must be viewed as furnishing, if possible, a more commanding testimony."[48] The Indian-Israelite identification confounded popular deism, vindicated God, and proved the Bible true.

The Pittsfield parchment story seemed to prove that the Indians had once possessed the Old Testament, and the story may have circulated in the Palmyra region years before Ethan Smith's second edition of 1825. Sylvester Larned and Elias Boudinot were two men responsible for the story's getting to Ethan Smith. Larned, a young, well-known preacher in the Congregational church, preached in the Canandaigua Congregational church in 1817 and 1818. Boudinot, long active in Indian affairs before he came to head the American Bible Society in 1816, used the Indian-Israelite identification in his *Star in the West* to combat deism, and was certainly influential in western New York.

Joseph Smith in his teens was, according to his mother, a thoughtful youth inclined to ponder life's issues. He could take current topics of interest and entertain others with them. He recited stories about Indians, their fortifications, customs, and life as if he had lived among them.[49] Years later Smith would see the Book of Mormon as a morality play with the ancestors of the American Indians cast in the leading roles. This is particularly evident in the book of Alma. The name of God given there is the Great Spirit, who is identified with the God of the Bible, the world's creator. There we read of Indians waging endless tribal warfare. They had tremendous battles in which tens of thousands were slain and built fortification mounds topped with palisades and towers with moats in front.

Religious and moral issues were at stake in Book of Mormon warfare, as well as European anxiety. Once a Book of Mormon tribe was converted to Jesus, it had to decide whether to continue fighting or to throw down its arms and risk being slaughtered: "They became a righteous people; they did lay down the weapons of their rebellion, that they did not fight against God any more, neither against any of their brethren" (Alma 23:6). "They began to be a very industrious people; yea, and they were friendly" (vv. 17-18). "Now there was not one soul among all the people who had been converted unto the Lord that would take up arms against their brethren; nay, they would not even make any preparations for war; yea, and also their king commanded them that they should not" (24:6). They repented of their past murderous ways and refused to wage war even in self-defense (vv. 7-16).

The Book of Mormon people of Anti-Nephi-Lehi carried out this "no fight" policy when they were attacked by the Lamanites. One thousand of them offered themselves as sacrificial lambs in a passive resistance movement and shamed the slaughtering Lamanites. Repenting Lamanites "threw down their weapons of war, and they would not take them again, for they were stung for the murders which they had committed" (Alma 24:25). More than one thousand were brought to the Christian faith as a result of this supreme act of love on the part of those who were willing to die to show that war was not the way. Preaching to the Indians led them "to disbelieve the traditions of their fathers, and to believe in the Lord" (25:6). "They were perfectly honest and upright in all things; and they were firm in the faith of Christ, even to the end" (27:27).

What Book of Mormon Lamanites were to play out was the fulfillment of the government's dream for an ideal Indian policy. Christian mission efforts among native Americans had had some results, but these were few and slow. The Book of Mormon gave American natives a past and an identity as the people of God and reason to make peace with each other and anglos and to become exemplary Christians.

The Book of Mormon echoed what had appeared in contemporary books and newspapers, and the apologetic value for countering deists and rationalists which Ethan Smith saw in the Indian-Israelite theory was realized in the Book of Mormon as well.[50] According to its title page, the Book of Mormon was "to shew unto the remnant of the House of Israel how great things the LORD hath done for their fathers; and that they may know the covenants of the LORD, that they are not cast off forever." It was this book, not the Bible, which Joseph Smith wanted the Indians to accept as their long lost book of God.

NOTES

1. W. W. Phelps, "Israel Will be Gathered," *The Evening and the Morning Star*, June 1833, 101.

2. Lewis Copeland, ed., *The World's Great Speeches* (New York: Garden City Publishing Co., 1941), 266-68.

3. The development of the region is described in Orsamus Turner's *History of the Pioneer Settlement of Phelps and Gorham's Purchase* (Rochester: Wm. Alling, 1851).

4. *Palmyra Register*, 26 May 1819; *Western Farmer*, 18 Sept. 1821; *Palmyra Herald*, 14 Nov. 1822, 24 July 1822, 30 Oct. 1822; *Wayne Sentinel*, 3 Nov. 1824, 24 July 1829. See also Dan Vogel, *Indian Origins and the Book of Mormon: Religious Solutions from Columbus to Joseph Smith* (Salt Lake City: Signature Books, 1986), 26-27.

5. *Palmyra Herald*, 30 Oct. 1822; *Wayne Sentinel*, 24 July 1829; *Western Farmer*, 18 Sept. 1821; *Palmyra Herald* 19 Feb. 1823; *Palmyra Register*, 2 June 1819; *Wayne Sentinel*, 3 Nov. 1824.

6. *Palmyra Herald*, 30 Oct. 1822.

7. Ibid., 19 Feb. 1823.

8. *Palmyra Register*, 26 May 1819.

9. *Wayne Sentinel*, 3 Nov. 1824.

10. Timothy Dwight, *Travels; in New-England and New-York*, 4 vols. (New Haven: S. Converse, Printer, 1821-22), 4:131.

11. *Wayne Sentinel*, 3 Mar. 1826. "It is exclusively an American work—descriptive of American scenery, and American aboriginal character." Cooper pictured one of the Indian villains as a deist.

12. Ibid., 24 July 1829. American identification with the vanquished Mound Builder race included other assigned traits such as white skin, agricultural civilization, and Christian religion. See Vogel, 53-69.

13. Ibid.

14. This ambivalence is traced by R. Pierce Beaver, *Church, State, and the American Indians* (St. Louis: Concordia Publishing House, 1966), 7-52. Colonial and early American justification for taking Indian lands is discussed in Vogel, 53-56.

15. Ibid., 73, 76.

16. *Western Farmer*, 4 Apr. 1821.

17. *Palmyra Herald*, 30 Oct. 1822.

18. *Palmyra Register*, 7 July 1818.

19. Ibid., 4 Oct. 1820.

20. Ibid., 25 Aug. 1818.

21. *Palmyra Herald*, 30 Oct. 1822.

22. *Western Farmer*, 4 Apr. 1821.

23. Jedidiah Morse, *The American Universal Geography*, 2 vols. (Boston, 1793), 1:75. Morris's book was on sale at Pomeroy Tucker's bookstore in Palmyra, New York. See *Wayne Sentinel*, 5 May-7 July 1824. For a discussion and other sources dealing with the pre-Adamite theory of Indian origins and its use by unbelievers, see Vogel, 35-39.

24. While the Indian-Israelite theory was one among many, it nevertheless had a significant following. See Vogel, 35-69, for a detailed discussion, and 103-44, for an extensive annotated bibliography of numerous pre-1830 sources. Lynn Glaser, *Indians or Jews? An Introduction to a Reprint of Manasseh ben Israel's The Hope of Israel* (Gilroy, CA: Roy V. Boswell, 1973), surveys the changing shape of that belief over the centuries. Robert Wauchope, "Lost Tribes and the Mormons," in *Lost Tribes & Sunken Continents: Myth and Method in the Study of American Indians* (Chicago: University of Chicago Press, 1962), 50-68, gives a broader and more scholarly survey. Robert Silverberg presents the archaeological evidence and evaluates the Indian-

Israelite theory within developing archaeological understanding from the sixteenth through the twentieth centuries in *Mound Builders of Ancient America: The Archaeology of a Myth* (Greenwich, CT: New York Graphic Society, 1968).

25. See Manasseh ben Israel's *The Hope of Israel.*

26. James Adair, *The History of the American Indians* (London, 1775), 3, 11; see Vogel, 41-42.

27. Ethan Smith's *View of the Hebrews; or the Ten Tribes of Israel in America,* 2d ed. (Poultney, VT: Smith & Shute, 1825), was only one of many.

28. Elias Boudinot, *A Star in the West; or A Humble Attempt to Discover the Long Lost Ten Tribes of Israel Preparatory to the Return to their Beloved City, Jerusalem* (Trenton, NJ: Fenton, S. Hutchinson, and J. Dunham, 1816) made the identification. Samuel Latham Mitchill spoke for an Asiatic origin in his "The Original Inhabitants of America Shown to Be of the Same Family with Those of Asia," *American Antiquarian Society Transactions,* 1 (1820).

Samuel Farmer Jarvis challenged James Adair and Elias Boudinot in "A Discourse on the Relations of the Indian Tribes of North America: Delivered Before the New-York Historical Society, December 20, 1819," in *Collections of the New York Historical Society, for the Year 1821* (New York: Bliss & White, 1821), 183. After citing Boudinot's book and judging James Adair's *The History of the American Indians* (London: Edward and Charles Dilly, 1775) of "little use," Jarvis acknowledged Boudinot's advocacy, saying that his "exalted character renders every opinion he may defend a subject of respectful attention." Boudinot, Mitchill, M. M. Noah, and Jarvis are listed as historical society members in the *Collections* (pp. 11, 17).

29. *Wayne Sentinel,* 27 Sept. 1825.

30. Ibid.

31. His 1811 book on millennialism also spoke against deism.

32. E. Smith, 70-71, 78. This distinction is found throughout the work. He cites Isaiah 49:18-22; 56:8; 63:1-6 as proof passages.

33. E. Smith, 230-31, 74-75, 81. 2 Esdras 13:40-42 reads: "Those are the ten tribes, which were carried away prisoners out of their own land in the time of Osea the king, whom Salmanesar the king of Assyria led captive, and he carried them over the waters, and so came they into another land. But they took this counsel among themselves, that they would leave the multitude of the heathen, and go forth into a further country, where never mankind dwelt. That they might there keep their statutes, which they never kept in their own land." Joseph Smith used the Book of Mormon passage in Ether 2:4: "the Lord commanded them that they should go forth into the wilderness, yea, into that quarter where there never had man been."

34. E. Smith, 198-99, 173. Vogel has pointed out that most other versions of the Mound Builder myth postulated the migration of two separate groups and that Ethan Smith was perhaps original in suggesting

that a single migratory group divided into two distinct groups. See Vogel, 98-99.

35. E. Smith, 234. In support of his notion that the restoration would be a literal one (just as the expulsion had been), he cites Isa. 14; 18; 49:18-23; 60; 65; 66:20; Jer. 16:14-15; 23:6, 8; 30:3; Deut. 30; Hos. 2-3; Zeph. 3:10.

36. E. Smith, 77.

37. Ibid., 115.

38. Ibid., 130, 131.

39. The Pittsfield Parchment story is found in E. Smith (pp. 217-25) in the 1825 edition. That year Josiah Priest, *The Wonders of Nature and Providence* (Albany, 1825), 290, began a chapter "extracted from the Rev. E. Smith's *View of the Hebrews*, with some additional remarks." In 1837 Parley P. Pratt cited parts of the story in *A Voice of Warning and Instruction to All People* (Independence, MO: Zion's Printing and Publishing Co., 1943), 79. Mormon historian B. H. Roberts pointed to the Pittsfield Parchment story as proof for the Book of Mormon in *New Witnesses for God*, 3 vols. (Salt Lake City: Deseret Book Co., 1926), 2:49-50.

40. Larned had just finished Andover and was preparing to enter Cambridge. By the time he preached in Canandaigua in 1817 and 1818, he had known the story for several years. See William Sprague, *Annals of the Congregational Pulpit*, Vol. 2, *Annals of the American Pulpit* (New York: Robert Carter & Brothers, 1869), 556-71.

41. The letter in E. Smith (p. 220) reads as follows: "Sir, I have examined the parchment manuscripts which you had the goodness to give me. After some time and with much difficulty and assistance I have ascertained their meaning, which is as follows; (I have numbered the manuscripts.) No. I is translated by Deut. vi. 4-9 inclusive. No. 2, by Deut xi. 13-21 verses inclusive. No 3, Exod. xiii, 11-16 verses inclusive. I am &c. SYLVESTER LARNED"

42. E. Smith, 223.

43. Ibid., 224. For evidence that the Pittsfield phylacteries probably came from contemporary Jews, see Lee M. Friedman, "The Phylacteries Found at Pittsfield, Mass.," *Publications of the American Jewish Historical Society*, No. 25 (1917): 81-85, and I. Herold Sharfman, *Jews on the Frontier* (Chicago: Henry Regnery Co., 1977), 210-11, in Vogel, 92n88.

44. Ibid., 229-30, 127. Boudinot in *A Star in the West* wrote in the same vein: "Who knows but God has raised up these United States in these latter days, for the very purpose of accomplishing his will in bringing his beloved people [the Israelites] to their own land" (p. 297). Boudinot (1740-1820) was an attorney active in the Revolutionary War. He served in Congress from 1777-84 and was a strong Federalist supporter of Washington. His three books before *A Star in the West* involved the deistic controversy.

45. E. Smith, 246-55.

46. Ibid., 253. Boudinot (pp. 279-80) appreciated this earlier than Ethan

Smith. He wrote: "What could possibly bring greater declarative glory to God, or tend more essentially to affect and rouse the nations of earth, with a deeper sense of the certainty of the prophetic declarations of the holy scriptures, and thus call their attention to the truth of divine revelation, than a full discovery, that, these wandering nations of Indians are the long lost tribes of Israel . . . ?"

47. E. Smith, 264.

48. Ibid., 266-67.

49. Lucy Mack Smith, *Biographical Sketches of Joseph Smith, the Prophet, and His Progenitors for Many Generations* (Liverpool: S. W. Richards, 1853), 84, 90.

50. See Fawn M. Brodie, *No Man Knows My History: The Life of Joseph Smith*, 2d ed. (New York: Alfred Knopf, 1971), 44-49, and Vogel, for the way Indian lore is woven into the Book of Mormon. David Marks, *The Life of David Marks to the 26th Year of His Age* (Limerick, ME: Office of the Morning Star, 1831), demonstrated that the impression created by the Book of Mormon on those who had heard it seemed to offer insights into Indian antiquities. "When I was in Ohio, I had quite a curiosity to know the origin of the numerous mounds and remains of ancient fortifications that abound in that section of the country; but could not find that any thing satisfactory was known on the subject. Having been told, that the '*Book of Mormon*' gave a history of them, and of their authors, some desire was created in my mind to see the book, that I might learn the above particulars" (p. 341). See David Marks, *The Life of David Marks to the 26th Year of His Age* (Limerick, ME: Office of the Morning Star, 1831), chap. 1, n12, who thought that the Book of Mormon might offer insight into Indian mounds and fortifications.

6.

Ezekiel's Two Books

Say, our Savior came through the tribe of Judah, and the Jews kept the record of the bible . . . and then, that the Redeemer shall come the second time, in the tribe of Joseph; and they have also written and kept a record, called the Book of Mormon, . . . and who can mistake what Ezekiel meant by the Two Sticks? They are the Lord's reading sticks (or records) for the benefit of Israel.

—W. W. Phelps,[1] an early Mormon apologist

The advice to "Go west, young man," guided America long before Horace Greeley. Immediately after the Revolutionary War, west meant to New Englanders the stretch of terrain from New York to Niagara Falls. Out there the Indians were fighting the ever-encroaching whites. Out there the boundaries of a surging nation claimed still more land. Out there, beyond the Falls, was Cincinnati and St. Louis—gateway to the new frontier. By the late 1820s the westernmost boundary had moved 250 miles from St. Louis to what is now the Kansas-Missouri border. Beyond that lay Indian territory.

Government policy toward Indians tended more and more toward removal. One church official advised their displacement beyond the Mississippi River where the whites would leave them alone, and vice versa.[2] Treaties made with the red men would not be kept. Tribes from the south and north over the years were forced out of the settled eastern regions—themselves to settle and displace other Indians.

In Palmyra this process was carefully watched. People read of Indian uprisings in the south due to government disregard of treaty obligations. Seminoles, Creeks, and Cherokees left their lands. Senecas sold over 80,000 acres near Buffalo to begin their retreat to a better place.[3] Many missionaries saw the retreat as a pilgrimage. Since whites could not be trusted, it was said, Indians would be better off beyond the reach of the United States.[4] Whatever part of the east they came from, the Indians were going to the center of the continent. Such a gathering had millennial overtones.

Another kind of gathering took place in the west in 1825. Mordecai Manuel Noah, self-appointed guardian of the Jews, founded a City of Refuge for oppressed Jews around the world. Situated on Grand Island in the Niagara River, the City of Ararat was dedicated in September 1825 as the reestablishment of the Jewish people as a nation. Laws were proclaimed, relations with the U.S. government were set up, and Noah's arms were opened to oppressed Jews everywhere.[5] A long story of the event was printed in the *Wayne Sentinel* accompanied by the claim that Indians and Jews were all descendants of Abraham. Ararat was to be temporary. The Jews would stay there until they could return to Palestine.

According to the Palmyra press, the Jewish influx had already begun. They came from the oppressive European governments which denied Jewish rights. Christian missionaries opened missions in Jerusalem.[6] The millennial picture was coming into focus, and the lens through which many saw it was Ezekiel 37.

Ezekiel 37 foretold the restoration of Jews to their land after their captivity in Babylon. It viewed them as a nation dead and gone which would take flesh and live again (vv. 1-10), much as bones in a grave stepping forth to new life (vv. 11-14). Ezekiel pictured it still another way: "The word of the LORD came again unto me, saying, Moreover, thou son of man, take thee one stick, and write upon it, for Judah, and for the children of Israel his companions; then take another stick and write upon it, For Joseph, the stick of Ephraim, and for all the house of Israel his companions. And join them one to another into one stick; and they shall become one in thine hand" (vv. 15-17). Then Ezekiel was to tell the people that they would return to Jerusalem and be reunited with the tribes of Israel, just as he held the two sticks united as one in his hand.

Elias Boudinot earlier had found the restoration theme of

Ezekiel 37 useful in exploring the connections between Indians and Israelites, and Ethan Smith used the passage to full advantage.[7] He quoted 37:11-14 as something to be fulfilled in the Millennium and not simply through the conversion of the Jews. "Lest any should say," he wrote, that "the prediction which here seems to foretell the restoration of the ten tribes, as well as that of the Jews, were accomplished in the restoration of that few of the Israelites, who clave to the Jews under the house of David, and the ten tribes are irrevocably lost; it is here expressed that the Jews and those Israelites, their companions, were symbolized by one stick; and Ephraim, all the house of Israel (the whole ten tribes,) by the other stick."[8]

Smith pointed to the continued existence of the Jews as an argument for a literal restoration. If the preservation of the Jews was literally intended by God—as their present existence evidenced—then Israel would be literally restored to one land, receive a new heart and spirit, and "the stick of Ephraim is to become one in the hand of the prophet, with the stick of the Jews." Smith further observed: "America was the land of Israel's outcast state. It was Israel's huge valley of dry bones . . . literal wilderness of thousands of miles, where the dry bones of the outcasts of Israel have for thousands of years been scattered . . . the most essential *pile* of the prophet Ezekiel's valley of dry bones." Israel's outcast condition presented a "volume of new evidence of the divinity of the Old Testament" and therein lay the importance of America as the valley of the dry bones.[9]

The restoration symbolized by Ezekiel's joining of the two sticks in his hand, Smith cautioned, had received neither a partial nor a complete fulfillment. None of the tribes, whose names were "written on the second stick, in the hand of the prophet, have ever yet been recovered. The whole passage is intimately connected with the battle of that great day, which introduces the Millennium."[10]

Finally, Smith related the "way-preparer" of Isaiah 40 to Ezekiel 37. John the Baptist may have fulfilled the former passage in its most immediate sense, but if the American Indians were the lost tribes of Israel, then its fullest completion would come in connection with the Millennium. "The voice, which restores Israel, is heard in the *vast wilderness of America*," and "is to have a kind of literal fulfillment upon a much greater scale, in the missions, which shall recover the ten tribes."[11]

Ethan Smith's literalistic application of Old Testament prophecies of restoration for Judah and Israel depended on the notion that Israel was not yet restored. The Book of Mormon presents the same view of the Indians: they were to be restored in fulfillment of God's promise to Israel. But the Book of Mormon contributes an important innovation. The Indians are presented as members of only one Israelite tribe—that of Joseph as represented through the half-tribes of his sons Ephraim and Manasseh.[12] Joseph Smith based this identification of the Indians as members of the tribe of Joseph on Ezekiel 37:16-17 and on Ethan Smith's use of the passage, although he never literally quoted it.

Another innovation by Joseph Smith in the use made of this passage came in his interpretation of the "sticks" of 37:16 as "books" or "records" of the tribes of Joseph and Judah.[13] The Book of Mormon makes clear the existence of two parallel records from the two tribes. In the vision of 1 Nephi 13, for example, Nephi saw the Gentiles who would come to America and scatter his descendants. The Gentiles had a book which was the record of the Jews, the Bible, but many of the important parts of that book had been omitted by the great and abominable church which was among the Gentiles. The Europeans brought the truncated Bible to America and to the Indians. Later on, an additional record would come to them: "And they must come according to the words which shall be established by the mouth of the Lamb; and the words of the Lamb shall be made known in the records of thy seed, as well as in the records of the twelve apostles of the Lamb; wherefore they both shall be established in one; for there is one God and one Shepherd over all the earth" (1 Ne. 13:41). In other words, the Nephites would be given a separate record through which Christ would make known his words. It would parallel and equal the record of the Jews, and would also restore many missing portions of the Bible.

The second record would be the record of the descendants of the biblical Joseph. The Book of Mormon includes Lehi's death-bed blessing to his last-born son Joseph, which makes this clear and foretells important details about the production of that record in the last days. According to the Book of Mormon, Joseph in the Bible was told by God that one of his descendants would minister to the rest of humankind. He would be another Moses. "But a seer will I raise up out of the fruit of thy loins; and unto him will I give power to bring forth my word unto the seed of thy loins—and not to the bringing forth of my word only, saith the Lord, but to the convincing them of my words, which shall have already gone forth among them. Where-fore, the fruit of thy loins shall write; and the fruit of the loins of Judah shall write; and that which shall be written by the fruit of thy loins, and also that which shall be written by the fruit of the loins of Judah, shall grow together, unto the confounding of false doctrines and laying down of contentions, and establishing peace among the fruit of thy loins" (2 Ne. 3:11-12). Like the biblical Joseph, the seer would be named Joseph, as would his father. Like Moses, he would receive the writing of God and have a spokesman. The writing to come from biblical Joseph's descendant would refute false doctrine, settle disputes, and establish peace among Joseph's posterity.

In 2 Nephi 29 God assures Lehi's son Nephi that God would remember their posterity "and that the words of your seed should proceed out of my mouth unto your seed" (the words of the Nephites would go to the Lamanites-Indians): "Thou fool, that shall say: A Bible, we have got a Bible, and we need no more Bible. Have ye obtained a Bible save it were by the Jews? Know ye not that there are more nations than one? Know ye not that I . . . bring forth my word unto the children of men, yea, even upon all the nations of the earth? Wherefore murmur ye, because . . . that I remember one nation like unto another? Wherefore, I speak the same words unto one nation like unto another. And when the two nations shall run together the testimony of the two nations shall run together also" (vv. 3-8). God was again affirming to Nephi that the Bible does not contain all the words of the Lord; more would come. Every nation shall have its own book out of which it would be judged.

In the Book of Mormon then Ezekiel 37 is implicitly called up to indicate that the Bible was to come from the Jews, the tribe of Judah. The Old and New Testaments were to be viewed as one book. The Nephites would be given a separate record through which Christ's words would be made known. It would equal and parallel the biblical record of the apostles and prophets. The Bible would be given to the Gentiles, and then the abominable church would remove some sections. After that, the Gentiles would bring the deficient book to the Indians.

A latter-day Joseph from the tribe of Joseph would write the Lord's words to give to the Indians. This writing, the Book of Mormon, would convince the Indians of the Bible's authenticity and would be used with the Bible together as one unit. Two nations then would become one, and their respective records one record. Their united testimony would make more of an impact than the testimony of only one people and of only one record. Every nation would have its own God-given record or scripture. All the tribes of Israel would produce scriptures. At the time of Israel's restoration all the different scriptures, including the records of the Jews and the tribe of Joseph, would be joined together into one great scripture.

Joseph Smith's implicit use of Ezekiel 37 had apologetic value in his defense of God. He gained the benefit of proof for God's existence, as he saw it, for there were two records in different parts of the world testifying to God's being and activity. God's justice and impartiality were upheld by making provision for each nation and tribe to have its own God-given record. God's unchanging way of dealing with humanity was maintained by having the different records contain the same essential message (2 Ne. 29:8). Ongoing revelation was asserted. By calling fools all who fought to uphold the Bible as the only written revelation, the idea of a closed biblical canon was denied.

The Book of Mormon may not have literally quoted Ezekiel 37:16-17, but early Mormons did.[14] Joseph Smith himself made explicit use of the passage in a revelation which was amended after 1833 and before 1835. Jesus spoke to Smith about his mission "to reveal the Book of Mormon, containing the fulness of my everlasting gospel, to whom I have committed the keys of the record of the stick of Ephraim" (D&C 27:5).[15] Smith's interest in the restoration of the Indians continued after the publication of the Book of Mormon.[16] Often discoveries or theories which might suggest that Smith's interpretation of "stick" as "book" or "record" corresponded with Indian tradition were printed in Mormon periodicals.[17] In his preaching Smith interwove this interpretation of Ezekiel 37 with his equally distinctive interpretation of another biblical passage—Isaiah 29. Ezekiel 37 had established the Book of Mormon as equal to the Bible. Isaiah 29, as Joseph Smith viewed it, predicted important events related to the discovery and translation of the book. Both confirmed God's preparation for the coming forth of the new record.

NOTES

1. *The Evening and the Morning Star*, Nov. 1832.

2. R. Pierce Beaver, *Church, State, and the American Indians* (St. Louis:

Concordia Publishing House, 1966), 95; see chap. 3, "The Missions and Indian Removal," 85-122.

3. *Wayne Sentinel*, 14 Feb., 17 Mar., 9, 23 June 1826; 8 Feb., 15 Aug. 1828; 6 Apr., 19 July, 16 Aug. 1825; 2 Feb. 1827; 8 Sept. 1826.

4. Beaver, chap. 3.

5. *Wayne Sentinel*, 27 Sept., 4, 11 Oct. 1825. See Abram Leon Sacher, *A History of the Jews*, 4th ed., rev. & enlarged (New York: Alfred Knopf, 1953), 396, for a description of the dedication ceremony; and *Wayne Sentinel*, 15 Nov. 1825.

6. Letters from Levi Parsons and Pliny Fisk, Presbyterian missionaries to Jerusalem, were often featured: *Palmyra Register*, 9 Dec. 1818; 11 Oct. 1820; *Western Farmer*, 20 June, 1 Aug. 1821; 31 Feb. 1822; *Palmyra Herald*, 17 July 1822; *Wayne Sentinel*, 24 Dec. 1823. Articles appeared on modern Jerusalem (*Western Farmer*, 20 June 1820) and the Holy Land (1 Aug. 1821).

7. Elias Boudinot, *A Star in the West* (Trenton, NJ: D. Fenton, S. Hutchinson, J. Dunham, 1816), 46, comments on Ezekiel 37:16: "It appears by this chapter, that there are some few of the Israelites still with Judah; but all are again to become one people at a future day. It also appears that the body of the house of Israel are remote from Judah, and are to be brought from distant countries to Jerusalem, when they are to become one nation."

8. Ethan Smith, *View of the Hebrews* (Poultney, VT: Smith & Shute, 1825), 53.

9. Ibid., 247, 79, 257, 266.

10. Ibid., 54.

11. Ibid., 257. The Shakers had identified Ann Lee as the voice in the wilderness. Mormons were to see Joseph Smith as the voice. Parley Pratt wrote that he was "the Elias, the Restorer, the presiding Messenger, holding the keys of the 'Dispensation of the fulness of time.'" *Key to the Science of Theology* (Liverpool, 1855), 77.

12. Lehi, patriarch of the Book of Mormon, came from a family of the tribe of Joseph which escaped the dispersion of the ten tribes in 721 B.C. by fleeing to Egypt. Lehi returned to Jerusalem, only to flee again with his family as the Babylonian invasion was imminent. Lehi was of the half-tribe Manasseh. Ishmael, who went with Lehi, was later said to be of the tribe of Ephraim. Still another fugitive, Zoram, was of unknown tribal origin.

By marrying Ishmael's daughters, Laman and Nephi provided America with a branch of the tribe of biblical Joseph. The restoration of the ten tribes of Israel will take place in Jerusalem, but the restoration of the tribe of Joseph—including those of Ephraim and Manasseh and the Book of Mormon tribes of Laman and Nephi—will happen on the American continent.

13. The best explication of this view is that of Hugh Nibley, "The Stick of Judah," *Improvement Era* 56 (Jan.-June, 1953), a somewhat technical treatment of the anthropological evidence of the use of writing sticks in

several cultures. A simplified version of the series is found in *An Approach to the Book of Mormon* (Salt Lake City: Deseret New Press, 1964), 257-72. Hundreds of years of French missionary influence, however, were not considered for the Indians of the northeastern region of the North American continent, nor Spanish and Portuguese missionary influence for the South American continent.

14. See Joseph Smith et al., *History of the Church of Jesus Christ of Latter-day Saints*, 7 vols. (Salt Lake City: Deseret Book Co., 1927), 1:84; 2:41, 390; 3:53; *New-Hampshire Gazette* (Portsmouth, NH), 25 Oct. 1831; *The Evening and the Morning Star*, June 1832, 6. These are representative; there are many more.

15. Other allusions are found in D&C 33:16; 35:17; 128:19-20.

16. Mormon publisher Phelps started a tradition which was continued in early Mormon newspapers. In *The Evening and the Morning Star*, Dec. 1832, he reported that 400 Shawnees "passed this place for their inheritance a few miles west, and the scene was at once calculated to refer the mind to the prophecies concerning the gathering of Israel in the last days." From his vantage point in Independence, Missouri, Phelps rejoiced "that the great purpose of the Lord are fulfilling before eyes." Routine reports of Indian movements were occasions to consider the fulfillment of prophecy.

17. "Israel Will Be Gathered," *The Evening and the Morning Star*, June 1833.

7.

Isaiah, Buried and Sealed

"I don't believe there's an atom of meaning in it," [said Alice.] "If there's no meaning in it," said the King, "that saves a world of trouble, you know, as we needn't try to find any."

—Lewis Carroll, *Alice in Wonderland*

Because of preoccupation with the Bible in early nineteenth-century America, Eduard Meyer argued, any new church would require a book to focus its claims and catalog its interpretations.[1] In the case of Mormonism, a generation of speculation had prepared a book which would disclose the origin of the Indians and confirm the revelatory activity of God.

Ethan Smith drew extensively from Isaiah to show that a literal restoration of Israel was predicted for the last days.[2] Joseph Smith made even greater use of Isaiah. One-tenth of the Book of Mormon comes from Isaiah, and Isaiah 29 stands out above all others in importance because the Book of Mormon interprets this portion to foretell the discovery and translation of the Book of Mormon itself. In the Book of Mormon, Isaiah 29 also gives Joseph Smith, Jr., his credentials as translator of Egyptian hieroglyphics and makes him subject of biblical prophecy.

Isaiah 29:3-5 talks of being brought low to the dust. The traditional interpretation has these verses refer to Jerusalem's destruction. But the Book of Mormon sees in this imagery the hiding in the

73

ground of the golden plates after the destruction of the Nephites. Nephi, father of the Nephites, wrote: "[A]nd now, my beloved brethren, all those who are of the house of Israel, and all ye ends of the earth, I speak unto you as the voice of one crying from the dust: Farewell until that great day shall come" (2 Ne. 33:13). Another Book of Mormon prophet, Moroni, similarly wrote: "I exhort you to remember these things; for the time speedily cometh that ye shall know that I lie not, for ye shall see me at the bar of God; and the Lord God will say unto you: Did I not declare my words unto you, which were written by this man, like as one crying from the dead, yea, even as one speaking out of the dust?" (Moro. 10:27).[3]

Entire Chapters of Isaiah in the Book of Mormon

Isaiah	*Book of Mormon*
2-14	2 Nephi 12-24
29	2 Nephi 27
48-49	1 Nephi 20-21
50-51	2 Nephi 7-8
52	3 Nephi 30
53	Mosiah 14
54	3 Nephi 22

A book buried by Hebrew forebearers and discovered in the 1820s needed translating to be of use. Isaiah 29:11-12 provided a pattern to follow. The passage depicts God denouncing the prophets and seers of Jerusalem who had closed their eyes to him. So completely did they lose their vision that they were like scholars trying to read a sealed book: "And the vision of all is become unto you as the words of a book that is sealed, which men deliver to one that is learned, saying, Read this, I pray thee: and he saith, I cannot; for it is sealed: And the book is delivered to him that is not learned, saying, Read this, I pray thee: and he saith, I am not learned."

For early Mormons, these verses foretold a literal historical event—Martin Harris's visit to Professor Charles Anthon of Columbia University to examine Book of Mormon hieroglyphics. In December 1827, according to Joseph Smith, Harris gave him fifty dollars to move from Manchester, New York, to Susquehanna County, Pennsylvania. Once there Smith copied a number of characters from the golden plates, translated them, and sent the sample

Isaiah 29 in the emended, or corrected, manuscript of Oliver Cowdery's printer's copy of the Book of Mormon. (Reproduced by permission of the Reorganized Church of Jesus Christ of Latter Day Saints, Independence, Missouri.

transcript with Harris to Anthon for scholarly evaluation.

When Harris returned he supposedly told this story: "I went to the city of New York, and presented the characters which had been translated, with the translation thereof to Professor Anthony, a gentleman celebrated for his literary attainments:—Professor Anthony stated that the translation was correct, more so than any he had before seen translated from Egyptian. I then showed him those which were not yet translated, and he said they were Egyptian, Chaldeac, Assyriac, and Arabac; and he said they were true characters. He gave me a certificate, certifying to the people of Palmyra that they were true characters, and that the translation of such of them as had been translated was also correct. I took the certificate and put it into my pocket, and was just leaving the house, when Mr. Anthony called me back, and asked me how the young man found out that there were gold plates in the place where he found them. I answered that an angel of God had revealed it unto him. He then said to me, 'let me see that certificate.' I accordingly took it out of my pocket and gave it to him, when he took it and tore it to pieces, saying that there was no such thing now as ministering of angels, and that if I would bring the plates to him he would translate them. I informed him that part of the plates were sealed, and that I was forbidden to bring them. He replied, 'I cannot read a sealed book.' I left him and went to Dr. Mitchell, who sanctioned what Professor Anthony had said respecting both the characters and the translation."[4]

Since Mormon theology, not to mention Book of Mormon prophecy, rests to some degree on this account of biblical interpretation, it may be worth examining it more closely. The official account asserts that Harris first visited Anthon and then consulted a "Dr. Mitchill." This is a minor point, but more initially set off to consult Mitchill rather than Anthon.[5] Samuel Latham Mitchill would have been a name known to Harris for his service in state and national legislatures from 1791 through 1813. Dating from his appointment in 1798 as a commissioner to purchase land in western New York from the Six (Indian) Nations, he was known as an authority on native Americans. He was also considered learned in science, history, higher education, medicine, and land development.[6] Mitchill's name appeared without explanation in Palmyra's newspapers at least fifteen times between 1821 and 1826.

In contrast, Charles Anthon was known primarily in New York City. He was admitted to Columbia College when just a boy and

Samuel L. Mitchill (from E. Watson, *History of the Western Canals*, p. 172; courtesy New York State Library).

recognized as a genius by the age of fourteen. The state supreme court accepted him to the bar when he was twenty-two. A year later in 1820 he became adjunct professor of Greek and Latin at Columbia College. He was also proficient in French and German. Although he was well known in educated circles for his edition of Lempriere's *A Classical Dictionary*, in 1828 his fame lay primarily in the future.[7]

In addition to Mitchill and Anthon, Harris apparently consulted Luther Bradish as well. Bradish went abroad as a special trade emissary of U.S. Secretary of State John Quincy Adams in 1820. He visited in countries bordering the Mediterranean, traveling in Turkey, Egypt, Syria, Tunisia, and Europe where he studied the "language, manners, and antiquities" of those nations. In 1827 he was elected to the state assembly as a Whig.[8] Joseph Smith, Sr., Pomeroy Tucker, and John Gilbert said that Harris consulted Bradish en route to New York City.[9] W. W. Phelps indirectly supported that claim.[10] Bradish was known in the Palmyra area because he had relatives there.[11] Harris probably tried to see him in his home in Utica, a stopping place on the Erie Canal, but went on to Albany when he found him absent.

The various accounts about what actually happened when Harris reached New York City differ as to important details of the consultation, but almost all of these—including the Book of Mormon account in 2 Nephi 27—contradict Joseph Smith's official version of events. One focus of dispute concerns whether or not Anthon (or others) was able to identify the language or characters which Harris had with him. Smith's recital has Anthon and Mitchill say that the transcript characters were "true characters" from Egyptian, Chaldaic, Assyriac, and Arabic. This assertion would confirm the Book of Mormon's own claims that the ancient Nephites used "reformed Egyptian," an altered form of Hebrew. Hebrew writing had been changed by the ancient Nephites so that "none other people knoweth our language" (Morm. 9:32-34).

Certain sources affirm that some characters were identifiable. An Episcopal minister, John Clark, saw one letter which may have been Hebrew, but he otherwise was ignorant "of the characters in which this pretended ancient record was written."[12] In 1834 Anthon spoke of Greek, Roman, and Hebrew letters, but by 1841 he concluded that "the marks in the paper appeared to be merely an imitation of various alphabetical characters." Joseph Smith, Sr., reported Anthon as saying that "with few exceptions, the characters

THE LATE CHARLES ANTHON, LL.D., OF COLUMBIA COLLEGE.—[PHOTOGRAPHED BY BRADY.]

Charles Anthon (engraved from a photograph by Matthew Brady, *Harper's Weekly* [1861]).

were Arabic," but that there was "not enough to make anything out."[13]

W. W. Phelps and David Whitmer supported Smith in saying that the scholars identified the characters as "shorthand" or "reformed" Egyptian.[14] Of course, the scholars would not have known reformed Egyptian if they saw it, since knowledge of this language had disappeared with the Nephites. They might identify an abbreviated script, except that in 1834 Anthon wrote that the characters were "anything but 'Egyptian hieroglyphics.'" In 1841 he denied that he had pronounced "the Mormonite inscription to be 'reformed Egyptian hieroglyphics.'"

Smith repudiated Anthon's statement that the characters were Greek, Roman, and Hebrew. In 1843 he wrote that "there was no Greek or Latin upon the plate from which I . . . translated the Book of Mormon."[15] Anthon and Mitchill might have compared these characters to existing alphabets,[16] but Smith excluded those which Anthon named.

During the summer of 1829 Smith told Martin Harris's brother Henry that the transcript was taken from "italic letters written in an unknown language."[17] In 1835 Cowdery wrote that Smith was denied the plates in 1823 "because they cannot be interpreted by the learning of this generation."[18] And in 1843 Smith wrote James Arlington Bennett that "I translated the Book of Mormon from hieroglyphics, the knowledge of which was lost to the world."[19] Charles Butler, an attorney in Geneva, New York, said that Harris told him Mitchill thought the characters were "of a nation now extinct which he named" but which Harris did not name.[20] But Harris also told Butler that Anthon "did not know what language they were,"[21] just as he had earlier told John Clark that Anthon "could not decide exactly what language" the characters "belonged to."[22]

If the scholars could not identify the language or the characters, they certainly could not have translated the transcript. Yet the official version has Anthon declare that Smith's sample translation of the transcript "was correct, more so than any he had seen before translated from the Egyptian." This claim cannot be supported by the sources. Ironically the Book of Mormon account of Isaiah 29:11-12 in 2 Nephi 27 does not deal with how well Anthon and Mitchill were able to translate the "sealed" transcript characters, because it was the words "which are not sealed" that were delivered

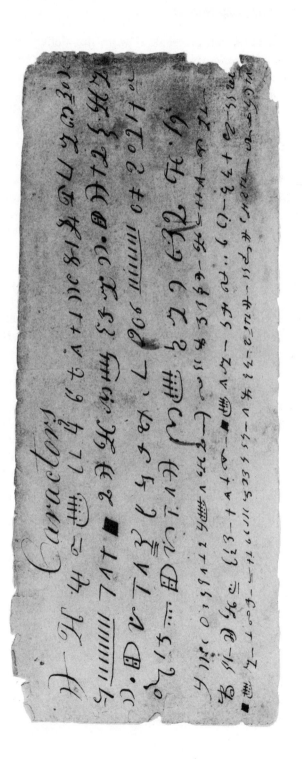

The Anthon Transcript, characters said to have been copied from the golden plates of the Book of Mormon. (Reproduced by permission of the Reorganized Church of Jesus Christ of Latter Day Saints, Independence, Missouri.)

to Anthon; the words "which are sealed" were not delivered. The "learned" (Anthon) neither confirms nor denies that he *can* read the transcript characters that Smith sent along with Harris. Instead he asks to see the "book" (golden plates) before he will *try* to read the characters. Harris (identified only as "another"; 2 Ne. 27:9, 16) told the "learned" (Anthon) that the "book" (plates) is "sealed" to all but the one who is "not learned" (Smith). The "learned" (Anthon) then responded that he "cannot read" a book he cannot see, but he is referring to the "book" (plates), not to the transcript characters.

Smith gave his clearest portrayal of the Harris-Anthon consultation in an unfinished history he began in 1832. He wrote that the Lord directed Harris to "go to New York City with some of the characters so we proceded to copy some of them and he took his Journey to the eastern City and to the learned saying read this I pray thee and the learned said I cannot but if he would bring the plates they would read it but the Lord had forbid it and he returned to me and gave them to me to translate and I said I cannot for I am not learned but the Lord had prepared spectacles for to read the Book therefore I commenced translating the characters."[23] There is no confusion here. Harris asked Anthon to translate the characters. Anthon could not decipher them and asked to see the plates. Smith could not translate the characters by his own ability but could after he donned the glasses. This account is clearer than both the Book of Mormon and official versions which have Anthon ask to see the plates and being denied. In these accounts Anthon does not say he cannot read the transcript but only asks to see the plates. In this 1832 account Smith says clearly that the scholars could not translate the characters. If they had translated the transcribed characters that would have been a problem for Harris, for only Smith had the spectacles needed to translate them.

Oliver Cowdery's 1835 history claims "the words of a book, which were sealed, were presented to the learned." "Sealed" is used to mean that the *language* was indecipherable to the learned but not to the unlearned. Orson Pratt used "sealed" in the same way when he wrote that the characters were a "sealed writing to the learned professor—the aboriginal language of Ancient America could not be deciphered by him."[24]

Other sources also rule out Anthon's ability to decipher the characters. For example, when the Smith party returned to Palmyra in June 1829 to find a printer, *Wayne Sentinel* publisher E. B. Grandin refused the contract but published the Book of Mormon title page in his paper along with his comment: "[M]uch speculation has existed, concerning . . . an ancient record, of a religious and divine nature and origin, written in ancient characters, impossible to be interpreted by any to whom the special gift has not been imparted by inspiration."[25] Similarly in August 1829 the *Palmyra Freeman* reported that Harris "took some of the characters interpreted by Smith, and went in search of some one, besides the interpreter, who was learned enough to *English* them; but all to whom he applied (among the number was Professor Mitchell, of New York,) happened not to be possessed of sufficient knowledge to give satisfaction!"[26] A week later a similar report in the *Rochester Gem* concluded that Harris "found that no one was intended to perform that all important task but Smith himself."[27]

David Whitmer, one of the Three Witnesses of the Book of Mormon, reported that when Smith opened the plates he discovered "divers and wonderful CHARACTERS; some of them large and some small, but beyond the wisdom of men to understand without supernatural aid."[28] Fifty years later Whitmer said that after Anthon and Mitchill had examined the transcript, "they pronounced the characters reformed Egyptian, but were unable to read them."[29]

In 1830 Joseph Smith, Sr., said that Luther Bradish "could not read the strange characters" and that Anthon could not "make any thing out" of the "Arabic" letters.[30] John Gilbert, Book of Mormon typesetter, wrote that "Martin returned from his trip satisfied that 'Joseph' was a 'little smarter than Professor Anthon.'"[31] In other words, Smith could read what Anthon could not. Gilbert's colleague, Pomeroy Tucker, wrote that the scholars "scouted the whole pretense as too depraved for serious attention."[32] Attorney Charles Butler reported Harris as saying that Anthon "admitted that he could not decypher them," and Mitchill gave a "learned dissertation" upon the characters but did not translate them.[33]

In 1837 Mormon apostle Parley Pratt said that Anthon examined the characters "but was unable to decipher them correctly," and in 1838 he said that Isaiah 29:11-12 was fulfilled because the "learned" (Anthon) received "the words or characters" but "could not read them."[34] In 1840 Orson Pratt echoed his brother's words of 1837,[35] and noted in 1848 that the characters were "a sealed writing to the learned professor—the aboriginal language of Ancient America could not be deciphered by him."[36] In a debate with Parson Hall in

Johnson County, Tennessee, in 1841, John D. Lee said that the Book of Mormon had been intended to appear "in a language unknown to men." The characters "were taken to Professor Anthon, of New York City, for translation. He replied that he could not translate them, that they were written in 'a sealed language, unknown to the present age.' This was just as the prophet Isaiah said it should be."[37]

Charles Anthon expressly denied that the transcript could be translated. According to his 1834 letter, "Dr. Mitchell confessed that he had been unable to understand. . . . I soon came to the conclusion that it was all a trick." Seven years later he reiterated that the characters "had, in my opinion, no meaning at all connected with them."

Support for the official version first came from W. W. Phelps in a letter dated 15 January 1831 to E. D. Howe. According to Phelps, the characters "were shown to Dr. Mitchell, and he referred to professor Anthon, who translated them and declared them to be the ancient shorthand Egyptian."[38] A few years later Joseph Knight, Sr., wrote that Martin Harris found men in Albany, Philadelphia, and New York who could translate some of the characters, although he said of Anthon and Mitchill, there were some characters "they could not well understand."[39] In 1870 Martin Harris recalled that his impression from the experts had been that "the characters were translated correctly."[40] When Anthony Metcalf interviewed him in 1873, Harris told him that Anthon "said the characters were translated correctly."[41] Nevertheless the nearly unanimous witness—from Mormon and gentile—is that the scholars could not translate the transcript.[42]

The confusion over whether or not Anthon or the other scholars could verify a translation is compounded by a contradiction over whether Harris even took a translation with him on his visits to the scholars. According to the official version, Harris took a transcription of characters along with a translation, which Anthon declared "was correct, more so than any he had before seen translated from the Egyptian." In contrast Anthon wrote in 1834 that "no translation had been furnished at the time by the young man with the spectacles."

Support for the official version came from the Pratt brothers who in 1837 and 1840 wrote that "a few of the original characters were accurately transcribed and translated by Smith, which, with the translation . . . were presented to . . . Anthon." Pomeroy Tucker wrote that Harris took the transcript "together with the translation in his possession" to New York but noted that Harris may not have given Anthon the translation.[43] Indirect support might be found in the two letters of Anthon. In the first he wrote of *copies* of the characters whereas the second has *copy*. John Clark wrote that Harris had left Anthon "with some of the manuscripts that Smith furnished him."[44] The first letter does not allow for a translation, only a transcript of characters; the second allows for a translation.

Not until 1870 did Martin Harris write anything about the sample translation: "[T]he translation that I carried to Prof. Anthon was copied from these plates."[45] Here the language is ambiguous about whether Harris refers to a translation or the characters. In 1873 Harris finally spoke clearly when he told Anthony Metcalf that Anthon "said the characters were translated correctly."[46] After Simon Smith spoke with Harris in 1875, he wrote that Harris "by command, took part of the manuscript with the translation thereof to one Professor Anthon . . . to get his opinion in regard to the language and translation."[47]

Those who knew Smith and Harris in the early years—including family members, close associates, and non-Mormons—made no mention of a translation when they spoke or wrote of the consultation with Anthon. The sample translation was not an element of the original story. One must therefore choose between the story that developed and the opposite word of Anthon, although Harris accommodated himself to the official version in 1853 and again in 1859.[48]

A final disputed detail is the certificate which Anthon supposedly wrote to the citizens of Palmyra verifying the characters and the transcript translation. The official version concerns itself primarily with this certificate, but it is mentioned nowhere else by Smith or others. In fact, Smith's 1832 account undermines the claim in insisting that Anthon could not translate the characters. If Anthon could not identify the characters or language and could not translate, then there would have been no certificate.

The official version has Anthon tear up the certificate. This serves the same purpose as having an angel remove the plates from Smith. It made comparison impossible and kept the focus on the message Smith brought rather than on the medium through which it came. But again, Anthon contradicts such a claim. According to Anthon, he gave a written opinion that the marks on the transcript were meaningless.[49]

Joseph Knight, Sr., recalled that Anthon could allegedly translate a few characters but not others. Therefore he "rote a very good piece to Joseph and said if he would send the original he would translate it."[50] It was this piece of paper which Anthon tore up according to Knight. Both Knight's and Anthon's versions are plausible, whereas Smith's version is contradicted by Smith himself.

The official version says nothing about why Harris decided to consult the scholars or whose idea the trip was. But such questions are important, both in helping to make sense of Harris's response to the "failure" of his trip and also in helping to see what was at stake in the attention Smith gave to the consultation. Harris returned eager to see the book translated and published and willing to help finance the venture. Clearly, securing such support from Harris was an important part of what had been at stake all along in this consultation of the scholars.

A number of sources suggest that Harris's concerns were both religious and pragmatic. He wanted to know if the proposed translation was from God or from Satan and whether he should advance money for printing the book. But he was also concerned about whether he would get his money back on the investment.[51] Harris first heard about the plates when his brother, Preserved Harris, spoke of them "about the first of October, 1827."[52] Soon afterwards Smith sent his mother to tell Harris that he wanted to see him. At an angel's direction, Smith looked into the glasses which were found with the plates and saw the man who was to help place the translation before the world. Harris was the man.

Harris was cautious. "If the Lord will show me that it is his work," he told Smith, "you can have all the money you want." He went home to pray about it, and then God "showed me that it was his work, and that it was designed to bring in the fulness of the gospel. . . . He showed this to me by the still small voice spoken in the soul. Then I was satisfied that it was the Lord's work, and I was under a covenant to bring it forth."[53] Thus Harris followed Smith from New York to Pennsylvania, got the transcript, returned to Palmyra, and called on Father John A. Clark of Palmyra's Episcopal Church before heading east.[54]

Clark heard that "a great flood of light was about to burst upon the world, and that the scene of divine manifestations was to be immediately around us." A golden Bible had been found "as would settle all religious controversies and speedily bring on the glorious millennium."[55] Charles Anthon later heard the same story. The contents of the gold Bible "would, as he had been assured, produce an entire change in the world and save it from ruin." It contained "very great truths, and most important revelations of a religious nature."[56]

Anthon wrote that Harris was under pressure to publish the translation and came to him "as a last precautionary step."[57] Harris had to convince himself more "clearly that there was no risk whatever in the matter, and that the work was actually what it claimed to be . . . and satisfy him[self] as to the perfect safety of the investment."[58] Harris told Pomeroy Tucker at the *Wayne Sentinel* office that the forthcoming translation would be of God but that he did not want to bear alone the publication costs. Nevertheless, Harris "sought out the 'wisdom of learned'" to see if the discovery and revelation were genuine.[59]

Martin Harris followed a well-worn route for those who had hieroglyphic writings in hand. In 1819 the *Palmyra Register* told of a rock in Dighton, Massachusetts, which had hieroglyphic inscriptions. Two copies of the characters were sent off to several universities in the United States and to the University of Edinburgh but were not deciphered until much later.[60] In 1823 the *Palmyra Register* printed the translation of a facsimile of a rock in Pompey, New York, and explained several symbols of the inscription. The article concluded that the inscription was written by a Roman Catholic in 1520 and suggested how the stone might have gotten to Pompey.[61]

"Deciphering of Hieroglyphics," which appeared in the *Wayne Sentinel* in 1827, described the work of Professor Seyffarth of Leipzig, who was translating Egyptian antiquities in Rome. Seyffarth "found the picture of a Jew in bonds, and other allusions to the state of slavery to which the Jews were reduced. He added, that he had found the old and new testaments in the Sefitic, and the Pentateuch in the Memphitic dialect; and a Mexican manuscript in hieroglyphics, from which he inferred, that the Mexicans and Egyptians had intercourse with each other from the remotest antiquity, and that they had the same system of mythology."[62]

Accounts from the period provide conflicting testimony about who first proposed the consultation. Many suggest that it was Smith's idea. His mother Lucy wrote that Harris's intense interest in the plates led her son to agree to the consultation even before he left for Pennsylvania.[63] Edward Stevenson, Smith's close friend in later years, said that it "was manifested" to Smith to send Harris east.[64] In 1875 Harris told Simon Smith that he went east "by command."[65]

More than a year before Harris went to New York City, however, Smith had been thinking about prophetic fulfillment in terms of Isaiah 29 and the golden plates. Emily M. Austin knew Joseph and Emma Smith in January 1827 at Colesville, New York, at the time the couple was married. She wrote that Smith "declared an angel . . . told him of golden plates . . . containing a history . . . which Isaiah the prophet had spoken of; a vision which should become as the words of a book that is sealed."[66]

Joseph Smith's testimony on the subject is ambiguous. 2 Nephi 27:15-18 indicates that the Lord would have commanded Smith to send Harris. When Smith began a draft of his history in 1832, however, he credited Harris with a vision in which Jesus told him to get the characters and consult the scholars.[67] According to Oliver Cowdery, the angel in Smith's 1823 vision said that the "scripture must be fulfilled before it is translated, which says that the words of a book, which were sealed, were presented to the learned."[68] Harris in this version of events pressed for the consultation, and Smith let him go in order to gain his support.[69]

An important clue as to who was controlling events might be seen in Harris's mood on his return. His enthusiasm to publish the book seems strange in view of what he had learned, that the scholars could not translate the transcript characters. In fact, Harris was even more convinced of Smith's divine commission after his visit with the eastern sages. John Clark reported that Harris was willing to "take of the spoiling of his goods . . . though it consumed all his worldly substance" to help Smith publish the book, because Harris thought it was "the work of the Lord."[70]

If Harris had gone expecting the scholars to confirm the authenticity of the transcript, if his only model had been the one often replayed in contemporary newspapers—taking a new find to scholars for explanation and clarification—then he would have returned disappointed. Luther Bradish told Harris that there was not enough "to make anything out." Anthon told him that the transcript was a "trick, perhaps a hoax," that it was "part of a scheme to cheat the farmer of his money" that "some cunning fellow had prepared the paper in question, for the purpose of imposing" upon him.[71] When Harris returned to Palmyra he told Clark that Anthon could not pinpoint the language of the characters.

But these results did not discourage Martin Harris. On the contrary, according to Clark, "Martin had now become a perfect believer. He said he had no more doubt of Smith's commission, than of the divine commission of the apostles. The very fact that Smith was an obscure and illiterate man, showed that he must be acting under divine impulses. It was in vain I endeavoured to expostulate. I was an unbeliever, and could not see afar off." Clark added, "My intimations . . . in reference to the possible imposition that was being practiced upon him . . . were indignantly repelled."[72]

Given Harris's joy at scholarly ignorance and disregard of their warnings, one can only conjecture that Harris had been prepared for such reactions. Smith must have forewarned Harris that the scholars' failure would be a sign that Smith's story was true. Harris said that he did not know that he was fulfilling Isaiah 29 until he returned from the consultation. Anthony Metcalf asked him in 1873 if he had known about the passage, and Harris replied that "Joseph Smith had shown that chapter to him after his return."[73] Smith apparently had told him—and he believed—"that Smith was to prepare the way for the conversion of the world to a new system of faith, by transcribing the characters from the plates and giving translations of the same."[74] But after the fact Harris explained the scholars' failure to translate the characters with a paradox: since the scholars failed, Smith must be right.[75]

Tending to confirm that he was prepared to interpret ignorance as proof, Harris even at the start of his eastward journey told Clark that Clark's ignorance of the characters was "new proof that Smith's account of the divine revelation made to him was entirely to be relied on."[76] Such sentiment is also behind John Gilbert's report that "Martin returned from his trip east satisfied that 'Joseph' was a "little smarter than Professor Anthon." Smith could "read" the characters which were "sealed" to the "learned." According to Pomeroy Tucker, Harris regarded "these untoward results merely as 'proving the lack of wisdom' on the part of the rejecters, and also as illustrating the truth of his favorite quotation, that 'God hath chosen the foolish things of the world to confound the wise.' This was always his self-convincing argument in reply to similar adversity in his fanatical pursuit."[77]

Smith sent Harris to Mitchill and Anthon not to get their translation but to convince Harris to go through with financing publication of the translation. Mormon writer Hugh Nibley has suggested that it was to give the leading scholars the opportunity "to speak their piece," so that no one could charge that Smith was afraid to display "his mythical manuscript to *real* scholars."[78] But Smith knew that they would not, could not—as Nibley also admits—translate the characters.

The Harris-Anthon consultation was suggested by Isaiah 29, but another source had demonstrated that evidence in hand was not necessary to promote faith. Ethan Smith's Pittsfield Parchment story told of his belief that there was an Indian parchment with Hebrew characters on it, but he never found the parchment. He believed it only on the basis of a translation and the testimony of two sets of witnesses. Thus the Harris-Anthon consultation connected the translation of the Book of Mormon and the launching of the restoration church to prophetic fulfillment. It was an initial step in the commonly accepted progression of events which millennialists believed would signal the second coming of Jesus Christ.

Smith fleshed out Isaiah 29:11-12 with his interpretation of the Harris-Anthon consultation. The biblical scenario dictated that Smith ("him that is not learned") would read what Anthon ("one that is learned") could not—namely, the transcribed characters ("the words of a book that is sealed").[79] The issue of time was important: the "sealed" book could not be translated before it was presented to the "learned." Smith had been talking about these conditions since his marriage to Emma in January 1827. In his 1832 draft Smith told of the consultation, the scholars' failure, Harris's return and request that Smith translate the characters, and his reply to Harris: "I cannot for I am not learned." Smith went on to tell of translating the characters with the aid of the glasses and then commented: "and thus the prophecy of Isaiah was fulfilled which is written in the 29 chapter concerning the book."[80] This evidence that Smith was fulfilling prophecy is strengthened by the Cowdery account three years later, where emphasis is placed on appropriate procedure: first the scholars had to see the characters and then the translating could begin.[81]

Soon after the translation work, the identity of what Charles Anthon could not read was changed in the Book of Mormon account; instead of the transcript characters he held during the consultation with Harris, the Book of Mormon account identifies the plates as that which he was not allowed to see. After that, changes in the story Joseph Smith first told in 1828 about the Anthon consultation can be seen to fall into several stages. Originally (1) Harris visited the scholars, found that they could not translate the characters, and went home. Later, possibly as early as the summer of 1829, (2) Harris visited the scholars and found they could authenticate but not translate the characters. Then, in late 1830 or early 1831, (3) Harris visited the scholars and found that they could identify and translate the characters. Finally, in 1838 the story had evolved to the point that (4) Harris visited the scholars, found that they could authenticate the characters, identify the language, and verify Smith's sample translation. Harris received Anthon's certificate to the Palmyrans and then saw Anthon tear it up. Also, the account expanded talk about reformed Egyptian characters to a discussion of the Egyptian, Chaldaic, Assyriac, and Arabic alphabets.

In 1838 Smith stayed for a time with George and Lucinda Morgan Harris.[82] Lucinda was the widow of William Morgan, whose 1826 disappearance was the immediate cause of the anti-Masonic excitement in New York. (Smith would later marry Lucinda polygamously.) William Morgan had received only the Royal Arch degree of Masonry, and in 1829 David Bernard had added the Royal Arch to his reprint of Morgan's exposé of Masonry's first three degrees, including the Royal Arch word for God, said to have been known to ancient Hebrews, lost during the Babylonian exile, and restored when the temple was rebuilt in Jerusalem. The holy word, JAH-BUH-LUN, was compounded from "three different languages, (i.e. Hebrew, Chaldaic, and Syriac.)"[83] Bernard had also added a secret alphabetical code, some letters of which correspond to characters on the Anthon Transcript.[84] Bernard's enormously popular book found its way into many Palmyra homes. By further identifying the characters as he did in 1838, Smith appealed to those with Masonic backgrounds. As the next chapter will show, he later made the appeal more openly.[85]

The story of the Anthon consultation was important in early Mormon missionary efforts. In 1834, if not earlier, Mormons used Anthon's name and authority to claim that the transcript characters were "reformed Egyptian hieroglyphics"[86] and were still doing it in New York in 1841.[87] In Brooklyn in 1836 Mormons held a meeting in which "they were to prove by the scriptures that the Book of Mormon was of divine authority." When they came to Isaiah 29, the speaker "strove to make his bearers believe that the prophet had this book in mind."[88] On a Mississippi steamer in 1842, according to

Daniel Kidder, Mormons used the consultation story in missionary work, claiming "that the prophecy of Isaiah was literally fulfilled in the origin of the book before us."[89] Today it has become one of the staples of Mormon folklore.[90]

The importance of tying biblical prophecy to contemporary events in dismissing critics cannot be overestimated. The conclusion that the Harris-Anthon consultation had no important missionary use and no "great practical value" is simply not born out by the evidence. The episode convinced Martin Harris to finance publication of the Book of Mormon. Joseph Smith used Isaiah 29:4 to show that the Book of Mormon was the lost book of the Indians, buried through the ages, and recovered by him from the side of Cumorah Hill near his home. Isaiah 29:11-12 was used to establish the book as written in a lost script which defied the efforts of the best known scholars of New York. It provided for Smith to translate the book as one foreseen by prophecy and to set the stage for the Millennium.

NOTES

1. Eduard Meyer, *Ursprung und Geschichte der Mormonen mit Exhursen über die Anfänge des Islams und des Christentums* (Halle: Max Niemyer, 1912), 28-34.

2. He cited in whole or in part chaps. 5, 7, 10, 11, 14, 18, 26, 42, 43, 48, 51, 60, 65, and 66. He regarded chapters 48-49 as predictions of the restoration in the "latter days." So did Joseph Smith, as he expressed it through Nephi in 1 Ne. 20-21.

3. Other passages also are used to make the Book of Mormon a subject of prophecy (1 Ne. 13:35), a buried book (2 Ne. 26:15, 17), and a book "out of the earth" (Morm. 8:23, 26). See 2 Ne. 26:15-18, where Isa. 29:3-5 is applied to the destruction of the Nephites, and 3 Ne. 8-9, which describes the destruction of Jerusalem.

4. *Times and Seasons*, 2 May 1842. Also in Joseph Smith et al., *History of the Church of Jesus Christ of Latter-day Saints*, 7 vols. (Salt Lake City: Deseret Book Co., 1927), 1:19-20; hereafter HC.

5. At least eight sources do not refer to names of the scholars. Some mention only Anthon. Four have the order of Mitchill, then Anthon. Anthon specifically said that Mitchill sent Harris to him.

6. "Samuel Latham Mitchill," *Dictionary of American Biography*, 13:69-71.

7. "Charles Anthon," *Dictionary of American Biography*, 1:313-14.

8. "Luther Bradish," *Dictionary of American Biography*, 2:467-68.

9. Fayette Lapham, "The Mormons," *Historical Magazine* (New Series), 7 (May 1870): 307, interviewed the prophet's father before 1831. Pomeroy

Tucker, *The Origin, Rise, and Progress of Mormonism* (New York: D. Appleton and Company, 1867), 42; Memorandum of John H. Gilbert, 8 Sept. 1892, Palmyra, New York (typescript copy, archives, Church of Jesus Christ of Latter-day Saints, Salt Lake City, Utah).

10. In his 15 Jan. 1831 letter to E. D. Howe (*Mormonism Unvailed* (Painesville, OH, 1834, 273), Phelps said that Harris took the characters to Utica, Albany, and New York City. Bradish lived at Utica and was serving in the state legislature in Albany in 1828. Two additional sources mention Philadelphia as one of the cities visited: Joseph Knight, Sr., and William R. Hine. See Dean C. Jessee, "Joseph Knight's Recollection of Early Mormon History," *Brigham Young University Studies* 17 (Autumn 1976): 34; and "W. R. Hine's Statement," *Naked Truths About Mormonism* 1 (Jan. 1888): 2. Knight's recollections were written in the 1830s. Both Knight and Hine lived in Colesville, New York, and knew Smith before publication of the Book of Mormon. Knight became a follower. Hine did not.

11. Stanley B. Kimball, "The Anthon Transcript: People, Primary Sources, and Problems," *Brigham Young University Studies* 10 (Spring 1970): 330, points out that Harris may have known about Bradish's travels, may have known Bradish himself since Bradish had relatives around Palmyra.

12. John A. Clark, *Gleanings by the Way* (Philadelphia: W. J. & J. K. Simon, 1842), 228.

13. Lapham, 307.

14. Phelps, in Howe, 273. Whitmer in an interview in the *Kansas City Daily Journal*, 5 June 1881.

15. *Times and Seasons*, 15 May 1843.

16. Kimball, 335.

17. Howe, 253.

18. *Messenger and Advocate*, Oct. 1835, 198.

19. Joseph Smith to James Arlington Bennett, Nauvoo, 13 Nov. 1843. *Reply of Joseph Smith to the Letter of J. A. B.–of A–n House* (New York and Liverpool, 1844); referred to in *Latter-day Saints' Millennial Star*, Feb. 1844, 160.

20. Leonard J. Arrington, "James Gordon Bennett's 1831 Report on 'The Mormonites,'" *Brigham Young University Studies* 10 (Spring 1970): 362. Arrington published the article referring to Butler along with the notes which Bennett took and used to write the article (p. 355). The notes were dated 7-8 Aug. 1831.

21. Ibid., 352.

22. Clark, 229.

23. This unfinished history first came to public view in Paul R. Cheesman, "An Analysis of the Accounts Relating to Joseph Smith's Early Vision," M.A. thesis, Brigham Young University, 1965. Dean C. Jessee then published portions of it in "The Early Accounts of Joseph Smith's First

Vision," *Brigham Young University Studies* 9 (Spring 1969): 275-94.

24. Orson Pratt, "Divine Authority, or the Question, Was Joseph Smith sent of God?" *Doctrines of the Gospel* (Salt Lake City: Juvenile Instructor Office, 1884), 9. This is a reprint of *A Series of Pamphlets* published from 1848-51 with some portions deleted.

25. *Wayne Sentinel*, 26 June 1829.

26. *Rochester Advertiser and Telegraph*, 31 Aug. 1829.

27. *Rochester Gem*, 5 Sept. 1829. The similarity of wording suggests that the editor of the *Gem* took his account from the *Advertiser*, published a few days earlier, or from the *Freeman* itself.

28. *Palmyra Reflector*, 19 Mar. 1831.

29. *Kansas City Daily Journal*, 5 June 1881.

30. Lapham, 307.

31. Gilbert, 4.

32. Tucker, 42.

33. Arrington, 362.

34. Parley P. Pratt, *A Voice of Warning and Instruction to All People* (Salt Lake City: Deseret News Steam Printing Establishment, 1874), 72; *Writings of Parley Parker Pratt* (Salt Lake City, 1952), 205-206.

35. Orson Pratt, *An Interesting Account of Several Remarkable Visions and of the Late Discovery of Ancient American Records* (New York City, 1841), 6-7. First published in Edinburgh in 1840.

36. "Divine Authority," 9.

37. John Doyle Lee, *Mormonism Unveiled: or the Life and Confession of the Late Mormon Bishop John D. Lee* (Omaha: F. H. Rogers, 1891), 119-120.

38. Howe, 273.

39. Jessee, "Joseph Knight's Recollection," 33.

40. Martin Harris to Mr. Emerson, Smithfield, Utah, 23 Nov. 1870; *Saints Herald* 22 (1875): 630.

41. Anthony Metcalf, *Ten Years Before the Mast* (Milad, ID, 1888), 71.

42. Mormon scholars recognize that the official version claims too much. B. H. Roberts, *New Witnesses for God*, 3 vols. (Salt Lake City: Deseret Book, 1926), 2:95-96; Hugh Nibley, "A New Look at the Pearl of Great Price: Part I. Challenge and Response," *Improvement Era* 71 (Feb. 1968): 17; and Kimball, "The Anthon Transcript," 335-36, have agreed that the scholars could not translate Egyptian at that time because the Rosetta Stone had only recently been decoded. There had not been sufficient time to learn the language. They suggest that Anthon and Mitchill may have compared the characters to various styles of writing or said that they were authentic characters but nothing more. Kimball also suggests that Harris was eager to fulfill a prophecy and that he might have mistaken "translation" for "transcription." Harris, however, said that he did not know of the prophecy until Smith showed it to him upon his return from the east.

43. Tucker, 42-45.

44. Clark, 229.

45. Martin Harris to Mr. Emerson.

46. Metcalf, 71.

47. Simon Smith to Joseph Smith III, 30 Dec. 1880. *Saints Herald*, 1 Feb. 1881, 43.

48. See David B. Dille, *Latter-day Saints' Millennial Star* 34 (20 Aug. 1853): 545-46; Joel Tiffany, "Mormonism No. II," *Tiffany's Monthly*, Aug. 1859, 163.

49. Two possible contradictions in Anthon's two letters led Mormon scholars to favor Harris's account over Anthon's. Kimball (p. 339) concluded that Anthon was an "uncritical, emotional man," not a "detached scholar," a description which better fits Martin Harris.

Nevertheless, when Howe asked Anthon for his version of the consultation, Anthon asked him "to publish this letter immediately, should you find my name mentioned again by these wretched fanatics." But in his introduction to the 1841 letter, T. W. Coit wrote that Anthon had not yet thought it "worthwhile to say anything publicly on the subject."

Second, in the 1834 letter Anthon states that he declined to give Harris an opinion in writing, while in his 1844 letter he says that Harris asked for an opinion in writing, to which he replied in writing that the marks on the paper "had in my opinion no meaning at all connected with them." *The Church Record* 1 (24 Apr. 1841): 231.

Wesley P. Walters offered a plausible explanation for the apparent contradictions. First, when Howe asked Anthon for his version of the consultation, he appeared not to have told Anthon it was for publication, since Anthon asked him "to publish this letter immediately, should you find my name mentioned again by these wretched fanatics." In his introduction to the 1841 letter, T. W. Coit wrote he had asked Anthon for a public statement. Anthon, therefore, replied that no one had previously asked for his statement in "writing," that he had not thought it "worthwhile to say anything publicly on the subject." Second, the 1834 letter restates Harris's story about the spectacles enabling the person who used them to examine the plates and fully "understand their meaning." Harris came to get Anthon's opinion "about the meaning of the paper," but Anthon refused to give a "learned opinion" about a "hoax." Harris, however, may have wanted a written statement that the characters "had in my opinion no meaning at all connected with them." Walters to Hullinger, 8 Jan. 1975. This is likely, since Harris most probably expected the scholars to fail.

50. Jessee, "Joseph Knight's Recollection," 33.

51. The sources reveal different estimates of Harris. Some saw Harris as deluded but absolutely honest in his persuasion. Others, including his wife, saw his involvement as a potentially profitable venture. Still others saw

a mixture of both motives. Clark (p. 224) reported Harris as "intent upon the pecuniary advantage . . . as upon the spiritual light" the newly discovered Nephite book "would diffuse over the world." See also Tucker, 55, and Orsamus Turner, *History of the Pioneer Settlement of Phelps and Gorham's Purchase* (Rochester: William Ailing, 1851), 215.

52. Tiffany, 167. The prophet's mother said that her husband told Harris about the plates at least a couple years before (Lucy Mack Smith, *Biographical Sketches of Joseph Smith, the Prophet, and His Progenitors for Many Generations* [Liverpool: S. W. Richards, 1853], 109).

53. Tiffany, 168. Turner (p. 215) supported Harris's story that Smith made the first contact in seeking Harris's support. Lucy Smith (pp. 113-14) said that her son asked her to arrange a meeting between him and Harris. Joseph Knight, Sr., also credits Smith with the initial impetus to contact the scholars. Compare Jessee, "Joseph Knight's Recollection," 33. It is clear that Smith wanted the meeting.

54. Clark (pp. 228-29) is the source for Harris's return to Palmyra before he left for New York City. Clark (p. 222) wrote that Harris had occasionally "attended a divine service in our church."

55. Ibid., 223-24.

56. From a letter to E. D. Howe in Howe, 170-72, cited hereafter as the 1834 letter.

57. Letter to Rev. T. W. Coit, Rector of Trinity church, New Rochelle, West Chester County, New York; in *The Church Record* 1 (24 Apr. 1841): 231-32. It appeared in Clark (pp. 233-38) and will be cited hereafter as the 1841 letter.

58. Tucker, 41-42.

59. Ibid., 55.

60. *Palmyra Register*, 2 June 1819.

61. *Palmyra Herald*, 19 Feb. 1823.

62. *Wayne Sentinel*, 1 June 1827. After their marriage on January 18, Smith and Emma stayed at the Smith home in Manchester until about December 1827. HC 1:20.

63. Lucy Smith, 109, 113-14.

64. *Reminiscences of the Prophet Joseph* (Salt Lake City, 1983), 28-29. In William E. Berrett and Alma P. Burton, *Readings in LDS History from Original Manuscripts*, 3 vols. (Salt Lake City: Deseret Book, 1953), 1:26.

65. Simon Smith to Joseph Smith III.

66. Emily M. [Colburn] Austin, *Mormonism; or Life Among the Mormons* (Madison, WI: M. J. Cantrell Book and Job Printer, 1882).

67. See Cheesman; Jessee, "Early Accounts."

68. *Messenger and Advocate*, Feb. 1835, 80. The trustworthiness of Cowdery's account on some particulars was debated by Wesley P. Walters and Richard L. Bushman in "The Question of the Palmyra Revival,"

Dialogue: A Journal of Mormon Thought 4 (Spring 1969): 59-100. Bushman criticized Walters's reliance on Cowdery's version because his evidence was "hearsay" and—because he was physically distant from Smith—"close cooperation was impossible" (pp. 85-86). Walters (p. 95) reviewed the evidence showing the frequency with which Cowdery and Smith spent time together to support Cowdery's claim to have had "authentic documents" and Smith's help.

69. Forty of the first seventy-two revelations demonstrate the following pattern. Some person or circumstance initiated—or presented—a question, challenge, or need to Smith. To respond, Smith began a dialogue with God. The impression which came to Smith's mind revealed the way to respond to the person, challenge, or need.

70. Clark, 230.

71. 1834 letter.

72. Clark, 230, 224.

73. Metcalf, 71.

74. Clark, 228.

75. Ibid., 230, and Tucker, 42, noted the paradox.

76. Clark, 230.

77. Tucker, 42.

78. Nibley, "A New Look," 17.

79. 2 Ne. 27:15-19. This account does not have Smith translate the characters, but finally he can, since he translated the plates from which the transcript was taken.

80. Cheesman, appendix D. See also Scott H. Faulring, *An American Prophet's Record: The Diaries and Journals of Joseph Smith* (Salt Lake City: Signature Books and Smith Research Associates, 1987), 7.

81. The Pratt brothers spread this thinking: the *words* of a book had to be delivered to the learned (who would be unable to read them), while the book itself was delivered to the unlearned (who would be able to read it with the aid of the glasses). That fulfilled the text. See Parley P. Pratt in *Mormonism Unveiled—Truth Vindicated* (1838). See *Writings of Parley Parker Pratt* (Salt Lake City, 1952), 205-206.

82. Ibid., 9. Smith arrived at Far West, Missouri, on 14 March 1838 and began dictating his *History* on April 27 (p. 25). He was still dictating on May 1-4 (p. 26). He did enough to cover the material of the official version in the first few days after having been with the George Harris family for over a month. The official version is found in Smith's Manuscript History, Book A-I, 9, in LDS archives.

83. David Bernard, *Light on Masonry* (Utica: William Williams, 1829), 138-39. Also reproduced in the "Report of Seceding Freemasons, or, A Summary of Freemasonry," *The Proceedings of the United States Anti-Masonic Convention, Held at Philadelphia*, September 11, 1830 (New York: Skinner

and Dewey, 1830), 45-46. See "The Royal Arch Key" illustration (p. 109) since Bernard's book and the "Report" appeared during the years that Smith was dictating and publishing the Book of Mormon, and Bernard's book was widely available. Smith may have seen it before his stay with the Harris family at Far West.

It is an interesting sidelight that the ritual as Bernard knew it mentioned only three languages. Although the official version mentions four, as does modern Masonic ritual, it appears that this was one of the variations to be found in Masonry in the 1820s and 1830s. Martin Harris mentioned only three languages in his interview with David B. Dille in 1853, although he later spoke of four. For a modern ritual with the context of the four languages in the Mystical Lecture of the First Chair of the Royal Arch and its modern spelling of the Sacred Names as JAH-BUL-ON, see Walton Hannah, *Darkness Visible: A Revelation & Interpretation of Freemasonry* (London Augustine Press, 1952), 181.

84. Bernard, 138-39; "Report of Seceding Freemasons," 45. See "The Royal Arch Key" illustration, 109.

85. Reed C. Durham, Jr., "Is There No Help for the Widow's Son," Presidential Address for the Mormon History Association, 20 Apr. 1974, Nauvoo, Illinois. In *Mormon Miscellaneous* 1 (Oct. 1975): 11-16. Durham finds many parallels between the developing Mormonism of the late 1830s and 1840s.

86. Howe, 273.

87. Coit, *The Church Record*, 231.

88. James McChesney, *An Antidote to Mormonism* (New York, 1838), 21.

89. Daniel P. Kidder, *Mormonism and the Mormons: A Historical View of the Rise and Progress of the Sect Self-Styled Latter Day Saints* (New York: G. Lane and P. P. Sanford, 1842), 305.

90. It is a faith-promoting story taught to children, similar to the story of the pilgrims in teaching patriotism to American children. See Austin and Alta Fife, *Saints of Sage and Saddle: Folklore Among the Mormons* (Bloomington, IN: Indiana University Press, 1956), 38-39.

8.

Masonic Ritual and Lore

In answer to our question, as to what it was that Joseph had
thus obtained, he said it consisted of a set of gold plates
about six inches wide, and nine or ten inches long. They were
in the form of a book. . . . On the next page were repre-
sentations of all the masonic implements, as used by masons
at the present day.

—Fayette Lapham,[1] citizen of Wisconsin

As the third decade of the nineteenth-century began, an anti-
Masonic movement had surfaced among some eastern churches.
In 1820 Baptists at Hamilton College in Clinton, New York, had
mounted a resistance to Freemasonry.[2] The Presbyterian Pitts-
burgh Synod had declared in early 1821 the Masonic Lodge
unfit for Christians, and the same year the General Methodist
Conference forbade its Pennsylvania clergy to be Masons.[3] Nevertheless, Freemasons were solidly part of the American establishment. Earlier fears that Freemasonry was connected to deism
and Jacobism had largely been assuaged.[4] Significant numbers
of the order were church members, and many Protestant clergy
served as chaplains of local lodges. Hence a Masonic sermon at
the close of the 1810s could demonstrate the same regard for
the Bible as a pietistic Christian sermon might: "Take from
Masonry the validity of the Bible . . . and total darkness will
ensue. If the unhallowed feet of the deist, presumes to step

upon the pavement, spurn him from thence. No DEIST OR STUPID LIBERTINE CAN BE A MASON."[5]

In 1825 the Masonic Lodge of New York had a membership of 20,000 in 480 lodges, and there were additional irregularly organized or not yet recognized lodges.[6] In the United States Masons represented nearly one-ninth of American voters. Nearly half of the lodges were in New York.[7] That is why the nation could hardly have anticipated the explosion of rage which followed William Morgan's abduction and disappearance just after he had published an exposé of Masonry. New York governor De Witt Clinton, himself a high-ranking Mason, offered a reward for information leading to the arrest and conviction of the kidnappers and for information about the whereabouts of Morgan.[8] Clinton's abhorrence of the affair was widely shared by Masons, who joined non-Masons in community meetings to draw up resolutions urging that justice be done.[9]

The kidnappers were tried in Canandaigua,[10] but the public was convinced that their sentences were too light and that others had been involved. The press covered the trial, and every paper carried an increasing number of stories about the Masonic controversy.[11] Public interest was so intense, however, that forty-six anti-Masonic papers sprang up in New York, and seventy others appeared in Pennsylvania, Ohio, Massachusetts, and a few other states.[12] By 1829 anti-Masonic papers were in Lyons, Canandaigua, Waterloo, Troy, and Seneca Falls. In 1828 the anti-Masonic *Palmyra Freeman* came on the scene.[13]

Anti-Masonic conventions convened already in 1826, and twenty such conventions were held in New York in 1827. Half of them were in West Bloomfield, Bloomfield, Manchester, Farmington, Seneca, Vienna, and Victor (all hosting one), and Canandaigua (hosting three).[14] Manchester and Farmington were close to the Joseph Smith, Sr., home. In October an anti-Masonic convention appointed Martin Harris to the Palmyra "committee of vigilance,"[15] and the Wayne County convention resolved not to elect to public office any Mason or one who did not treat seriously Morgan's abduction.[16] A distinct feature at the conventions was the enactment and parody of Masonic ritual by ex-Masons for the sake of lampooning Masonic "secrets."[17]

Lodges in western New York condemned the abduction, and chapters in Canandaigua and Pultneyville disavowed it publicly.[18] Soon after, Palmyra Lodge No. 112 published its repudiation.[19]

Manchester Lodge No. 169 with over 100 members dissolved in December 1828, the same month when all lodges in Monroe County disbanded.[20] Lodges in Richmond and Naples, Ontario County, followed suit by March 1829.[21] From 1827 to 1834 the number of lodges reporting to the Grand Lodge of the state of New York had diminished to between ninety and fifty lodges.[22]

Church bodies and individual congregations divided over the Masonic question. Baptist churches convened at Milton, New York, 27 September 1827 and adopted a fifteen-point condemnation of the Freemasons.[23] In January 1828 the Baptist Society Convention at Le Roy, New York, resolved to ask all members who were Freemasons to leave the lodge or face eventual excommunication.[24] In June the Genessee Consocation resolved: "That the Consocation will neither license, ordain, or install those who sustain any connexion with the institution of Masonry, or who will not disapprove and renounce it; nor will we give letters of recommendation in favor of such persons to preach in any of the churches in our connexion."[25] Baptists around Palmyra were at war with each other.[26] Revivalists who had united in camp meetings were divided over the lodge. Methodist Lorenzo Dow and Presbyterian Charles Finney were on opposite sides, while others, including Free-will Baptist David Marks, were perplexedly undecided.

The first edition of Morgan's exposé appeared in 1826 from Batavia, and in 1827 English editions were printed in New York City, Rochester, and York, Canada. A French edition was published in Boston in 1827 and a German edition in Waterloo, New York (twenty-five miles from Palmyra), in 1828. The *Rochester Daily Advertiser* said of the Canadian run on Morgan's book: "McKenzie at York, published an edition, with a sort of historical preface, and sold a couple hundred copies the first day. M. McFarlane, of the Kingston Chronicle, had still greater success, having disposed of 1733 in four days."[27]

Appeals for Morgan's family were published far and wide. A letter published in Batavia several weeks after Morgan disappeared reappeared in a number of papers and expressed the typical sentiment: "His distressed wife and two infant children, are left dependent on charity for their sustenance. . . . All persons who are willing to serve the cause of humanity, and assist to remove the distressing apprehensions of his unfortunate wife are earnestly requested to communicate to one of the committee."[28] McFarlane at the *Kingston*

Chronicle intended to donate the proceeds from his printing to Mrs. Morgan.[29] The same concern surfaced in the Book of Mormon: "Yea, why do you build up your secret combinations to get gain, and cause that widows should mourn before the Lord, and also the book of their fathers and their husbands to cry unto the Lord from the ground, for vengeance upon your heads?" (Morm. 8:40)

The charge of "secret combinations" had been hurled at the Masonic Lodge for years. In fact, there were several points developed against the Masons and repeated over and over in the anti-Masonic conventions, town assemblies, books, and newspapers, most of which appeared in the Book of Mormon. (1) The Masonic Lodge was one of those combinations which George Washington had warned the country about in his presidential farewell address.[30] (2) The Masons were a secret society, but to what end now that their secret rituals were known?[31] (3) Masonic oaths were blasphemous in themselves but also pledged Masons to carry out institutionally authorized murder.[32] (4) Masons had taken over the judicial system, which meant that a Masonic judge could not be counted on to mete out justice to any Mason who was guilty or party to a case.[33] (5) Masons claimed the right to judge and punish their members by their own laws.[34] (6) Freemasons had usurped power, controlled the government, and proposed to destroy it.[35]

All the fearful aspects of the Infidel International were revived in Masonry, and Morgan's fate could have been anyone's. The image of the Masonic Lodge as a deistic, subversive, and terroristic society with dark ritual came once again clearly into focus. The Jacobins were back and they were wearing lambskin aprons.

But Joseph Smith revealed that all this had happened before. A secret society had subverted the early Jaredite civilization, and the Gadianton band brought the later Nephite and Lamanite societies to ultimate ruin. Sworn to secrecy by oaths, known to each other by signs, loyal to each other even though guilty of heinous crimes, in control of the judiciary and making their own laws, the early secret societies destroyed good government and true religion.[36] Their secrets were so seductive that people easily could be tempted to want them for themselves. Neither their secrets nor charitable works should be known among good people, but the consequences of their influence should be broadcast as a warning not to get involved.[37] As an example that this devil-led[38] activity could not be assumed to be dead simply because it was ancient, it was foretold that when the

Justice Albert Neely's bill establishes Joseph Smith's involvement with money digging and his 1826 court appearance. The third item above reads:

same [i.e., The People]
    vs
Joseph Smith   Misdemeanor
The Glass Looker
March 20, 1826

                To my fees in examination
                of the above cause 2.68

Book of Mormon came to light the same activity would be causing problems among the populace (Eth. 8:18-26).

The Book of Mormon not only condemned "secret combinations," it included stories and objects and rituals which drew on and seemed to confirm certain Masonic beliefs. In 1826 at the time the Morgan story broke and the anti-Masonic movement was building momentum, Joseph Smith, Jr., was ending a six-year career as a "money-digger"—a career which drew on popular folk magic notions. In the years immediately after Morgan, Smith's interest in ancient power and ritual drew increasingly on Masonic lore instead. Money-digging was an activity which people in New England and New York had pursued for some time. In 1825 Vermont's *Windsor Journal* complained that "even the frightful stories of money being hid under the surface of the earth, and enchanted by the Devil or Robert Kidd, are received by many of our respectable fellow citizens as truths."[39]

At the Smiths' earlier home in Tunbridge, Vermont, a man was told in a dream of a treasure chest buried on an island in Agre's Brook near Randolph. He took a crew to the site, dug a hole fifteen feet square and eight feet deep, and allegedly found the chest lid. One of the crew pierced it and cried out: "'There's not ten dollars a piece.' No sooner were the words out of his mouth, than the chest moved off through the mud."[40] In the late 1840s the Smithsonian Institute and the New York Historical Society jointly sponsored an exploration of the mounds in western New York. The explorer reported that "most of them have been excavated under the impulse of an idle curiosity, or have had their contents scattered by 'money diggers,' a ghostly race, of which, singularly enough, even at this day, representatives may be found in almost every village."[41]

The stories and court testimonies about the Smiths' money-digging activities show the same characteristics as stories about such activities in general. Joseph Jr. used his seerstone to locate a cache at some distance. Then he accompanied a crew which included his father and brother Hyrum to dig it up. They enacted a magic ritual consisting of drawing a circle around the site and marching around it, and are said to have sacrificed a dog or sheep and sprinkled its blood on the ground to nullify the effect of the charm which kept them from the treasure. But someone in the crew usually spoke at the wrong time or enacted the ritual incorrectly, and the chest moved off through the ground out of their reach and sight.[42]

During 1825-26 young Joseph worked as a money-digger for Josiah Stowell in Harmony, Pennsylvania, and boarded with Isaac Hale nearby. He often spoke of his activities when he went to Colesville, New York, a little way across the state line. William R. Hine of Colesville recalled that Smith spoke about his seerstone and money-digging activities, claiming "that he could see lost or hidden things through it. He said he saw Captain Kidd sailing on the Susquehanna River during a freshet, and that he buried two pots of gold and silver. He claimed he saw writing cut on the rocks in an unknown language telling where Kidd buried it, and he translated it through his peepstone."[43]

In later years Smith's mother recalled her son's use of magic rites in his youth and told her intended public: "let not my reader suppose that . . . we stopt our labor and went at trying to win the faculty of Abrac drawing Magic circles or sooth saying to the neglect of all kinds of business we never during our lives suffered one important interest to swallow up every other obligation."[44] Abrac, from Abracadabra and Abraxis, is a magic word or formula used on amulets to work magic charms.[45] Eighteenth-century Masons were said to know how to conceal "the way of obtaining the faculty of Abrac, which implied that they knew how to get it."[46] Hyrum Smith was a member of the Mount Moriah Lodge, Palmyra Lodge No. 112, sometime previous to 1827, and may have provided this Masonic lore in the pre-Morgan era.[47]

As 1827 dawned and the Morgan trials heated up, Joseph Smith returned to his father's house at Manchester with his new bride, Isaac Hale's daughter Emma. Within a few weeks anti-Masonic conventions came to Farmington and Manchester. Smith still practiced money-digging in 1827,[48] but he also spoke of golden plates which he had located with his seerstone.[49] By August Smith had decided to discontinue his money-digging.[50] In September he recovered the plates from which he would read in 1829 that God had cursed the land so that the riches, weapons, and tools of long-ago people behaved just like the objects of New England treasure hunters: "Yea, we have hid up our treasures and they have slipped away from us, because of the curse of the land" (He. 13:33-36); "the inhabitants thereof began to hide up their treasures in the earth; and they became slippery, because the Lord had cursed the land, that they could not hold them, nor retain them again" (Morm. 1:18).

Oliver Cowdery indicated that Smith had found the plates in

1823 within this same context of treasure hunting. Smith tried three times to get the chest containing the plates, but his motives were impure and he was shocked away and deprived of his strength: "What was the occasion of this he knew not—there was the pure unsullied record, as had been described—he had heard of the power of enchantment, and a thousand like stories, which held the hidden treasures of the earth."[51]

Smith's early money-digging activity was not unrelated to his career as translator and prophet. In 1827 he began to tell stories about his ability with the stone to see golden plates buried in the earth. After he had received the plates, his stories began more and more to display characteristics of Masonic lore. When Cowdery described Smith's recovery of the chest containing the golden plates, he listed the contents of the box. There was a breastplate used as chest armor. Three small pillars stood upright and upon them "was placed the record of the children of Joseph and of a people who left the tower far, far before the days of Joseph." The pillars "were not so lengthy as to cause the plates and the crowning stone to come in contact."[52] Lucy Mack Smith spoke of four pillars.[53] Joseph Smith also listed the glasses which he called the Urim and Thummim, the Sword of Laban, and the ball or compass.[54]

Each of these objects would have had special significance for Masons, including the pillars. In the Explanation of the First Degree Tracing Board, the newly Entered Apprentice Mason learns that three pillars support the Masonic lodges. They are called Wisdom, Strength, and Beauty and represent Solomon, King of Israel; Hiram, King of Tyre; and Hiram Abiff. The Second Degree Tracing Board Lecture teaches that Solomon's Temple at Jerusalem had two great pillars at the entrance. They were cast from molten brass, made hollow, contained the constitutional rolls, served as the archives, and were topped by two spherical balls on which maps of the terrestrial and celestial globes were represented.[55]

One use of the pillars in Masonry is found in the Enoch Legend of the Royal Arch Degree.[56] The degree teaches that the Christian world owes to Masonry the preservation of the Book of the Law (the five books of Moses) and its rediscovery when it was lost.[57] Enoch, the seventh from Adam, foresaw the flood of Noah's time. He had an underground temple built and erected two pillars over the entrance. One was of brass to withstand water. The other was of marble to withstand fire. On the marble pillar Enoch engraved hieroglyphics which told of treasure concealed in the underground temple. (A variant ritual had the marble pillar describe a history of the Creation and the Secret Mysteries.[59]) On the brass pillar Enoch engraved the principles of Masonry and events connected with the Tower of Babel.[58]

The brass pillar survived the Flood, but the marble pillar was broken up. When Solomon sent three Master Masons to explore the ruins of Enoch's temple, they found some marble fragments engraved with hieroglyphics and took them to Solomon, who had the pieces assembled and placed them in the Sacred Vault—a room beneath his temple known only to him, to Hiram of Tyre, to Hiram Abiff, and to the three Master Masons.[60] The Book of Mormon makes reference to plates of brass containing a history of the Creation down to the Tower of Babel, plus the "mysteries of God."[61]

The Royal Arch taught that three other Master Masons lived through the Babylonian captivity and were released by Cyrus to return to Jerusalem. When they came to the pavilion near the temple ruins, they offered themselves to Haggai, Joshua, and Zerubbabel as assistants in rebuilding the temple. They set to work clearing away the ruins of Solomon's temple and discovered his secret vault. They found a box on a pedestal and took it to the Grand Council, which opened the box and found the Ark of the Covenant. On the lid in a triangular form were three characters. Inside the box were the long lost Book of the Law, the pot of manna from Sinai, Aaron's rod, and a key to the characters on the lid. The council used the key to decipher the box lid characters, which were sacred characters spelling the name of God.[62] This fits with the Masons' claim to have preserved the highest respect for the name of God, to have the *true* name of God in both its written and pronounced forms.

The early stories from 1828 and 1829 tell of Smith's warning all that any one who saw the plates would incur God's displeasure and probable death. In June 1829 he revealed that three could see the plates and live (D&C 17). This is similar to the Enoch Legend in the Royal Arch degree. After the three Master Masons were allowed to see the gold plate engraved with the forbidden name of God, a band of workers was impatient to discover the secret for themselves and went to the ruins of Enoch's temple, descended through the nine arches into the secret chamber, and died as the arches collapsed upon them.[63] Only three who were worthy could see the characters and live. So it would be with Smith and the golden plates.

David Whitmer said that when he and Oliver Cowdery viewed the plates (Martin Harris could not see them at first but would only a few minutes later be visited by the angel), they were overwhelmed by a brilliant light: "In the midst of this light, but a few feet from us, appeared a table, upon which were many golden plates, also the sword of Laban and the directors."[64] This sword—with a hilt of pure gold (which had rusted away by the time Smith found it[65])—had been used in the Book of Mormon to decapitate Laban (1 Ne. 4:7-18). In Masonic legend, a mason decapitated one of the assassins of Hiram Abiff. As in the Book of Mormon, the Masonic protagonist found his nemesis asleep and killed him with his own sword.

Another artifact in the Palmyra chest—the Liahona or compass—also seems related to Masonic lore. The pillars of the Second Degree Tracing Board were topped by globes, one of the earth and one of the universe. In the Enoch Legend the brass pillar was topped by a metal ball containing maps, "directions of the world and of the universe, and which also acted as a sort of oracle."[66] The "directors" which Smith listed as one of the relics in the stone chest contained two spindles, one of which pointed the way for Lehi and his family through the wilderness (1 Ne. 16:10). As occasion demanded, writing appeared on the ball to inform the refugees of the Lord's ways according to their "faith and diligence."

The final object, the breastplate, was also Masonic. The Royal Arch Degree provided for the installation of the Grand Council, whose principals following the return from Babylon were Joshua, Haggai, and Zerubbabel. Their priestly, prophetic and kingly offices continue in the Masonic Lodge. During the installation of the Joshua-elect, the candidate kneels before the chair of his office while biblical passages are read describing Moses instituting the Aaronic priesthood. Over Aaron's robe Moses bound an ephod over which he put a breastplate. He put the Urim and Thummim in the breastplate and then put a turban upon Aaron's head and a golden plate upon the turban to make a holy crown (Lev. 8:7-8). Many of the stories about Smith's translating the golden plates indicate that he sometimes wore the breastplate with the glasses (Urim and Thummim). In Masonry, the Most Excellent High Priest of the Royal Arch wears "a breastplate of cut glass, consisting of twelve pieces to represent the twelve tribes of Israel." One objection that the Saratoga Baptist Association had against Masons was "their wearing garments in simulation of those worn by the Jewish High Priests;

making and carrying in procession a mimic representation of the ark of the covenant; making and wearing similar representation of the breastplate; inscribing on mitres, 'Holiness to the Lord.'"[67]

The Book of Mormon describes the breastplate and other artifacts as relics of authority passed down from leader to leader.[68] Smith also used the relics to help establish the authority he needed to defend God, but once established he needed them no longer. This is seen by the fact that long before the translation process was completed, Smith had substituted the seerstone for the glasses. It performed exactly the same function. The angel reclaimed the spectacles and plates after the translation process was completed at the end of June 1829. Smith kept the stone.

Though the relics of succession were only used by Smith in the beginning, the Melchizedek priesthood, important also to Masonry, eventually became a permanent part of Mormonism. During Masonic observances regarding the Order of High Priest in the Royal Arch, Bible passages which dealt with the priesthood of Melchizedek were read.[69] The Aaronic priesthood came by heredity, but that of Melchizedek by special dispensation from God. In July 1828 an article designed "to show that Masonry is a religious institution" listed as one of its points that "its priests are consecrated High Priests forever, after the order of Melchizedek."[70]

Joseph Smith and Oliver Cowdery are said to have received the Aaronic priesthood on 15 May 1829 when they were baptized at the hands of John the Baptist, who was acting on the orders of Peter, James, and John, who held a higher priesthood.[71] When Smith completed the translation process he received the Melchizedek priesthood.[72] Carrying the mantle of a dual priesthood, possessing the relics of succession, and having in hand the translation of the golden plates, Smith was now in proper position to defend God.[73]

The Book of Mormon established a claim to the Melchizedek priesthood in Alma 13, maintaining that the "Lord God ordaineth priests after his holy order, which was after the order of his Son." A person who exercised "exceeding faith and good works" was "called with a holy calling" and could be "ordained unto the high priesthood of the holy order of God." "This high priesthood being after the order of his Son, which order was from the foundation of the world; or in other words, being without beginning of days or end of years, being prepared from eternity to all eternity, according to his foreknowledge of all things." Melchizedek "was also a high priest after this same order . . . who also took upon him the high priesthood forever." In Smith's later book of Moses, Adam, Abel, Seth, and Enos had the same priesthood, as did Enoch.[74] They also all had instruments for seeing into the future, making them "seers."

It should be noted that in 1829 and still in 1830 the Melchizedek priesthood for Smith was a symbol of authority and nothing more. Not until June 1831 did Smith induct others into this higher priesthood and begin to make of this order the administrative hierarchy it was later to become.[75] David Whitmer supports this observation in his comment that early Mormonism had no Melchizedek priesthood.[76]

The Mormon notion of temples also borrowed from Masonic ritual, based on biblical accounts that God revealed a new, divine name to Moses (Ex. 6:3) and said that this name would dwell in a temple to manifest his presence.[77] The Nephites in the Book of Mormon built temples. Using Laban's sword as a model, Nephi armed his people so that they could protect themselves from hostile Lamanites while building an edifice. With tools of masonry in one hand and swords in another, Nephi's workmen built a temple like Solomon's, though less imposing.[78]

The Masonic Enoch foresaw that an Israelite would discover the buried treasure after the Flood, which he also foresaw. The Book of Mormon indicated that Joseph Smith was an Israelite, a descendant of the biblical Joseph (2 Ne. 3:6-7, 15) and a seer (Mosiah 8:13; 28:11-16). From June to December 1830, Smith dictated a vision in which Enoch, high atop a mountain, saw a vision of many biblical and Book of Mormon events (Moses 6:35-36; 7:3, 38-43, 69). Enoch was a seer (Moses 6:35-36), and all signs indicated that the descendant he saw in vision was Joseph Smith. In March 1832 Smith revealed that he was Enoch (D&C 78:1), and he would carry that identification into his death

Joseph Smith's interest in Egypt was also connected to Masonry. Even before Smith's Canandaigua trial for glass-looking in January 1828, John Sheldon had reportedly written a letter in Masonic hieroglyphics to General Solomon Van Rensselaer, the Revolutionary War hero.[79] At the time it sensationally underlined the claim of the Explanation of the First Degree Tracing Board: "the usages and customs of Masons have ever corresponded with those of the Egyptian philosophers, to which they bear a near affinity . . . . they concealed their particular tenets . . . under hieroglyphical figures."[80]

The Saratoga Baptist Association at Milton, New York, in 1828 took that claim seriously, charging in the second of its fifteen-point indictments that Masonic rites "correspond with the Egyptian."[81] The Egyptian obelisks upon which Champollion and Seyffarth had recently turned public attention were said to have been inscribed with Masonic hieroglyphics.[82] Combining the Egyptian on the marble pillar fragments, which Solomon could not translate, with the unknown script in which God's name was written on the gold plate in the Royal Arch might produce "reformed Egyptian," which could only be translated with a key which worked by revelation. Like Solomon, Smith received revelation in the manner of a Masonic priest.

Joseph Smith condemned current expressions of Masonry but nevertheless accepted Masonry as a truly ancient form confirming God's relationships with humans from Adam on. He restored a Masonry unencumbered by the corruptions and heresies of the lodges and churches in western New York.[83] The high percentage of ex-Masons among Smith's early converts in the 1830s, when the anti-Masonic conflict was still fresh, indicates that many were looking not for rejection but for reform. Masonic legend provided support for Christian tradition and a rich lode to mine in combating deism. Joseph Smith took what he felt was true and transformed it for his own use.[84]

NOTES

1. Fayette Lapham, "The Mormons," *Historical Magazine* (New Series), 7 (May 1870): 307.

2. S. H. Goodwin, *Additional Studies in Mormonism and Masonry* (Salt Lake City: Grand Lodge of F. & A. M. of Utah, 1932), 15-16. A notice that a Baptist clergyman in Illinois had been dismissed because he was a Freemason was captioned as "Bigotry." *Wayne Sentinel*, 12 July 1825.

3. Alphonse Cerza, *Anti-Masonry* (Fulton, MO: The Ovid Bell Press, Inc., 1962), 35.

4. See John Robison, *Proofs of A Conspiracy Against All the Religions and Governments of Europe, Carried on in the Secret Meetings of Free Masons, Illuminate, and Reading Societies: Collected from Good Authorities*, 3rd ed. (Philadelphia: T. Dobson, 1793). Abbe Barruel, *The Anti-Christian and Antisocial Conspiracy* (Lancaster, PA: Joseph Ehrenfried, 1812).

5. *Palmyra Register*, 19 Mar. 1819, in a column entitled "The Moralist."

6. Henry Wilson Coil, *Masonic Encyclopedia* (New York: Macoy Publishing & Supply Company, 1961), 58.

7. James C. Odierne, *Opinions on Speculative Masonry* (Boston: Perkins & Marvin, 1830), 198.

8. *Wayne Sentinel*, 13 Apr. 1827.

9. Ibid., 22 Dec. 1826, "Monroe County Meetings."

10. Ibid., 6 Apr. 1827.

11. Ibid., 2 Feb. 1827, carried the following advertisement just two weeks after the Canandaigua trial ended: *"Trial of the Conspirators*: 'an account of the Trial of the Conspirators, on an indictment for carrying away WILLIAM MORGAN, from the jail of Ontario county, on the evening of the 12th of Sept. 1826; together with Throop's Address. Jan. 19.'"

12. Goodwin, 17.

13. *Wayne Sentinel*, 14 Mar. 1828, carried the notice that an anti-Masonic paper called the *Palmyra Freeman* would start publication soon.

14. Rob Morris, *William Morgan: or Political Anti-Masonry, Its Rise, Growth and Decadence* (New York: Robert Macoy, 1883), 183-84. The sequence is listed as follows (pp. 347-48): Bloomfield, 11 Dec. 1826; Seneca, 13 Jan. 1827; Lewiston, 25 Jan. 1827; Canandaigua, 31 Jan. and 16 Feb.; West Bloomfield, 27 Feb.; Vienna, 12 Mar.; Manchester, 15 Mar.; Farmington, 16 Mar.; Victor, 2 Aug.; and Canandaigua, 19 Sept.

15. Richard L. Anderson, "Martin Harris, the Honorable New York Farmer," *Improvement Era* 72 (1969): 20.

16. *Wayne Sentinel*, 5 Oct. 1827.

17. See "Marks of Masonry," in ibid., 8 Dec. 1826.

18. *Wayne Sentinel*, 10 Nov. 1826. See "The Batavia Affair," 22 Dec. 1826, for an editorial typical of the period. It is restrained and not overtly anti-Masonic but still calls for Morgan's release.

19. *Wayne Sentinel*, 24 Nov. 1826. The text follows: "Whereas, much excitement has been caused throughout the community, on the subject of certain imputed, improper and illegal conduct, by certain individuals said to be connected with this ancient Fraternity, towards a man called 'Morgan.' Therefore, *Resolved unanimously*, That this Lodge, impressed with emotions of deep regret, that any imputations against the conduct of persons connected with us in the solemn ties of Masonic Brotherhood, should have been made, which can be by any possible implication regarded as a violation of the laws of the government under which we so happily live, and to support which is one of the principal tenets of our order, do cordially agree with and approve of the resolution adopted by 'The Ontario Masters' Lodge, No. 23.'"

20. Charles F. Milliken, *A History of Ontario County, New York and Its People*, 2 vols. (New York: Lewis Historical Publishing Company, 1911),

1:414.

21. *Wayne Sentinel*, 27 Mar. 1829.

22. Coil, 58.

23. Morris, 289. Morris may be mistaken about the date. David Bernard identifies the meeting as that of the Saratoga Baptist Association, prints the fifteen resolutions in full, and gives the date as 12-15 Sept. *Light on Masonry* (Utica: William Williams, 1829), 361-66.

24. *Wayne Sentinel*, 25 Jan. 1828.

25. Goodwin, 18.

26. *Palmyra Reflector*, 2 Dec. 1829, notes that the Rev. Henry Davis, anti-Masonic pastor of the Baptist church in Macedon, was leaving a congregation which was suffering from internal strife. On 22 and 30 January 1830, the *Reflector* states that the local Baptist church was anti-Masonic.

27. *Wayne Sentinel*, 25 Jan. 1828.

28. Ibid., 13 Oct. 1826. The letter was signed by a committee of ten men, one of whom signed himself "Ja's Smith" (probably James), but the letter was reproduced in many papers and in some it was signed simply as "J. Smith." On this basis Reed C. Durham, Jr., "Is There No Help for the Widow's Son, "*Mormon Miscellaneous* 1 (Oct. 1975): 11-16, mistakenly identified the signatory as the Mormon prophet. The committee was formed of citizens from Batavia, however, and the letter is found in many forms and publications. See John E. Becker, *A History of Freemasonry in Waterloo, New York, 1817-1942* (Waterloo, NY: Seneca Lodge No. 113, F. & A. M., 1942), 22-23.

29. *Wayne Sentinel*, 4 May 1827.

30. He warned against "all combinations and associations . . . with the real design to direct, control, counteract, or awe the regular deliberation and action of the constituted authorities," because they destroyed the democratic process ("Farewell Address," *The World's Greatest Speeches*, Lewis Copeland, ed., 252-53). "Combinations" became synonymous with Freemasonry. See Goodwin, 27-29. Freemasonry was called a "combination" in *Wayne Sentinel*, 18 July 1828, and a "secret combination" in *Palmyra Farmer*, 10 Nov. 1829.

31. Secret oaths, secret plans, secret words, secret combinations, secret signs, secret abominations, secret band, secret work, secrets—all were anti-Masonic epithets of the time. The *Albany Daily Advertiser* ran a column debating the use of the term "secret societies," which suggests the tenor of the rhetoric: "whether Washington meant *secret societies or political parties* . . . is of little consequence; . . . the sentence—*Beware of secret societies*, is unexceptional—and will last for a freeman's motto, as long as a freeman's blood stains freemasonry." Reprinted in the *Ontario Phoenix*, 31 Mar. 1830. Masonry was called a "secret society" in *Wayne Sentinel*, 18 July 1828, and *Palmyra Farmer*, 2 Dec. 1828. See also *Palmyra Farmer*, 10 Nov. 1829.

32. The oaths to the first three degrees all involved the candidate's vowing never to reveal in any way the Masonic secrets, "under no less penalty than to have my throat cut across, my tongue torn out by the roots, and my body buried in the rough sands of the sea at low water-mark, where the tide ebbs and flows twice in twenty-four hours." This is the oath taken in the Entered Apprentice, or first degree. From William Morgan, *Illustrations of Masonry*, reprinted as *Morgan's Freemasonry Exposed and Explained* (New York: L. Fitzgerald, 1882), 19. The oath was also printed in *Wayne Sentinel*, 10 Nov. 1826. *Wayne Sentinel*, 14 Mar. 1828, has the obligations and penalties of the Mark Masters through the Knight's Templar degrees.

In Smith's Book of Moses, 5:29-32, Satan and Cain enter into an oath-bound pact to kill Abel. Cain says: "Truly I am Mahan, the master of the great secret, that I may murder and get gain. Wherefore Cain was called Master Mahan, and he gloried in his wickedness." Cain's descendant, Lamech, also entered into a covenant with Satan and became a Master Mahan. Here Smith injects the Morgan episode and his alleged murder: "Irad, the son of Enoch, having known their secret, began to reveal it unto the sons of Adam; Wherefore Lamech, being angry, slew him, not like unto Cain, his brother Abel, for the sake of getting gain, but he slew him for the oath's sake" (vv. 49-50).

33. The Knight's Templar candidate swore "to advance my brother's best interest by always supporting his military fame, political preference in opposition to another" (*Wayne Sentinel*, 14 Mar. 1828). In the same issue the Royal Arch obligation for the candidate for the degree is printed: "Furthermore do I promise and swear, that I will vote for a companion Royal Arch mason before any other person of equal qualifications." Again, the candidate swore "that a companion Royal Arch mason's secret given me in charge as such, and I knowing him to be such, shall remain as secret and inviolate in my breast as in his own, when he communicated it to me, *Murder and Treason*, not excepted."

William L. Stone, *Letters on Masonry and Anti-Masonry, Addressed to The Hon. John Quincy Adams* (New York: O. Halsted, 1832), 75, wrote that the pledge in favor of political preferment and the word "not" in italics were interpolations but that this was the way the obligation was given in western New York.

The New York County sheriffs had the power to select and summon grand juries for courts in their jurisdiction. In those counties where the Morgan incident took place and in which there were trials, the sheriffs were all Masons, possibly all Royal Arch Masons. The Genessee County grand jury met in February 1827, where the foreman was a Knight Templar and so were several jury members. In Niagara County, where Eli Bruce was sheriff, sixteen Masons and several friendly to the Lodge were summoned for jury selection in January 1827. In April Bruce summoned the grand jurors—of twenty-one members present several were friendly to the Lodge and sixteen were Masons—the Niagara County court of Oyer and Terminer. Two of the jurors were themselves later indicted for the Morgan conspiracy. A majority of Masons were on the jury at the May session and half of the September session jurors were Masons.

34. See Goodwin's documentation of the charge (p. 34). See also *Wayne Sentinel*, 9 Nov. 1827, 14 Mar. 1828, 18 July 1828.

35. Goodwin, 34-35. See *Wayne Sentinel*, 23 Mar. 1827, 7 Mar., 18 July 1828, 26 Sept. 1828; and *Palmyra Farmer*, 1 Dec. 1828.

36. The following are some of the passages which deal with these topics. Combinations: 2 Ne. 9:9; 26:22; Alma 37:21-32. Secret oaths and covenants: 2 Ne. 26:22-23 (compare the contrast that Smith draws with God, who opens his courts to all, vs. 24-30); Alma 37:27, 29; Hel. 6:25; 4 Ne. 42. Masonic secrets already revealed and known: Alma 37:23-26; Ether 8:20; 2 Ne. 30:17; Mosiah 8:17, 19. Masonry out to take over and destroy the government and all freedoms: Alma 10:27; Hel. 6:39; Ether 8:9-25; 9:1, 5-6, 26; 10:33; 11:7; 3 Ne. 6:21-30. Masonic judges control the courts: Alma 11:20; Hel. 6:21, 23; Mosiah 29:28-32; 3 Ne. 6:21-30. Masons claim the right to punish their members according to their own laws and not the laws of the land: Hel. 6:21-24.

37. Hel. 1:27, 29; 6:25-30, 38; Ether 8:20.

38. 2 Ne. 9:9; 26:22; Alma 37:30-31; Hel. 3:23; 6:21; 3 Nel. 6:6, 9; Morm. 8:27; Ether 8:18, 22, 24, 25; 9:1, 6; 11:15, 22; 13:18. In 3 Ne. 6:10-30 Satan caused class divisions within the church over educational, financial, and professional differences. He used the upper class desire to get ahead as a temptation to gain power and thereby managed to get the lodge started in and among church members. Compare Moses 5:29-50.

39. *Wayne Sentinel*, 16 Feb. 1825.

40. Ibid.

41. E. G. Squier, "Report upon the Aboriginal Monuments of Western New York," *Proceedings of the New York Historical Society* (New York: William Van Norden, 1849), 54. See "Money Digger," *Palmyra Herald*, 24 July 1822, which was reprinted from the Montepelier, Vermont, *Watchman*. The article reported that "digging for money hid in the earth is a very common thing; and in this state is even considered an honorable and profitable employment. We could name, if we pleased, at least five hundred respectable men, who do, in the simplicity and sincerity of their hearts, verily believe, that immense treasures lie concealed upon our Green Mountains; many of whom have been for a number of years, most industriously and perserveringly engaged in digging it up."

42. See D. Michael Quinn, *Early Mormonism and the Magic World View* (Salt Lake City: Signature Books, 1987).

43. Arthur Deming, *Naked Truths about Mormonism* 1 (Jan. 1888): 2.

44. Lucy Mack Smith, preliminary manuscript, photocopy, [46,] archives, Church of Jesus Christ of Latter-day Saints, Salt Lake City, Utah.

45. See Quinn, *Early Mormonism and the Magic World View.*

46. James Hardie, *The New Free-Mason's Monitor* (New York: George Long, 1818), 203. Henry Dana Ward, *Free Masonry. Its Pretensions Exposed in Faithful Extracts of Its Standard Authors* (New York, 1828), 104-105, ridiculed the details of the Hiram Abiff allegory. "This is truly Free Masonry; the art of finding new arts, and the way of winning the faculty of Abrac." Ward's comment upon the way Hiram Abiff met his death at the hands of the assassins: "What a wonder! The Master of 'the art of foresaying things,' did not foresee his danger; the master of 'the art of wonder-working,' did not even draw a magic circle; the master of 'the way of winning the faculty of abrac,' did not utter a syllable of magic, did not spit out one mouthful of fire, did not make the slightest attempt to conjure a spirit to his rescue; but alas! forgetful of all his masonic defenses, he died; he basely died!"

47. Mervin B. Hogan, "The Founding Minutes of Nauvoo Lodge," *Further Light in Masonry* (Des Moines: Research Lodge No. 2), 8, shows that Hyrum Smith was transferred into the Nauvoo Lodge from Mount Moriah, No. 112, New York. Grand Lodge of Free and Accepted Masons of the State of New York, New York, NY, "Return of the Mount Moriah Lodge No. 112 held in the Town of Palmyra in the County of Wayne and State of New York from June 4th AL 5827 [1827] to June 4th AL 5828 [1828]," lists Hyrum Smith, but a record of his initiation has yet to be found.

48. Joseph Capron met Smith's father in 1827. According to Capron, Joseph Jr. had a stone by which he located a chest of gold watches near Capron's house. The chest was in possession of an evil spirit. Joseph Jr., therefore, got a polished sword and marched around the treasure site with Samuel Lawrence to fend off satanic assaults. Eber D. Howe, *Mormonism Unvailed* (Painesville, OH, 1834), 258-60.

49. As early as June 1827, Joseph Smith, Sr., reportedly told Willard Chase that Joseph Jr. had had a vision of the plates. Chase's statement is found in Howe, 240-48. Martin Harris said that Smith discovered the site by using his stone; Joel Tiffany, "Mormonism No. II," *Tiffany's Monthly*, Aug. 1859, 163, 169. The Smith family told Harris the same thing.

50. Peter Ingersoll said that he was hired by Smith in August 1827 to take him to Harmony, Pennsylvania, to pick up Emma's furniture. Isaac Hale remonstrated with Smith to give up his money-digging, and Smith promised to do so. But on the return trip to Palmyra, Smith told Ingersoll that that would be hard to do, since others would pressure him to use the stone. Howe, 232-37. Isaac Hale also stated that Smith told him he "had given up what he called 'glass looking.'" *Susquehanna Register*, 1 May 1834. By the time Smith told Harris about this decision, the reason he gave for quitting the money-digging business was that an angel had told him to;

Tiffany, 169.

51. Oliver Cowdery to W. W. Phelps, *Latter-day Saints' Messenger and Advocate*, Mar. 1835, 197.

52. Ibid., 196-97.

53. Lucy Mack Smith, preliminary manuscript, [47].

54. *Latter-day Saints' Messenger and Advocate*, Mar. 1835, 196-97. If one objects that Cowdery's record is from the mid-1830s, there are earlier sources that mention the stone chest relics. Willard Chase, Joshua M'Kune, and Abigail Harris refer to the breastplate, Sword of Laban, the compass, and the glasses; see Howe, 240-48, 253, 267. Although Chase dated the time he heard of the breastplate, sword, and plates as 1829, the fact that he said Emma Smith was to give birth in June dates the time as 1828. M'Kune lived in Susquehanna County, Pennsylvania, and claimed to have known Harris and Smith when they were in Harmony—from April to June 1828. Abigail Harris's altercation with her husband, Martin, over his involvement with Smith also took place in 1828. Joseph Smith, Sr., told Fayette Lapham in 1830 that his son had found a gold hilt and chain of a large sword, a gold ball with two pointers, the spectacles, and plates. Lapham, 307. Finally Smith listed the relics in June 1829 (D&C 17).

55. Walton Hannah, *Darkness Visible: A Revelation & Interpretation of Freemasonry* (London: Augustine Press, 1952), 111, 125, 127.

56. The legend is found in Thomas S. Webb, *The Freemason's Monitor; or Illustrations of Masonry* (New York: Southwick and Crooker, 1802), 246-60. Henry Dana Ward's *Freemasonry* extracted parts of the Enoch legend from Webb. The *Wayne Sentinel* bookstore ran ads for Webb's *Monitor*, 24 Nov. 1826, and for Dana's book, 4 Sept. 1829. Another popular work, Jeremy Cross, *The True Masonic Chart, Or Hieroglyphic Monitor*, was advertised 14 Feb. 1826.

Albert G. Mackey, *The History of Freemasonry: Its Legends and Traditions; Its Chronological History*, 7 vols. (New York: The Masonic History Company, 1950), vol. 1, traces the legend of the pillars from the writings of Josephus as it was transformed into the Masonic legend in the middle ages. Josephus attributed the pillars to the sons of Seth, who wanted to leave the world some memory of their learning and inventions when they pondered Adam's prediction that at one time the world would be destroyed by fire, at another by water. Therefore, "they made two pillars; the one of brick, the other of stone: they inscribed their discoveries on them both, that in case the pillar of brick should be destroyed by the flood, the pillar of stone might remain, and exhibit those discoveries to mankind; and also inform them that there was another pillar of brick erected by them. Now this remains in the land of Siria to this day." Josephus, "Antiquities of the Jews," Bk. 1, chap. 2, in *The Life and Works of Flavius Josephus*, trans. William Whiston (Philadelphia: John C. Winston Company, n.d.), 36.

57. Stone, 44-46, gives the Royal Arch teaching about the "book of the law" discussed in 2 Chron. 34 and 2 Kings 22, which was the "book of the law of the LORD given through Moses" (2 Chron. 34:14). Hilkiah, the priest, found the book during temple repairs. According to the teaching, Solomon had built a secret vault beneath his temple to keep the sacred treasure safe during the reigns of idolatrous kings, and only Masons knew it. After King Josiah's time the book was hidden again in the secret vault and survived the destruction of the temple at the hands of the Babylonians. After the Jews, with Cyrus's permission, rebuilt the temple, Ezra and Zerubbabel rediscovered the vault and the book. Then Ezra, the priestly scribe, "corrected, revised, and re-wrote some of the sacred books" of the Pentateuch (p. 45). Stone gives this as a variant tradition of the Royal Arch.

The Royal Arch tradition was unbiblical, since Ezra returned to Jerusalem from Babylon carrying in his hand "the law of Moses which the LORD the God of Israel had given," Ezra 7:6, 10, 14. In fact, the Royal Arch seems to have taken its tradition from the Apocrypha. According to 2 Esdras 14:18-48, Ezra completed the scriptural restoration thirty years after the temple. During a forty-day period, Ezra, inspired by God, dictated 94 books to his assistants and was told to publish the first twenty-four but to save the rest for "the Sages." The Book of Mormon quotes 2 Esdras 13:40-42.

When Joseph Smith translated the plates, he translated a portion but was forbidden to translate the "sealed" portion. His Nephite scribes also corrected, revised, and re-wrote the records which had come to them. Smith also kept a record which he called the Book of the Law of the Lord, which is preserved today in the office vault of the LDS First Presidency.

58. Webb, 247.

59. Durham's source shows some variations from Webb, but there were many variations in Masonic ritual in the United States.

60. Webb, 259-60. See Mos. 8:11-13.

61. 1 Ne. 3:12, 19-20, 24; 4:24, 38; 5:10-22; 13:23; 19:22; 1 Ne. 4:2; 5:12; Mos. 1:3-4; 28:20; Al. 37:3-12; 63:1, 11-14; 3 Ne. 1:2. This may be the missing connection between Ethan Smith's and Joseph Smith's separate uses of the Two Sticks of Ezekiel 37:16. In Ezekiel the Two Sticks refer to the nations of the northern kingdom (the Ten Lost Tribes) and the southern kingdom (Judah). Ethan Smith used it like that, but Joseph Smith transformed the meaning to refer to the two nations' records or histories. See notes 7-11, chap. 6. The Book of Mormon describes the brass plates as containing history from creation of the world to the Tower of Babel, plus "the mysteries of God." 1 Ne. 3:12, 19-20, 24; 4:24, 38; 5:10-22; 13:23; 19:22; 2 Ne. 4:2; 5:12; Mosiah 1:3-4; 28:20; Alma 37:3-12; 63:1, 11-14; 3 Ne. 1:2. The plates of Lehi and his descendants were made into two sets of plates by Nephi, the larger set telling of the Nephites' secular history and the smaller set telling of their religious history (1 Ne. 9:1-5; 19:1-6). The two sets together

also absorbed the brass plates, and the whole constitutes the "record of Joseph."

62. Stone, 45. See also Bernard, 138-43. Smith called the spectacles a "key," according to his mother, *Biographical Sketches of Joseph Smith, the Prophet, and His Progenitors for Many Generations* (Liverpool: S. W. Richards, 1853), 101-106.

63. Webb, 259.

64. *Kansas City Daily Journal*, 5 June 1881.

65. Lapham, 307.

66. Durham. Webb, 56, said that the metal globe was able to improve the mind and to give it "the most distinct idea of any problem or proposition." For another good study of the Enoch legend's relationship to Mormon origins, see J. N. Adamson, "The Treasure of the Widow's Son," *Mormon Miscellaneous* 1 (Oct. 1975).

67. Bernard, 141, 363.

68. 2 Ne. 5:12; Jacob 7:27; Jarom 1, 15; Omni 1, 9; Mosiah 1:15-16; 8:11-18; 28:10-20; Alma 37:1-4, 14, 16-18; 63:1, 11-13. These men all held the Melchizedek priesthood.

69. Webb, 197-99. He lists the passages read: Num. 6:22-26; Gen. 14:12-24; Heb. 7:1-5.

70. *Ontario Phoenix* (Canandaigua, NY), 31 Mar. 1830.

71. Although this date is well established in Mormon literature, it was not in the 1833 Book of Commandments. Oliver Cowdery referred to it in "Letters to W. W. Phelps," *Messenger and Advocate*, Sept. 1834, 15-16. D&C 13 appeared in the 1876 edition of the Doctrine and Covenants. See also Smith's description, Joseph Smith et al., *History of the Church of Jesus Christ of Latter-day Saints*, 7 vols. (Salt Lake City: Deseret Book Co., 1927), 1:39-41; hereafter HC.

72. The exact date is not clear, but several statements by Smith, Cowdery, and others suggest a time between 15 May and June 1829. See Lawrence C. Porter, "A Study of the Origins of the Church of Jesus Christ of Latter-day Saints in the States of New York and Pennsylvania, 1816-1831," Ph.D. diss., Brigham Young University, 1971, 157-64, for a discussion. It would have been the natural completion of the chain of events leading to Smith's having the proper credentials to defend God.

73. Fawn M. Brodie, *No Man Knows My History: The Life of Joseph Smith*, 2nd ed. (New York: Alfred Knopf, 1971), 111n, suggests that Smith may have borrowed the notion of a dual priesthood from James Gray's *Dissertation on the Coincidence between the Priesthood of Jesus Christ and Melchisedek* (1810).

74. Smith seems to have been expounding the book of Hebrews in Alma 13 and extended it in the Book of Moses. The following context of Alma reflects touches of Hebrews: Alma 12:7/ Heb. 4:12; Alma 12:27/ Heb.

3:4-4:9; Alma 13:14/ Heb. 7:1-4; Alma 13:7, 9/ Heb. 7:3.

75. Moses 6. For a time only Smith and possibly Cowdery had the high priesthood. No one else was involved with this priesthood until June 1831. For the evolution of the early Mormon concept of authority, see Dan Vogel, *Religious Seekers and the Advent of Mormonism* (Salt Lake City: Signature Books, 1988), 97-158.

76. David Whitmer said that the first high priests were ordained at Kirtland, Ohio, in June 1831: "To Believers in the Book of Mormon," part 2, chap. 3, *An Address to All Believers in Christ* (Richmond, MO, 1887), 36. Whitmer said that "we had no high priests, etc. in the beginning" until "after we had preached almost two years, and had baptized and confirmed about 2000 souls into the Church of Christ" (p. 57). David's brother John, one of the eight witnesses, was an early church historian appointed by Smith (D&C 47:69:2-8), 8 March 1831. He recorded that on 3 June 1831 the high priesthood was given to several men at a general church conference. Smith ordained Lyman Wight, who was commanded to ordain several others, including Smith, to the high priesthood, the Order of Melchizedek. *John Whitmer's History* (Salt Lake City: Modern Microfilm Company, n.d.), chaps. 7, 5.

77. Deut. 12:5, 21; 14:23-24; 1 Kings 8:16-20, 29; 2 Chron. 2:1; 20:8-9; 1 Chron. 22:7-8, 10, 19; 28:3; 29:16.

78. Temples in the Book of Mormon: Jacob 1:17; 2:2, 11; Mosiah 1:18; 3 Ne. 11:1. Durham examines how Smith carried out Masonic themes in the Kirtland and Nauvoo temples.

79. Stone, 196-97; Morris (pp. 140-41) noted that Averill was a seceded Mason.

80. Webb 1860 ed., 39.

81. Morris, 289.

82. Stone, 90.

83. Ibid.

84. Smith listed "priestcraft" as one of the evils which people needed to reject (3 Ne. 16:10; 21:19; 30:2). Observers have often noted that his use of the term probably referred to the Roman Catholic priesthood and less emphatically to the Protestant clergy.

Smith may also have had the Masonic priesthood in mind: "priestcrafts are that men preach and set themselves up for a light unto the world, that they may get gain and praise of the world; but they seek not the welfare of Zion" (2 Ne. 26:29). Candidates for Masonic degrees are said to be seeking "light," but the high fees, expensive uniforms, and perceived collusion with politics were unsavory to the dispossessed.

9.

A God of Revelation

The God that others worship is not the God for me;/ He has no parts nor body, and cannot hear nor see;/ But I've a God that lives above—/ A God of power and of Love—/ A God of Revelation—oh, that's the God for me!

—Old Mormon Hymn (in Arbaugh, *Revelation in Mormonism*)

Deists had perfected the argument that the God of Christianity was capricious and that a lack of modern revelation proved him so. To convince Gentiles otherwise, Joseph Smith demonstrated that God still dealt with humanity as he had in the past. Smith regarded revelation and charismatic gifts as necessary and urged readers to accept them on the basis that God is unchangeable.[1] A typical assertion of this was advanced through a Book of Mormon sermon by Moroni: "And again I say unto you who deny the revelations of God, and say that they are done away, that there are no revelations nor prophecies, nor gifts, nor healing, nor speaking with tongues, and the interpretation of tongues; behold I say unto you, he that denieth these things knoweth not the gospel of Christ; yea, he has not read the scriptures; if so, he does not understand them. For do we not read that God is the same yesterday, today, and forever, and in him there is no variableness neither shadow of changing? And now, if ye have imagined up unto yourselves a god who doth vary, and in whom there is a shadow of changing, then have ye imagined

121

up unto yourselves a god who is not a God of miracles. But behold, I will show unto you a God of miracles, even the God of Abraham, and the God of Isaac, and the God of Jacob; and it is that same God who created the heavens and the earth, and all the things that in them are" (Morm. 9:7-11).

Christians played into the hands of skeptics, argued Book of Mormon writer Nephi, when they denied present-day revelation and miracles or when they said, "Behold there is no God today, for the Lord and the Redeemer hath done his work, and he hath given his power unto men . . . for this day he is not a God of miracles; he hath done his work" (2 Ne. 18:5-6). For a thousand years Christians gave such an explanation for the cessation of revelation and charismatic gifts. Smith insisted that they denied God's power (28:6). In his opinion miracles could not cease, nor could angels cease appearing, nor had God kept from people the power of the Holy Ghost: "Wherefore, if these things have ceased wo be unto the children of men, for it is because of unbelief, and all is vain . . . if these things have ceased, then has faith ceased also" (Moro. 7:27-38).

Christians who did not accept the validity of charismatic gifts in the life of the church then were responsible for the suspension of revelation and miracles. Moroni in his farewell sermon to the Lamanites elaborated this view and enumerated the gifts of the Spirit: "All of these gifts of which I have spoken, which are spiritual, never will be done away, even as long as the world shall stand, only according to the unbelief of the children of men . . . if the day cometh that the power and gifts of God shall be done away among you, it shall be because of unbelief" (Moro. 10:19, 24).

The Book of Mormon confirmed that God does not change. God produced the Book of Mormon "that I may prove unto many that I am the same yesterday, today, and forever" (2 Ne. 29:6-9). By ushering the new scripture into the world, God proved "to the world that the holy scriptures are true, and that God does inspire men and call them to his holy work in this age and generation, as well as in generations of old; Thereby showing that he is the same God yesterday, today, and forever. . . . By these things we know that there is a God in heaven, who is infinite and eternal, from everlasting to everlasting the same unchangeable God, the framer of heaven and earth, and all things which are in them" (D&C 20:11-12, 17).

This emphasis on God's unchanging nature is behind the consistent pattern in the Book of Mormon of equating the creator of the world with the God of the Old Testament with Jesus Christ. The emphasis on consistency is both an appeal and an answer to deists who believed that the God of nature was different from the God revealed in the Bible. The Book of Mormon clearly demonstrated that God was not some remote being unmoved by human experience. For example, in a passage predicting the crucifixion of Jesus, all the forces of nature are pictured in upheaval: "And the rocks of the earth must rend; and . . . many of the kings of the isles of the sea shall be wrought upon by the Spirit of God, to exclaim: The God of nature suffers" (1 Ne. 19:12).

No deist could accept such response, for such feelings made God a changeable being. Deism had drawn upon arguments used against Christian theology by Neo-Platonic, Stoic, and Neo-Pythagorean philosophers of the second and third centuries A.D. They too were offended by the human characteristics of Jesus, who was identified as God-in-the-flesh. Christian theologians adopted Greek categories to explain their faith and had seemingly met those objections with the doctrines of the Trinity and the two natures of Christ—human and divine.

The Unitarian message denied the Trinity doctrine but still held to special revelation as long as it was reasonable.[2] Joseph Smith adopted the Unitarian point of view of Christ[3] but emphasized on-going revelation. He chided Christians who denied present revelation for playing the skeptics' game. According to Smith, denying contemporary revelation meant ascribing a change to God, if only in the manner of his relating to people. If "he hath done his work" then "there is no God today" (2 Ne. 28:5-6) argued Smith in the Book of Mormon. The alternative was atheism and nihilism.

Rather than ascribing the change to God, Smith declared humanity responsible for the break in communication. Present unbelief, he held, accounted for the lack of on-going revelation and charismatic gifts within and without the churches. God had always related to humanity on the basis of faith, and any other terms would indeed make God mutable.[4]

In the Book of Mormon this controversy among evangelicals, rationalists, and skeptics is particularly striking in the allegory of 1 Nephi 8-15. An angel led Nephi out of a dark and dreary wasteland to see a tree laden with fruit. He tasted it and was filled with joy, so he invited his family to eat the fruit. While they ate, Nephi noticed a river near the tree. There was also a straight and narrow path leading to the tree but separated from the river by an iron railing or rod. Crowds of people walked the path toward the tree, but many missed their way when a dark mist surrounded them. Others, however, held the iron rod and safely reached the tree. Once there, they ate the fruit but felt only shame because many scoffers were ridiculing them. These fell away. Still others abandoned the path and iron rod and made their way across the river into the company of the scoffers, joining them in a huge building high in the air. The river separated the tree from the building. While the skeptics were celebrating in their sky-high building, it suddenly fell into the river, carrying its occupants to their destruction.

The allegory suggests that life is aimless without communion with God. The tree of life represents this communion, for it stands for the love God showed in reaching out to people through Jesus' ministry. To eat of the tree's fruit is to know the joy of fellowship with God. Countless multitudes seek this fellowship, but it can be found only by walking the path of life guided by the quality of virtue. A virtuous life, however, is not enough to bring one to fellowship with God. Many hazards await the seeker: temptation and terrors (the dark mist); a real, existential hell (the river); the approval of the sophisticated, which seems more attractive than the tree (the scoffers in the great building); or an existence lost on the broad roads which lead away from the tree to nowhere. Only by holding on to the word of God (the iron rod) can one make contact with God. Yet even some who reach the tree and eat the fruit feel shame when scorned by scoffers and choose to join forces with those scoffers. Others, however, eat the fruit and ignore the jeers. The scoffers represent the world which rejects Christianity because of pride in scientific knowledge and human reason. In the final showdown between unbelievers and the disciples of a Christianity which accepts on-going revelation and spiritual gifts, the worldly wise will be humiliated (1 Ne. 11:36; see 10:19; 16:38).

The allegory makes several points about life with God. How is it found: by God's on-going guidance, by some other means, or not at all? Book of Mormon prophet Nephi believed that he could receive the same vision his father had on the basis that God does not change: "For he that diligently seeketh shall find; and the mysteries of God shall be unfolded to them, by the power of the Holy ghost, as well in these times as in times of old, and as well in times of old as in times to come; wherefore, the course of the Lord is one eternal round" (1 Ne. 10:9). Other points made are (1) present-day revelation is an essential ingredient of fellowship with God. (2) People must let the Bible (the iron rod) guide them or they will lose contact with God or become his enemy. (3) The history of this continent, from the time of the Tower of Babel to the present and into the future Millennium, is one of conflict between those who accept present-day revelation and spiritual gifts and those who deny them or deny Christ and God. Christians who deny these points of the allegory wind up supporting the anti-clerical Laman and Lemuel, who presented the deistic position: "Now, he says that the Lord has talked with him and also that angels have ministered unto him. But behold, we know that he lies unto us . . . and he worketh many things by his cunning arts, that he may deceive our eyes, thinking perhaps, that he may lead us away into some strange wilderness; and after he had led us away, he has thought to make himself a king and ruler over us, that he may do with us according to his will and pleasure" (16:38).

Smith believed that holy living opens one to revelation through voices, dreams, visions, angelic announcements, theophanies, prophecy, and written records. The voice of the Lord may speak forgiveness to the mind (Enos 5, 10). The Divine Presence may appear as a reward for faith and lead to knowledge (Ether 3:18). In dreams God may speak his commands and warnings (1 Ne. 2:1-2, 3:2; Ether 9:3). In visions one may see the future portrayed (1 Ne. 1:6-14). There is no discernible difference between dreams and visions. Nephi says of the allegory of the tree of life: "Behold, I have dreamed a dream; or, in other words, I have seen a vision" (8:2, 4, 36).

In the Book of Mormon visions are usually previews of history. When Lehi was carried away in vision he saw Jesus and his apostles, Jerusalem's destruction, and the Babylonian captivity (1 Ne. 1:6-14). Although his wife complained that he was a "visionary man," Lehi saw a vision which warned of Jerusalem's impending disaster (5:4) and another which confirmed Jerusalem's destruction (2 Ne. 1:4; Hel. 8:19-22).

Nephi, Lehi's son, said that God "hath given me knowledge by visions in the nighttime" (2 Ne. 4:23). Like Paul, Nephi saw things too great for humans to see and was forbidden to write them down (v. 25). A typical prophetic vision is found in 1 Nephi 13. There Nephi sees the Virgin Mary in Nazareth swept away by God's Spirit and returned with an infant: "And the angel said unto me: Behold the Lamb of God, yea, even the Son of the Eternal Father" (1 Ne. 11:21). Nephi also saw Jesus' ministry, John the Baptist baptizing Jesus and attendant theophany, Jesus' trial and crucifixion for the world's sins, the world drawn up to battle against the twelve apostles, and finally the world's defeat.

The Book of Mormon provides considerable insight into angelic ministrations. Angels are sent to rebuke disobedience to divine commands (1 Ne. 3:29-31), comfort the sorrowing (Alma 14-15), instruct men and women as to what they should do (8:14-15, 20; 10:7-8), clarify doctrinal matters (40:11-15), interpret dreams or visions (1 Ne. 11:25, 35-36; 12:16; 14:29), reveal the future (Mosiah 3:2-27; 1 Ne. 11; 13; 2 Ne. 6:11; 10:3; 25:19), declare repentance (Alma 13:22), attest to God's power (Mosiah. 27:14), and warn of impending destruction (Hel. 13:7). Seeing an angel or hearing his message motivates humans to obey. If an angel says something, there is no room for doubt (Mosiah 27:14-15; 1 Ne. 4:3; Alma 10:9; 11:31; 21:5). This is true because "angels speak by the power of the Holy Ghost; wherefore, they speak the words of Christ" (2 Ne. 32:2-3). They may speak to men, women, and children (Alma 32:23). Angels fail to visit the earth only because faith is lacking; as Moroni explained, "it is by faith that angels appear and minister unto men" (Moro. 7:37).

Signs are also important in the Book of Mormon. An angel may give a sign to confirm a vision (1 Ne. 11:7). The Lord may give one to warn of the impending Millennium (3 Ne. 21:1-7). More often, a sign is given by a prophet to attest to his authenticity (Hel. 9:24-41), to help people recognize when a prophecy is about to be fulfilled, or to detect when an event has been prophesied.[5] Signs may not be demanded by skeptics as proof of God's message or existence (Alma 32:17-18, 21). They may be granted when asked for but with dire results. Sherem demanded a sign of the power of the Holy Ghost and received first a scolding and then an affliction which led to his death. Korihor asked for a sign to prove God's existence and was offered the works of creation as proof. Unsatisfied, Korihor was struck dumb and eventually met a terrible death (30:43-59).

The Book of Mormon is especially clear about the importance of written records of God's interaction with humans. In contrast to the Bible, no book of the Mormon scripture has an unknown author and each writer has a genealogy. A detailed calendar is provided with times for the composition of each book.

The most ancient record in the American scripture is found in the book of Ether. This book tells of Jared and his family leaving the Tower of Babel with their language unchanged. Jesus—not yet born into the world—appeared to them and commanded Jared's brother to record what he heard and saw during this visit. The record and two stones by which it could be translated were to be kept sealed until after Jesus' crucifixion: "And the Lord said unto him: Write these things and seal them up, and I will show them in mine own due time unto the children of men" (Ether 3:21-22, 27; 4:1). Generations later Ether, Jared's descendant, edited the record of Jared's brother and added to it (2:13). When he finished the record, Ether hid it "in a manner that the people of Limhi did find them" (15:33).

Centuries later another record was generated by Lehi's family which left Jerusalem just before the first Babylonian offensive in about 600 B.C. Lehi sent his sons into the city to secure from Laban the twenty-four brass plates which contained Lehi's genealogy, the law of Moses, and prophecies of Jeremiah, Jacob, and Joseph (1 Ne. 3:20; 3:3, 12, 24; 4:15, 38). To the twenty-four brass plates Lehi added his vision of Jerusalem's destruction, the advent of the Messiah, and the world's redemption, and recorded this along with other visions and prophecies (1:1-3, 16-17).

The most important records in the Book of Mormon for verifying the Bible were these brass plates. Since the Tower of Babel, the plates had been handed down along with the "interpreters." This enabled any future translator to understand the original language and eventually enabled Joseph Smith to translate. The plates informed God's people of his mysteries, records, and commandments, without which they would have "suffered in ignorance" (Mosiah 1:3). Through future generations the plates would be "preserved by the hand of the Lord until they should go forth unto every nation, kindred, tongue, and people, that they shall know of the mysteries contained thereon" (Alma 37:4). For that reason Lehi's family carried the plates to America (1 Ne. 5:21-22), and the Nephites often copied its contents into the records which became the Book of Mormon (2 Ne. 4:15).

Nephi made two sets of plates, the larger containing the secular history of the Nephites and the smaller their religious history.[6] Nephite editors and writers preserved and added to Nephi's records through the following centuries. Enos wanted to preserve a record for future Lamanites in the event of a Nephite apostasy from Jesus Christ. Two hundred years later, 121 B.C., King Benjamin passed the record to his son Mosiah, who kept the records from the general populace. Later the records were updated by King Limhi (Mosiah 1:1-6, 16). In 46 B.C. the records were again revised, to be eventually a sign to the gentiles of God's power (3 Ne. 3:3-18; 21:5). When the Savior visited the Nephites in 34 A.D., he commanded them to fill in past omissions and to update the records (23).

Mormon was one of the last surviving Nephites. He witnessed and recorded the destruction of almost all his people. Mormon abridged the large plates (the secular record) of Nephi and added to them, noting the fulfillment of prophecies recorded long before by Nephi, Lehi's son. By making his record available to posterity, Mormon hoped to bring the Lamanites back to the knowledge of God: "And now I, Mormon, proceed to finish out my record, which I take from the plates of Nephi. . . . And I, Mormon, pray to God that they may be preserved from this time henceforth. And I know that they will be preserved; for there are great things written upon them, out of which my people and their brethren shall be judged at the great and last day, according to the word of God which is written" (W of M). Mormon buried the records in the hill Cumorah in 385 A.D. to preserve them from his contemporaries and for future generations. Moroni finished his father's records (Morm. 8) and then edited the material of Ether, including only a portion of Ether's report of Jesus' visit to the Jaredites. Moroni again buried the records.

The next chapter in the record's transmission occurred in September 1827. Moroni, appearing now as an angel, committed the plates and the "interpreters" to Joseph Smith for translation. By identifying the records as the "Stick of Joseph" of Ezekiel 37:16 and the "sealed book" which cries "out of the dust" of Isaiah 29, the discovery of the plates was a fulfillment of prophecy.

In the contemporary climate of skepticism, Smith's discovery could be seen to bolster revealed religion in several ways. (1) The detailed genealogy provided by the book responded to Thomas Paine's criticism of the Bible: that books of testimony could not accurately be placed with their times or authors.[7] (2) By tracing the records back to Jared and asserting that prophecies from Adam's time were also available, the book provided evidence for an argument that people had always kept records as part of their relationship with God. (3) Again responding to Paine's criticisms, the book strengthened the value of hearsay reports of signs, wonders, and other historical events.[8] (4) Since the book provided accounts of unfamiliar events, it also met Paine's demand that revelation should communicate only previously unknown material.[9] (5) Christ's interest in bringing records up to date supported the contention that God reveals himself through human language and writing, which Paine also denied.[10] (6) The inclusion of "interpreters" with the plates demonstrated that God provided for accurate translation of the records. (7) The Bible was confirmed as revelation through the parallels and corrections provided by the newly translated Nephite scriptures. (8) The advantages enabled by the book could only be confirmed by admitting on-going revelations and spiritual gifts as a key feature of Christianity.

Joseph Smith thus regained a great deal of territory from deists and rationalists. Further, speculations about Indian origins then in circulation—theories that a lost Hebrew race pre-dated the Indians—were confirmed.

Willard Chase first heard of the discovery of hidden plates in June 1827[11] and Martin Harris in October.[12] Smith said that he "could see the place where the plates were deposited, and that so clearly and distinctly that I knew the place when I visited it." Moroni commanded Smith "to go to my father and tell him of the vision and commandment which I had received. I obeyed; I returned to my father in the field, and rehearsed the whole matter to him. He replied to me that it was of God, and told me to go and do as commanded by the messenger."[13] According to Smith, the vision was repeated each year until Smith finally got the plates in 1827.

This vision led Smith to new scripture and a new church. A vision was not a unique happening in the Palmyra region,[14] but Smith found a way to "prove" his claim which others had not and in the process strengthened the basis of faith in his new movement against objections by skeptics. Smith arranged for corroboration to come from three witnesses as early as March 1829. He received the following revelation: "And the testimony of three witnesses will I send forth of my word" (D&C 5:15). The following month Smith translated from the Book of Mormon: "by the words of three, God hath said, I will establish my word" (2 Ne. 11:3). Nephi was here speaking of his own testimony corroborating that of his brother Jacob and the ancient Isaiah. Within a few weeks, Smith translated

Nephi's prediction that the Book of Mormon "shall be hid from the eyes of the world, that the eyes of none shall behold it, by the power of God, besides him to whom the book shall be delivered; and they shall testify to the truth of the book and the things therein" (27:12). Moroni granted the future translator permission to show the plates to assistants: "And unto three shall they be shown by the power of God; wherefore they shall know of a surety that these things are true. And in the mouth of three witnesses shall those things be established; and the testimony of three, and this work, in the which shall be shown forth the power of God and also his work, of which the Father, and the Son, and the Holy Ghost bear record—and all this shall stand as a testimony against the world at the last day" (Ether 5:3-4).

Martin Harris, Oliver Cowdery, and David Whitmer were the three who became the witnesses for the book. For Martin Harris 1828 was an exciting year: his trip to Pennsylvania to get the characters, his return to Palmyra, his journey east to consult the scholars, his return home—all this climaxed by his return to Pennsylvania to take up duties as Smith's scribe. After three months Harris went back to Palmyra with the 116-page manuscript and lost it. God denounced Harris through a revelation to Smith.

Oliver Cowdery came to Palmyra[15] and heard of Smith's vision. At the beginning of April he went to Pennsylvania to see the young prophet. Smith surmised Cowdery's sincerity to learn the truth and told him of his "secret thoughts and all he meditated about going to see him, which no man on earth knew, as he supposed, but himself."[16] Two days after his arrival, Cowdery became Smith's scribe. Soon thereafter Cowdery wanted power to translate and was promised that he should "receive a knowledge of whatsoever things you shall ask in faith, with an honest heart, believing that you shall receive a knowledge concerning the engravings of old records, which are ancient, which contain those parts of my scripture of which has been spoken by the manifestation of my Spirit. Yea, behold, I will tell you in your mind and in your heart. Now, behold, this is the spirit by which Moses brought the children of Israel through the Red Sea on dry ground" (D&C 8:1-3). His attempt to translate failed, but the promise came that he would have another chance. When he tried again he was told that he should study "out in his mind" his proposed translation. If it was satisfactory his bosom would "burn" within him and he would "feel that it is right" (9:8-9).[17]

Cowdery was then told about the contribution he would make. He should consider his duty as scribe as "a witness unto thee—that the words of the work which thou hast been writing are true." A further witness was the peace and satisfaction he had sought and found about Smith's mission: "If I have told you things which no man knoweth have you not received a witness?" (D&C 6:14-17, 22-24). A second request for assurance about the plates brought out more explicitly the meaning of the "spirit of revelation." On condition that Cowdery "ask in faith, with an honest heart, believing that you shall receive a knowledge concerning the engravings of old records," the "spirit of revelation" would come upon him and speak in his mind and heart the assurance that he wanted concerning the plates (8:1-3).

On 15 May 1829 Smith and Cowdery received baptism and the Aaronic priesthood at the hand of an angel, who identified himself as John the Baptist (D&C 13).[18] In spite of the angelic visit, Cowdery's faith faltered a third time. Once again God reassured him (18:3-4).

David Whitmer took interest in Smith's mission when Smith came to the Whitmer home to finish translating the Book of Mormon. Whitmer was told to ask in faith, believing, and he would receive the Holy Ghost and stand "as a witness of the things of which you shall both hear and see" (D&C 14:8). Jesus declared that he was speaking in person and said: "thou are David . . . called to assist; which thing if ye do, and are faithful, ye shall be blessed both spiritually and temporally, and great shall be your reward" (v. 11).

When the three witnesses had been chosen and were eager to see the plates, they received another communique addressed to them jointly: "And it is by your faith that you shall obtain a view of them, even by that faith which was had by the prophets of old. And after that you have obtained faith, and have seen them with your eyes, you shall testify of them, by the power of God. . . . And ye shall testify that you have seen them, even as my servant Joseph Smith, Jun., has seen them; for it is by my power that he has seen them, and it is because he had faith. . . . And I, Jesus Christ, your Lord and your God, have spoken it unto you, that I might bring about my righteous purposes unto the children of men. Amen" (D&C 17:2-3, 5, 9).

On their way to view the plates, the four men prayed for the angel to appear and display them. Sure that his presence was a detriment because of doubt, Martin Harris withdrew. After the others had seen the plates and the angel, Smith went to Harris and prayed with him. Then Harris too saw the vision and gained the conviction that he had seen the angel and the plates.[19]

Joseph Smith had not chosen these three men randomly. All three had already accepted the reality of angelic visits before he chose them as witnesses. Oliver Cowdery had had visions before he came to New York from Vermont. During the winter of 1828-29, he stayed at the Smith home while teaching at the Palmyra Academy. According to the 1832 history of Joseph Smith, "the Lord appeared unto a young man by the name of Oliver Cowdery and showed unto him the plates in a vision and also the truth of the work and what the Lord was about to do through me his unworthy servant therefore he was desirous to come and write for me to translate."[20] Earlier in this account Smith had written of Martin Harris that "he had become convinced of the vision and gave me fifty dollars to bear my expenses and because of this faith and this righteous deed the Lord appeared unto him in a vision and showed unto him his marvelous work which he was about to do and immediately came to Susquehannah and said the Lord had shown him that he must go to New York City with some of the characters."[21] Rev. Diedrich Willers wrote on 18 June 1830 that Smith went to the home of David Whitmer with the purpose of "completing the translation" of the Book of Mormon because Whitmer claimed to have "seen an angel." He added that this was the eleventh place where Smith had "worked on the translation," that he could work only where others had had visionary experience.[22]

Thus all three witnesses believed that on-going revelation was an essential ingredient of true faith. It led them to expect visions, angelic visits, a sign to confirm faith, and the manifestation of spiritual gifts, and the understanding that any failure to experience these would be due to unbelief. All three had also demonstrated their need for acceptance by Smith and by God. Prior to the completion of the translation, Harris knew that he was in need of humility, prayer, recognition, and repentance of his sins.

The witnesses, thus specially chosen and prepared for their task, did not "see" the plates in an unambiguous sense—despite the confident language of their printed testimony. Joseph Smith received a revelation telling them that they were to see the plates "by your faith . . . as my servant Joseph Smith, Jr. has seen them for it is by my power that he has seen them" (D&C 17:2, 5). Anthony Metcalf,

John H. Gilbert, Reuben P. Harmon, and Rev. Jesse Townsend all said that the three witnesses viewed the plates with their "spiritual eyes."[23] In 1838 Martin Harris publicly stated that the three witnesses saw the plates in a vision but not with their natural eyes. He added that "he never saw them only as he saw a city through a mountain."[24]

Smith also seems to have chosen eight additional witnesses because they were spiritually receptive to new revelation. Rev. Diedrich Willers pictured the Whitmer family as believing in witches, for example. Four of the eight witnesses were Whitmers, and Willers included Hiram Page in the description.[25] Joseph Sr., Hyrum, and Samuel Smith had their own family tradition of visions.[26]

The written testimony of the eight witnesses differed from that of the three witnesses. They claimed no revelation. No "voice" declared to them that the "work is true." No "power of God" showed them the plates—just Joseph Smith. No "angel of God" laid the plates before them; no "voice of the Lord" told them to testify of what they saw. For that reason Eduard Meyer concluded that the testimony of the eight was written primarily as further evidence that Smith indeed had the plates rather than as a demonstration of modern-day revelation.[27] However, the eight did claim revelation in their conversations with others. When David Marks stopped at the Whitmers on 29 March 1830, the eight witnesses "affirmed, that an angel had showed them certain plates of metal, having the appearance of gold that were dug out of the ground by one Joseph Smith."[28] They explained to Marks certain basic points about the Book of Mormon and its contents but claimed to have viewed the plates in vision only.

In 1838 John Whitmer left the church and was confronted by Theodore Turley, who reminded Whitmer that he had "published to the world that an angel did present those plates to Joseph Smith." Although that is not what the testimony of the eight claims, Whitmer nevertheless affirmed that the plates "were shown to me by a supernatural power." But he could not vouch for the translation because he could not read the engravings on the plates.[29] Martin Harris publicly denied that the eight witnesses ever saw the plates. The eight paused before signing their testimony, he said, and signed only after much persuasion.[30]

In response to the testimony of these witnesses, and other signs of modern-day revelation associated with his movement, Smith challenged each person to receive his or her own testimony and affirm the reality of present-day revelation. Alexander Campbell expressed the frustration many felt with such a challenge. Campbell imagined a conversation with the three witnesses: "I would ask them how they knew that it was God's voice which they heard—but they would tell me to ask God in faith. *That is, I must believe it first, and then ask God if it is true.*" In other words those who did not affirm the testimony only proved their own unbelief blocking the witness.[31]

In 1834 Oliver Cowdery talked about the place of faith in the new church in a letter to his brother, a letter which makes clearer the context in which those involved interpreted events. People believed that "Jesus is the Christ" because they believed apostolic testimony about him. But people needed additional "assurance" in order to face the arguments of God's enemies. According to Cowdery, "revelation" was the rock upon which Christ would build his church, against which "the gates of hell should not prevail" (his interpretation of Matthew 16:15-18). No apostle's testimony could reveal this: "flesh and blood cannot reveal it—it must be the Father"; and if "men *Know* that Jesus is the Christ, it must be by revelation."[32]

This view of the possibility of personal revelation counters Thomas Paine's critique of traditional Christianity. Paine had written that the accurate prediction of an eclipse or transit of Venus proves that humans know the distance between heavenly bodies and their mass when they most closely approach each other. That is, the fact of accurate prediction proves the existence of true knowledge.[33] According to Mormons, the testimony of the witnesses provided such a verification of present-day revelation and validated the records contained in the Book of Mormon. Mormon and Book of Mormon prophet Moroni provided a guideline for receiving a personal revelation: "I would exhort you that when ye shall read these things. . . . that ye would ask God . . . if these things are not true; and if ye shall ask with a sincere heart, with real intent, having faith in Christ, he will manifest the truth of it unto you, by the power of the Holy Ghost, ye may know the truth of all things" (Moro. 10:3-5). Deists could run their own experiments and seek their own testimonies. If one must use scientific presuppositions to check the findings of science, then one must use spiritual guidelines to check matters of religion. If deists could not muster the interest to examine printed records with a believing mind, at least they could no longer rail against the adherents of revealed religion.[34] Mormons, like skeptics, could now deprecate faith based on hearsay evidence.

Instead they promoted a faith established by personal revelation, an experience which could be reproduced if certain principles were applied.

After his conversion Sidney Rigdon visited members of his congregation in Kirtland, Ohio, to win them over to his new faith. He argued that their faith was based on the Bible, which came to them only upon "human testimony." They denied this "and gave him reasons which he himself formerly urged against *deists*. He then said the *old* revelation was confirmed by miracles, but the Book of Mormon would never be; it was not designed to be thus confirmed."[35] Rigdon's reply is borne out in how the Book of Mormon deals with miracles. Although it speaks about miracles as a potential manifestation of the Spirit, actual mention of miracles performed is rare.[36] Joseph Smith would claim some miracles[37] for his new church, but miracles never became the final basis for faith. That was reserved for personally experienced revelation.

Choosing three witnesses proved to be a successful strategy. They frequently testified before large audiences.[38] And even when later developments clouded their testimony, the restored church rode out the storm. Eventually few in the church questioned the literal words of the testimony.

Deists rejected the deity of Jesus and the reliability of the New Testament gospels because they were based on human testimony. By prompting each convert to pursue his or her own personal revelation that Jesus is the Son of God, Smith removed the issue of secondary testimony. Now it was a matter of knowledge—knowledge communicated directly to the believer and meeting the criteria for revelation stated by Paine. The development of the Christian church in the Grecian east and the Roman west led to an interpretation of *Peter* as the "rock" of Matthew 16:18. Peter's successors were a visible guarantee that the church still had the faith delivered by Jesus Christ. The Protestant reformers of the sixteenth century interpreted Peter's *confession* that Jesus was "the Christ, the Son of the living God" as the "rock" on which Christ would build his church. The Roman Catholic claim to apostolic succession and ultimate papal infallibility and the Protestant claim to a succession of faith based on an infallible, inspired Bible were both undermined by the deistic polemic, many felt, because both claims were based on apostolic testimony or hearsay evidence. By interpreting *revelation* as the "rock," Smith defended God, the deity of Jesus Christ, and biblical revelation against deism in a way which Protestants and Catholics did not—in a way which seemed to give believers a sounder foundation for their faith.

NOTES

1. The argument is used for other matters as well. Redemption and salvation have been available since the Fall, "for the Spirit is the same, yesterday, today and forever" (2 Ne. 2:4). Little children need no baptism or repentance, and "if not so, God is a partial God, and also a changeable God, and a respecter to persons; for how many little children have died without baptism. . . . For I know that God is not a partial God, neither a changeable being; but he is unchangeable from all eternity to all eternity" (Moro. 8:11-12, 18).

This refers only to the manner of God's dealing with people, not to his essence. See *The Evening and the Morning Star*, Feb. 1833, 97, for a similar argument for the Book of Mormon. It contained the full gospel and proved to Jews and Gentiles that the Bible is true and that God still inspires people and calls them to do his work.

2. William Ellery Channing summed up this point in 1819 in his "Baltimore Sermon." He held to the inspiration of the Bible and set forth the "leading principle in interpreting scripture": "the Bible is a book written for men, in the language of men, and that its meaning is to be sought in the same manner, as that of other books . . . that God, when he condescends to speak and write submits, if we may so say, to the established rules of speaking and writing. How else would the Scriptures avail us more than if communicated in an unknown tongue." Vergilius Ferm, ed., *Classics of Protestantism* (New York: Philosophical Library, 1959), 245. Paine would have disowned this position as unworthy of God.

3. See George B. Arbaugh, "Evolution of Mormon Doctrine," *Church History* 9 (1940), in which he traces monistic tendencies in the Book of Mormon through tri-theism and then polytheism late in Smith's life. See also the earlier chapter in this book on Unitarianism, Universalism, and the Christian Connection.

4. Smith's concern to keep God unchangeable was to find an ironic development years later when he advanced the position that God progresses in his own development. The unchangeable aspect of God, as Smith and later Utah Mormonism saw it, was to be found only in his manner of relating to humanity.

5. Specific signs given include: Christ's birth from a virgin (2 Ne. 17:11, 14; cf. Isa. 7:11, 14); the appearance of a new star and a prolonged day at his birth (Hel. 14:2-6; 3 Ne. 1:15); Christ's crucifixion to be signaled by a three-day darkness (1 Ne. 19:10; Hel. 14:14).

6. 1 Ne. 9:1-5; 19:1-6. The small plates comprise the books of 1 Nephi, 2 Nephi, Jacob, Enos, Jarom, and Omni. See Hugh Nibley, *Since Cumorah* (Salt Lake City: Deseret Book, 1967), 143-52. His account of "The Transmission of the Record" lays out the parallels between the efforts of the Nephite editors and those of biblical Isaiah.

7. Thomas Paine, *The Age of Reason*, Moncure Danile Conway, ed. (New York: G. P. Putnam's Sons, 1898), 91-92. The genealogies of Lehi and Laban went back to biblical Joseph.

8. Ibid., 168, 183.

9. Ibid., 33.

10. Ibid., 38, 170.

11. See Brodie's discussion based on Howe. *No Man Knows My History: The Life of Joseph Smith*, 2d ed. (New York: Alfred Knopf, 1971), 437.

12. Joel Tiffany, "Mormonism—No. II," *Tiffany's Monthly*, Aug. 1859, 167.

13. Joseph Smith et al., *History of the Church of Jesus Christ of Latter-day Saints*, 7 vols. (Salt Lake City: Deseret Book Co., 1927), 1:13, 15; hereafter HC. Joseph Smith dated this vision to 1823. It often is confused with what is called the first vision, which he dated to 1820. No one knew about the first vision at this time and it was not a factor in winning the first converts of early Mormonism.

14. *Western Farmer*, 16 May 1821, contains a story of a Methodist preacher who asserted that he was one of the "prophets that was to come in the latter days—that the dawn of the millennium has commenced." The story of Asa Wild, *Wayne Sentinel*, 22 Oct. 1823, is also pertinent. He had a vision in which Jehovah "told me that the Millenium state of the world is about to take place; that in *seven* years literally, there would scarcely a sinner be found on earth. . . . above all, various and dreadful judgments executed immediately by God, through the instrumentality of the Ministers of the Millenial dispensation." All denominations had become corrupt, guided only by reason not by revelation as was the original church. But God would raise up that "class of persons" mentioned in Revelation 14:6-7, "of an inferior class, and small learning," who would be superior Christians in every way. All denominations constitute the New Testament Babylon. Wild had tried the Calvinist and Methodist churches but found them wanting. See Brodie, 22-23; also the visions of Solomon Chamberlain, early convert to Mormonism, in Lawrence C. Porter, "A Study of the Origins of the Church of Jesus Christ of Later-day Saints in the States of New York and Pennsylvania, 1816-1831," Ph.D. diss., Brigham Young University, 1971, 360-62.

15. Before coming to New York from Middleton, Vermont, Cowdery associated with a sect "apparently involving millennial expectations and direct revelation as well as some mysterious treasure hunting" (R. Whitney

Cross, *The Burned-over District: The Social and Intellectual History of Enthusiatic Religion in Western New York, 1800-1850* [Ithaca, NY: Cornell University Press, 1950], 38-39).

16. *Latter-day Saints' Millennial Star* 40 (1879): 772.

17. Cowdery had asked to translate and had been assured that he could do it (D&C 8:9-12, 9:1). But he failed for four reasons. First, Cowdery had "feared" and did not continue the translation (9:5, 11). Second, he had expected Christ to give him the translation (v. 7). Third, he was supposed to think through the translation until an inner burning would let him know that "it is right" (v. 8). Finally, he could have translated if he had known all this (v. 10), but no one had prepared him for the translation process; only after his failure was it revealed to him. Cowdery was then told why he should not soon try again: "I have taken away this privilege from you." This is similar to previous explanations for failure to find hidden treasure. When William Stafford let Smith and his father look for treasure, they went through an elaborate ceremony, "but as there was some mistake in the process, it did not have the desired effect." Brodie reprints this experience from Eber D. Howe, *Mormonism Unvailed* (Painesville, OH, 1834), 434. Smith's father-in-law, Isaac Hale, told of the time when Smith directed some money-diggers, "but when they had arrived in digging to near the place where he [Smith] had stated an immense treasure would be found—he said the enchantment was so powerful that he could not see" (Brodie, 439).

Mormon apologists have tended to discredit Hale's statement because it appeared in Howe's *Mormonism Unvailed*, but Wesley P. Walters's "Joseph Smith's Bainbridge, N.Y., Court Trials," *Westminster Theological Journal* 36 (Winter 1974): 151-52, shows that the statement was first published independently of Howe or Philastus Hurlbut (ex-Mormon collaborator with Howe). It appeared first in Hale's local newspaper, *The Susquehannah Register*.

18. In 1838 Cowdery would allow himself to be baptized a Methodist.

19. HC 1:54-55.

20. See Dean C. Jessee, "The Early Accounts of Joseph Smith's First Vision," *Brigham Young University Studies* 9 (Spring 1969): 275-94.

21. Ibid. Confirmed by Martin Harris; compare Tiffany, 163.

22. Willers to Mayer and Young. See D. Michael Quinn, "The First Months of Mormonism: A Contemporary View by Rev. Diedrich Willers," *New York History* 54 (July 1973): 317-31.

23. Anthony Metcalf, *Ten Years Before the Mast* (Malad, ID, 1888), 73-74, printed a letter from David Whitmer dated 2 April 1887: "of course we were in the spirit when we had the view, for no man can behold the face of an angel, except in a spiritual view, but we were in the body also, and everything was as natural to us, as it is at any time. . . . A bright light enveloped us where we were, that filled at noon day, and there *in a vision or in the spirit,*

we saw and heard just as it is stated in my testimony in the Book of Mormon."

Whitmer was not thoroughly consistent in the many statements he made about the event. See Hill, 92. Also in "Murphy and Mormonism," *The Kingston Times* (Caldwell County, MO), 16 Dec. 1887, John Murphy describes an interview with Whitmer, who reportedly said that seeing an angel was like having an impression, similar to the experience of a Quaker or Methodist in meditation; it was "being impressed with the truth and reality of it."

Jesse Townsend's letter to Phineas Stiles, dated 24 Dec. 1833, Palmyra, Wayne County, New York, spoke of the Book of Mormon translation being done in secret, and that Harris "claimed to have seen the plates with 'spiritual eyes'" (Pomeroy Tucker, *The Origin, Rise, and Progress of Mormonism* [New York: Appleton & Co., 1867], 290).

John H. Gilbert said "nobody but Joe himself ever saw the golden tablets or the far-seeing spectacles." In "Joe Smith," *Post & Tribune* (Detroit, MI), 3 Dec. 1877, 3. See also the citation in Hill, 92.

24. Stephen Burnett to Br. [Lyman E.] Johnson, 25 Apr. 1838, in Joseph Smith Letter Book, 2, archives, Church of Jesus Christ of Latter-day Saints, Salt Lake City, Utah.

25. Page said of his experience in becoming a Mormon that holy angels "came and showed themselves to me as I was walking through the field, to confirm me in the work of the Lord of the last days—three of whom came to me afterwards and sang a hymn in their own pure language." *The Ensign of Liberty of The Church of Christ*, 1 (Dec. 1847): 63; Hiram Page to William McLellin, 30 May 1847.

26. Lucy Smith, *Biographical Sketches of Joseph Smith, the Prophet, and His Progenitors for Many Generations* (Liverpool: S. W. Richards, 1853), 21-59.

27. Eduard Meyer, *Ursprung and Geschichte der Mormonen mit Exhursen uber die Anfange des Islams und des Christentums* (Halle: Max Niemeyer, 1912), 22.

28. *The Life of David Marks to the 26th Year of His Age* (Limerick, ME: Office of the Morning Star, 1831), 340.

29. HC 3:307-308.

30. See n24 above.

31. Alexander Campbell, *Delusions. An Analysis of the Book of Mormon . . . and a Refutation of Its Pretensions to Divine Authority* (Boston, 1832), 15. A debate between Tyler Parsons and Elder Freeman Nickerson demonstrates a similar argument. Nickerson "knew" that the Book of Mormon was a true revelation from God "by the power of God, for his voice had made it known to him, by his obedience to his commands." Parsons. "Do you know of his [Smith's] digging certain plates out of the earth, in the town of Manchester in the State of New York?" Nickerson. "I did not see

him dig them up." Parsons. "Then how dare you say in your statement to the audience, that you knew it was all true, for the voice of the Lord had declared it? What do you mean by the voice of the Lord?" Nickerson. "From hearsay; from those that knew it by the power of God." Parsons. "Mr. Nickerson, do you suppose Cowdery, Whitmer and Harris, the three witnesses that have testified to seeing these plates, have sworn by the same rules you have stated, viz: hearsay?" Nickerson. "I do not know" (*Mormon Fanaticism Exposed*, 5, 44).

32. Oliver Cowdery to W. A. Cowdery, *Latter-day Saints' Messenger and Advocate*, Nov. 1834, 26. At Joseph Smith's 1826 examination in South Bainbridge (now Afton), New York, his employer testified in his behalf: "He [Josiah Stowell] swore that the prisoner [Joseph Smith] possessed all the power he claimed, and declared he could see things fifty feet below the surface of the earth, as plain as the witness could see what was on the Justice's table, and described very many circumstances to confirm his words. Justice Neeley soberly looked at the witness and in a solemn, dignified voice, said, 'Deacon Stowell, do I understand you as swearing before God, under the solemn oath you have taken, that you *believe* the prisoner can see by the aid of the stone fifty feet below the surface of the earth, as plainly as you can see what is on my table?' 'Do I *believe* it?' says Deacon Stowell, 'do I believe it? No, it is not a matter of belief. I positively know it to be true.'" Account of W. D. Purple in the *Chanango Union* (Norwich, NY), 2 May 1877. Text in William Mulder and A. Russell Mortensen, eds., *Among the Mormons: Historic Accounts by Contemporary Observers* (New York: Alfred Knopf, 1958), 34-37. Smith was tried again in 1830 for money digging. The trial was reported in 1831 by A. W. Benton. Once more Josiah Stowell testified for Smith, and the questioning was reported by Benton: "Did Smith tell you there was money hid in a certain place which he mentioned? Yes. Did he tell you, you could find it by digging? Yes. Did you dig? Yes. Did you find any money? No. Did he not lie to you then and deceive you? No! the money was there, but we did not get quite to it! How do you know it was there? Smith said it was!" Reprinted in Jerald and Sandra Tanner, *Joseph Smith and Money Digging* (Salt Lake City: Modern Microfilm Company, 1970), 33.

33. Paine, 71.

34. Orson Pratt carried this strategy to its conclusion when he spoke of those who had gotten a witness: "This great cloud of witnesses know with the greatest certainty that the Book of Mormon is true. . . . The nature of their testimony is such that it precludes all possibility of their being deceived themselves. Before mankind can be justified in calling these thousands of witnesses impostors, they must prove that none of them have seen and heard as they boldly testify." "Divine Authority of the Book of Mormon," *Doctrines of the Gospel* (Salt Lake City: Juvenile Instructor Office, 1884), 43.

35. *Painesville Telegraph*, 15 Feb. 1831. The report to the paper came from a person identified only as M. S. C., who said that Rigdon asked for a sign a few days after talking with Cowdery. This seems to have been the asking of someone who had read and believed the Book of Mormon and now was asking for confirmation of what he already believed. M. S. C. identified himself as a member of the Church of Christ in Kirtland, perhaps a member of Rigdon's congregation.

36. Hel. 16:4, 13, reports a later leader performing signs, wonders, and miracles, "that they might know that the Christ must shortly come." 3 Ne. 17:7-10; 26:15 has Jesus performing some healing miracles because peoples' faith was "sufficient." 4 Ne. 5 sees Jesus' disciples do "great and marvelous works," and "healing, and all manner of miracles." There are a few additional references, but no appeal to any of them as the basis for believing.

37. The first miracle acknowledged by Smith as coming through the new church was his exorcism of a demon from Newel Knight in the middle of April 1830; HC, 1:82-83.

38. Reported by an early apostate, Ezra Booth, to the *Ohio Star*. His account later appeared in Howe's book and is quoted in Francis W. Kirkham, *A New Witness for Christ in America: The Book of Mormon*, 2 vols., 3rd ed. (Independence, MO: Zion's Printing and Publishing Co., 1951), 1:458.

10.

Prophecy Proves Revelation

> There are certain events plainly predicted in the Prophets, yet future, which, when fulfilled, will convince all the heathen nations of the true God, and they shall know that He hath spoken and performed it. And all the great and learned men of Christendom, and all societies, who put any other than a *literal* construction on the word of prophecy, shall stand confounded.
>
> —Parley P. Pratt,[1] a Mormon apostle

Prophecy was central to Joseph Smith's message. He traced prediction and fulfillment of prophecy back to Jared and the Tower of Babel, and noted that ancient prophecies were recorded on the brass plates of Laban (1 Ne. 3:30). Soon after publication of the Book of Mormon, Smith recorded prophecies from Adam himself.[2]

The Book of Mormon's notion of prophecy responded strategically to objections which had been raised by deists. For example, it detailed the case against prophecy through the person of Korihor, archvillain and anti-Christ of the Book of Mormon narrative. Korihor "began to preach unto the people against the prophecies which had been spoken by the prophets, concerning the coming of Christ" (Alma 30:6). He asked: "Why do ye look for a Christ? For no man can know of anything which is to come. Behold, these things which ye call prophecies . . . are foolish traditions of your fathers. How do ye know of their surety? Behold, ye cannot know of things which ye

143

do not see; therefore ye cannot know that there shall be a Christ. Ye look forward and say that ye see a remission of sins. But behold, it is the effect of a frenzied mind; and this derangement of your minds . . . lead[s] you away into a belief of things which are not so" (Al. 30:13-16). Asked why he spoke "against all the prophecies of the holy prophets," Korihor replied: "because I do not teach this people to bind themselves down under the foolish ordinances and perform-ances which are laid down by ancient priests, in ignorance . . . . Ye say that those ancient prophecies are true. Behold, I say that ye do not know that they are true" (Alma 30:23-26).

Unbelieving Nephites at the time of Jesus' coming articulated similar objections to prophecy. Samuel the Lamanite prophet pre-dicted particular signs of the coming of Christ. When the signs started to appear, unbelieving Nephites said that "Some things they may have guessed right, among so many; but behold, we know that all these great and marvelous works cannot come to pass, of which has been spoken" (Hel. 16:15-16).

Thus the Book of Mormon summarized the arguments against prophecy popularized by deists: Bible traditions are foolish and untrustworthy; foreknowledge is impossible; prophecy is a delusion used by corrupt priests to manipulate people; there is no way of knowing the truth of prophecy, since the law of averages allows for correct guesses. But the Book of Mormon also launched a counter-offensive to preserve prophecy as proof of revelation. On one level, the Book of Mormon affirmed a traditional view of prophecy. Its presentation of the prophetic gift and the means by which it was given were similar to views held by Protestant enthusiasts in western New York. But Mormon scripture went further and enlisted proph-ecy and revelation in its own cause.

Fulfilled prophecy was meant to inspire faith in future fulfill-ment. The Book of Mormon included both prophesied signs of the birth and death of Jesus Christ and notice of their accomplishment. Such accounts of the fulfillment of prophecy were meant to assure readers that God would yet fulfill his covenant to Israel by working through the predictions of the millennial agenda. Because of what the Bible and Book of Mormon describe as a sign of the last days—notably the discovery of a new book—readers were encouraged to believe that the signs leading to the winding up of this world's affairs were in the process of being fulfilled and that the Millennium would soon come. In turn such belief in prophecy would become part of what might enable the end. With other millennialists, Smith thought that human effort could help bring in the Millennium. If Smith could arouse the expectation of the faithful, God would come that much sooner to his temple. Prophecy was as much foreseeing the event as its cause (1 Ne. 10:13; Moro. 8:29).

This emphasis on the importance of worthiness for fulfilling prophecy—in the future as well as in the past—helped to answer one objection Thomas Paine had raised. He had scorned biblical prophets for giving predictions and then, when no fulfillment was forthcoming, explaining away the failure by supposing that God had "repented."[3] But the Book of Mormon did not include the notion that God "repented," and Smith edited this notion out of his Inspired Version of the Bible.

Conditional prophecy was a different matter, since its purpose was to effect repentance. Nephite prophets warned their nation to repent or be destroyed (1 Ne. 1:4). Abinadi preached repentance to the people and warned that God would allow their enemies to bring them into bondage if they refused to repent (Mosiah 11:20-26; 12:1-8). In Enos's time many prophets were required to proclaim forthcoming doom in order to keep the people in line: "I say there was nothing short of these things, and exceeding great plainness of speech, would keep them from going down speedily to destruction" (Enos 23). But indictment and threat were never without the accompanying promise of a Messiah from whom sinners could hope for reprieve.[4] Rather than representing God as capricious, conditional prophecy verified God's respect for human freedom. God would not violate human "free agency," but neither would he deny justice and withhold punishment, for that would make God inconstant.[5]

The Book of Mormon showed that people in all ages had had access to such notions about prophecy. Because of the doctrine that faith in Jesus Christ saves, critics had often asked about the status of those who lived before Jesus. The standard Christian response was that they too were saved by faith when they looked forward to the coming of the Messiah. Smith made prophecy prove that what was known of Jesus in 1829 A.D. was also known at the time of Adam (D&C 20:26-28). The content of doctrine in all ages was the same: repentance, baptism, faith, and continuing revelation. If anyone should wonder why this was so, he or she were told in the Book of Mormon: "And now I will ease your mind somewhat on this subject. Behold, you marvel why these things should be known so long beforehand. Behold, I say unto you, is not a soul at this time as precious unto God as a soul will be at the time of his coming? [Alma is speaking to his son, Corianton, about 73 B.C.] Is it not as necessary that the plan of redemption should be made known unto this people as well as unto their children? Is it not as easy at this time for the Lord to send his angel to declare these glad tidings unto us as unto our children, or as after the time of his coming?" (Alma 39:17-19). Thus the Book of Mormon assured modern believers that the ancients had full doctrinal faith.[6]

Virtually without exception, Smith made prophecy predictive, specific, and detailed.[7] The messianic prophecies designated aspects of Jesus' life and ministry, his doctrinal positions, the signs of his birth and death, and the exact number of years from the time of a prophecy to the date of his birth. In the Book of Mormon Isaiah 29 is deployed as a detailed prediction of the Harris-Anthon consultation and the coming forth of the American scripture. The three witnesses are predicted in several places. Even the name of the one to translate the records was known to the biblical patriarch Joseph, son of Jacob. These are not equivocal predictions which might fit circumstances other than those intended.

Smith's attitude toward prophecy was literalistic,[8] a feature he shared with conservative and millennialistic Protestants. In this they may have been partly reacting to the deistic call for allegorical rather than literal understanding of prophecy. But when Christians agreed to understand a prophecy allegorically, deists scorned them for their apparent embarrassment over literal interpretation. Smith's use of prophecy exhibits disdain for anything other than literal interpretation.[9]

The Book of Mormon provided detailed accounts of familiar prophecies which had been fulfilled and used similar detail to introduce fulfillment of prophecies which were not so familiar to traditional Christian readers. Messianic prophecy is particularly prominent in the Book of Mormon. In no other instance was Smith more precise than in describing the events and significance of Jesus' life as foreseen by those living before his time. The creation of a whole line of Nephite prophets who predicted the coming of Jesus to the exact year dramatically reaffirmed Christian claims that the messianic passages of the Old Testament had accurately pointed to the birth of Christ. In the Book of Mormon, even his many titles and names had been foreknown: Messiah, Savior, Redeemer, Son of

God, "Son" of Righteousness,[10] Only Begotten, Holy One of Israel, Mighty One, Father and Son, Good Shepherd, King of Heaven, and the Eternal Father of heaven and earth.[11]

Prophecy described to Book of Mormon characters far in advance what would happen at Jesus' birth and death. A new star and the sun shining for two days and a night would announce his birth. A three-day darkness accompanied by earthquakes would signal his death (Hel. 14). He would be born of a virgin named Mary (1 Ne. 11:18; Mosiah 3:8); be baptized by John (1 Ne. 11:27); be rejected (2 Ne. 25:12), mocked and scourged (Mosiah 15:5), lifted up on a cross (1 Ne. 11:33). He would break the bonds of death (Mos. 15:8) and rise from the dead (2 Ne. 15:13). He would atone for sin (Mosiah 3:11), would redeem his people (15:1), and satisfy the demands of justice (v. 9). He would be the means of salvation to the gentiles (2 Ne. 33:9); would bring about the resurrection of the dead (Alma 5:14); and would judge all humanity (2 Ne. 33:7, 11). Such knowledge was known by Adam (Book of Moses, revealed in 1830).

The Book of Mormon also prophesied of the fate of the Jews. Smith operated within a premillennial framework which considered the conversion of the Jews an indispensable part of the last days. Thus the Jews became part of the House of Israel which should be grafted onto an olive tree (1 Ne. 10:12-24). Because they had denied Christ (1 Ne. 19:13), the Jews had to be scattered over the earth (10:12) and be persecuted by other nations for many generations "until they shall be persuaded to believe in Christ" (2 Ne. 25:16; 1 Ne. 19:14). Eventually, assisted by the rulers and monarchs of the gentile world (2 Ne. 10:8-9), they would be gathered (v. 8) and once again occupy the "land of Jerusalem" (20:29). They would accept Christ and his atonement and no longer look for another Messiah. They would also believe the Book of Mormon (25:16). A place for God's people would then be established in the mountain tops. From there God's word would go forth. Jerusalem, along with Zion, would be world centers. Universal peace would prevail (2 Ne. 12:1-4/ Isa. 2:1-4; 2 Ne. 21:11-12/ Isa. 11:11-12).

The Book of Mormon spoke about the future of the Lamanites or native Americans as well. As an expression of God's wrath, they would be scattered and smitten by gentiles (1 Ne. 12:14). God would take away their land (2 Ne. 1:11) and cause them to be afflicted, slain, cast out, hated—to become a "hiss and a by-word" (3 Ne. 16:9). But they would survive (2 Ne. 3:3; Alma 9:16), and their fortunes would change for the better when they discovered their Israelite origins, learned of the restored gospel and how to be saved (1 Ne. 15:14). They would know that this knowledge comes from God, would rejoice (2 Ne. 30:6), and would come into the "true fold of God" (1 Ne. 15:15). They would be nourished by gentiles (22:8) who would share the records of the Jews and the Book of Mormon with them (2 Ne. 29:13). In future generations the Lamanites would become a "white and delightsome people" (30:6).[12] Together gentiles and Lamanites would build the New Jerusalem (3 Ne. 20:22; 21:22-23).

The Book of Mormon detailed other events in the gentiles' future. The Book of Mormon foresaw that they would scatter the Lamanites, possess the land of promise, and prosper because of the Spirit of the Lord (1 Ne. 13:14-15). God's blessing would make them a mighty nation (22:7; 3 Ne. 20:27). God would establish his church among them when they repented and obeyed him. He would give them much of his gospel "which shall be plain and precious" (1 Ne. 13:34; 3 Ne. 21:22). They would then take the "fulness of the gospel" to the Lamanites (1 Ne. 15:13) and to the Jews (3 Ne. 16:4). The restored gospel would divide the gentiles into two camps: those who accepted it and those who rejected it (1 Ne. 14:6-7). Those who rejected it would do so because they already had a Bible and would expect no other scripture (2 Ne. 29:3, 9). Some of the gentiles would pridefully consider themselves to be above all other nations and yet allow fraud, false religion, murder, and secret combinations to go unchecked. As a consequence, God would remove the "fulness" of his gospel from them (26:22; 27:1; 3 Ne. 16:10). Even then, if they would repent, they would once again be considered God's people (v. 13).

The Book of Mormon foretold its own appearance. It would appear when Nephites had disappeared and when Lamanites had been smitten by the gentiles and had lost the Nephite records. Gentiles would have many churches but would minimize God's power, would prefer human wisdom, support secret combinations, and keep the poor in poverty (2 Ne. 26:14-22). There would be "wars, rumors of wars, and earthquakes in divers places" (Morm. 8:26-30; cf. vv. 31-34). At just that time the gentiles would bring forth the Book of Mormon. Its appearance would demonstrate God's power (1 Ne. 13:35).

Joseph Smith's role was anticipated, as mentioned (2 Ne. 3:6-7, 15).[13] A seer would perform work which would be of great value for the Lamanites (vv. 7, 11). He would make his full-time career doing God's work (v. 8) and would be as great as Moses in the eyes of God (vv. 8-9; compare Moses 1:41). He would be made strong out of his weaknesses (2 Ne. 3:13). Although many would try to destroy him, his persecutors would be confounded, and instead of death he would receive God's blessing (v. 14). Like Moses, he would have a spokesman (v. 18).

The Book of Mormon thus contained many detailed predictions dealing both with ancient and contemporary events. Revelations which came in this early period but after the translation of the Book of Mormon—such as those recorded in the Doctrine and Covenants—were more reticent about predicting the new church's fortunes. The majority of revelations which do prophesy express general confidence in the eventual success of efforts undertaken to found the church. David Whitmer reported an early failed prophecy not recorded in the official edition of Smith's revelations—Smith's prediction that Hiram Page and Oliver Cowdery would be able to sell the copyright to the Book of Mormon in Canada.[14] Such a failure may suggest why Smith was thereafter cautious. His role as a prophet who could predict the future was more potential than actual before he left New York for Ohio in 1831.

Responding to deists' criticisms of unfulfilled prophecy, Smith furnished what he took to be abundant proof of fulfilled prophecy.[15] By showing that ancient prophecy dealt with matters of nineteenth-century concern and by demonstrating congruence with his theology, Smith strengthened the claim for the Book of Mormon's being a special revelation.

NOTES

1. Parley P. Pratt, *A Voice of Warning and Instruction to All People* (Salt Lake City: Deseret News Steam Printing Establishment, 1874), 20.

2. Adam prophecies in Moses 5:10; 6:8; Seth in 6:13; Enos in 6:13; Enoch in 7:2, 41-46; Methuselah in 8:3; and Noah in 8:16. The book of Moses was written June-December 1830; Pearl of Great Price.

3. Thomas Paine, *The Age of Reason*, Moncure Danile Conway, ed. (New York: G. P. Putnam's Sons, 1898), 82.

4. Used with individuals: 2 Ne. 5:22; Alma 5:51. Used with nations and peoples: 1 Ne. 14:5-7; 22:18; 2 Ne. 6:12; 28:17, 19; 31:13-14; Jacob 3:3; Mosiah 11:20-25; 29:19-20; Alma 8:16, 29; 10:20-23; 13:27, 30. This list is only partial.

5. See Hel. 14:29-31.

6. Smith explicitly stated that the plan of redemption had to be the same in all ages or else God had changed his plan. See *The Evening and the Morning Star*, Mar. 1834, 143-44.

7. Only in Alma 8:25 is prophecy found without the predictive factor. In D&C, only in section 34:6-10.

8. Especially in portions reproducing texts declared fulfilled by the New Testament. It is also true of those pertaining to the millennial scheme of events and those portraying the circumstances surrounding the emergence of the Book of Mormon. One important factor in this literalism was Smith's conviction that he could do something to fulfill a prophecy. This lay behind Smith's use of Isaiah 29:11-12. The literalism lent itself to strategies by which people could intentionally fulfill prophecy.

9. For example, see D&C 77:2 dealing with the "beasts" of Rev. 4. Joseph thought that the four beasts were real, saved from other worlds, and now living in heaven with real power over earth's inhabitants (Joseph Smith et al., *History of the Church of Jesus Christ of Latter-day Saints*, 7 vols. [Salt Lake City: Deseret Book Co., 1927], 5:340-44). Paul's "earthly" corresponding to the "heavenly" is touched on in D&C 128. Parley Pratt, *Voice of Warning*, 6-7, 25, later contrasted the literal prophetic fulfillment with what he called the modern system of "spiritualizing" of which, he felt, the biblical prophets knew nothing.

10. Apparently Smith meant to apply the title "Sun of Righteousness" from Mal. 4:2, which had been applied to Jesus early on in church history. When Cowdery heard the word "sun," he transcribed it "son." Smith used the rest of the verse ("with healing in his wings") to describe Jesus' resurrection from the dead (2 Ne. 25:13).

11. 1 Ne. 19:17; 13:40; 15:14; 2 Ne. 25:16; 26:9; Jacob 4; 1 Ne. 19:14; 21:26; Mosiah 15:2; Alma 5:38, 50; 11:39. One citation is given for each name or title. All but three occur many times.

12. Dark skin as a sign of God's displeasure is taught in 1 Ne. 12:23; 2 Ne. 5:21-23; Alma 3:6-9; Morm. 5:15. In W. W. Phelps's version of Joseph Smith's 1831 revelation, verse 4, Smith envisioned inter-marriage with the Indians as a way of making them "white and delightsome": "For it is my will, that in time, ye should take unto you wives of the Lamanites and Nephites, that their posterity may become white, delightsome and just, for even now their families are more virtuous than the gentiles." Martin Harris, Oliver Cowdery, Brigham Young, Phelps, and apostate Ezra Booth all knew about the revelation. Brigham Young's attitude on inter-marriage with native Americans during the early Utah years, when many Mormon men took Indian wives, carried out the principle established in the 1831 revelation. See Jerald and Sandra Tanner, *Mormonism Like Watergate?* (Salt Lake City: Modern Microfilm Company, 1974), 6-14. See also Richard S. Van

Wagoner, *Mormon Polygamy: A History* (Salt Lake City: Signature Books, 1986).

13. David Whitmer, one of the three witnesses, agreed that Smith was the "man who is not learned" of Isa. 29 but not that he was the choice seer. The seer was to be a descendant of Lehi through the youngest son, Joseph (2 Ne. 3), from whom the Indians descended, and the choice seer was to come from the Indians. *An Address to All Believers in Christ* (Richmond, MO, 1887), 26-27. See chap. 1, n12, for Whitmer's comment on Smith as the "choice seer."

14. *An Address*, 31. According to Whitmer, the prophecy was written on a piece of paper but was never printed.

15. Rejection of "spiritualizing" was to be an on-going weapon in Mormon polemics against Protestant interpretation of the Bible. Most millennialists agree with this position against mainline Protestant interpretation. Some passages, however, could have both a literal and a spiritual fulfillment. Compare 1 Ne. 22:1-3, 6, 27 with Isa. 48-49.

11.

Records of Revelation

Mr. R[igdon?]. with great show of good nature . . . spoke of the supernatural gifts with which he said Smith was endowed; He said he could translate from any language in which they were now extant, and could lay his finger on every interpolation in the sacred writings, adding, that he had proved him in all these things.

—*Painesville Telegraph*, 15 Feb. 1831

In defense of God, Joseph Smith assailed the natural revelation of deism, which excluded the supernatural, and the static revelation of traditional Christianity contained in a closed canon. But to enable revealed religion to overcome natural religion, Smith supported the deistic attack on the Bible's being complete and errorless. Rejection of the traditional view left him free to pursue special revelation specific to his own cause.

If revelation was only a phenomenon of the first century Christian church, if prophecy died with Jesus, deists pointed out, then God had changed his manner of relating to humanity. To avoid the force of that argument, Smith joined with critics in disparaging a book whose contents had been decided, as Thomas Paine saw it, by committee vote. Smith concurred with Ann Lee in urging continuing revelation as an effective counter to skepticism but went beyond the Shakers, providing a new scripture as well. Not only new visions, angelic ministration, and gifts of the Spirit were possible but also

153

new revealed scriptures. To defend the Bible's status as revelation, the Book of Mormon demanded the same status.

The Book of Mormon clearly affirmed the importance of the Bible. But how could revelation be valid and useful when there were so many variant interpretations? Protestants worked to develop a proper hermeneutic;[1] the Shakers' solution was to seek modern revelation while retaining the Bible. Smith believed that the Bible had once been a clearly understood book, affirming Protestant tradition that originally biblical writings were without error. According to the Book of Mormon, the Bible first came forth "from the Jews in purity unto the Gentiles, according to the truth which is in God" (1 Ne. 13:25). Originally it contained the "plainness of the gospel of the Lord" and was "plain unto the understanding of the children of men" (vv. 24, 29).

But Smith also believed that there were two major defects in the biblical text which had been caused by accidental as well as deliberate corruption. References to sources consulted in writing biblical books (such as the Book of Jashar, noted in Joshua 10) but not included in the current canon indicated the canon's incompleteness.[2] Smith blamed the Roman Catholic church, the "great and abominable" church of 1 Nephi 13, for the loss of biblical books and for additional corruptions in the remaining text (1 Ne. 13:26). The missing portions are those "which were plain unto the children of men, according to the plainness which is in the Lamb of God" (v. 29). Herein was an explanation for seemingly impossible problems with the Bible.

Smith also provided further information about the "abominable church." Satan, who was its head, decimated the Bible to pervert the "ways of the Lord" and to lead men astray (1 Ne. 13:27). He was successful: "Because of these things which are taken away out of the gospel of the Lamb, an exceeding great many do stumble, yea, insomuch that Satan hath great power over them" (v. 29). As a result gentiles are in an "awful state of blindness" and "stumble exceedingly" (vv. 32-34).

God's solution to the incomplete and corrupt Bible was to supply through the Book of Mormon what was missing: "I will be merciful unto the Gentiles in that day, insomuch that I will bring forth unto them, in mine own power, much of my gospel, which shall be plain and precious, saith the Lamb" (1 Ne. 13:34). By making the text obvious in meaning, Smith would deny skeptics the argument that the "unclear" words were unworthy of God and therefore could not be revelation.

The Book of Mormon preserved the authority of the Bible by affirming those portions which were essential and by clarifying those which had been corrupted. For example, the Book of Mormon affirmed that Genesis was authentic; that man was created in the image of God (Mosiah 7:27); that Adam and Eve were in the Garden of Eden, ate the forbidden fruit, and were expelled (Alma 42:2; 2 Ne. 2:18-19); that they were kept out of the garden by a flaming sword and cherubim so they could not eat and live forever (Alma 12:21). Evidence of the consequences of the Fall were found in Cain's murder of Abel; of the Flood covering the earth (Hel. 6:27); and of God's confusing the languages when he dispersed people from the Tower of Babel (Title Page; Omni 22; Mosiah 28:14; Hel. 6:28; Ether 1:3).

The Mormon record confirmed other important Old Testament events. Abraham paid tithes to Melchizedek, a king over Salem (Alma 13:14-19). Abraham's near sacrifice of Isaac,[3] God's covenants with Isaac and Jacob, and God's identification as the God of Abraham, Isaac, and Jacob[4] are all borne out. Isaac's son, Jacob, is mentioned frequently.[5] Joseph's torn coat is mentioned (46:23), as well as his brothers' selling him into bondage.[6] Moses had a rod and spokesman (2 Ne. 3:17); he divided the waters of the Red Sea (Hel. 8:11; 1 Ne. 4:2; 17:26-27); and he received the Law at Mt. Sinai (Mosiah 12:33-36; 13:12-24).[7] Support is found for the pillar of light leading the Israelites, the brazen serpent, the water from the rock, and the manna (1 Ne. 1:28-30, 41).[8] To convince the gentiles, God's command to destroy the Canaanites was corroborated (17:28-30),[9] as was David and Solomon's polygamy and keeping of concubines (Jacob 2:23-24), Zedekiah's reign,[10] the careers of Elijah, Jeremiah, and Malachi,[11] and both the career and writings of Isaiah.[12]

The Book of Mormon confirmed important New Testament events as well: John the Baptist's testimony about Jesus, Jesus' baptism by John (1 Ne. 10:7-10; 11:27; 2 Ne. 31:4-8), Jesus' choosing of John the Apostle, John's writing of the last days (1 Ne. 14:20-27), and the fourth Gospel's report of the misunderstanding that John the Apostle should tarry until Jesus comes again (3 Ne. 7:19). The Book of Mormon substantiated the events and significance of Jesus Christ's life. Mary conceived a child by the Holy Ghost, gave birth, and yet remained a virgin (Alma 7:10; 1 Ne. 11:13-20). Jesus chose twelve disciples, performed miracles, endured persecution, suffered, died by crucifixion, was buried, and rose from the dead on the third day.[13] He preached his Sermon on the Mount again in America (3 Ne. 12-14). Through his ministry he fulfilled the Mosaic Law and ended the law of circumcision (Moro. 8:8; 3 Ne. 15:5-8).

The Book of Mormon also solved a variety of serious problems associated with the Bible in the nineteenth century. It added, omitted, changed, interpreted, or reinterpreted words and clauses of unclear or contradictory biblical passages in order to make them logically or doctrinally more acceptable.[14] One miracle which seemed to contradict scientific knowledge involved Joshua telling the sun to stand still (Joshua 10:12-14). The Book of Mormon made the miracle more acceptable by up-dating the Ptolemaic assumptions of the biblical text: "Yea, and if he say unto the earth, move, it is moved; yea, if he say unto the earth, thou shalt go back, that it lengthen out the day for many hours, it is done; and thus according to his word, the earth goeth back, and it appeareth unto man that the sun standeth still; yea, and behold, this is so; for sure it is the earth that moveth, and not the sun" (Hel. 12:13-15).

In line with the intention to bring doctrinal peace to Christendom (D&C 10:44-63), the Book of Mormon clarified many issues of early nineteenth-century interest. In some cases the American scripture employed the weight of antiquity to endorse a doctrinal position; in others, it repudiated what was considered corrupt innovation. The doctrines thus clarified[15] found no final or unique settlement in the Book of Mormon, however, as a majority of them were later modified and developed by Smith and succeeding Mormon church leaders. Two examples will indicate the nature of such doctrinal clarification.

The Book of Mormon adopts the early Unitarian view in treating the Trinity, that "Christ was the God, the Father of all things" (Mosiah 7:27), and later gave a theological interpretation: "And now Abinadi said unto them: I would that ye should understand that God himself shall come down among the children of men, and shall redeem his people. And because he dwelleth in flesh he shall be called the Son of God, and having subjected the flesh to the Father, being the Father and the Son—The Father, because he was conceived by the power of God; and the Son, because of the flesh; thus becoming the Father and the Son—And they are one God, yea, the very Eternal Father of heaven and earth" (15:1-4). Smith affirmed this Unitarian position later in the dictation process: "Behold, I am Jesus Christ. I am the Father and the Son" (Ether 3:14).[16] Later developments were to see this original Unitarian position develop into a kind of tritheism and finally into polytheism.[17]

One of the questions millennialists never settled was the number of resurrections. Revelation 20 speaks of two. Alma 40:4-21 stressed that whether "there shall be one time, or a second time, or a third time, that man shall come forth from the dead, it mattereth not; for God knoweth all these things; and it sufficeth me to know that this is the case—that there is a time appointed that all shall rise from the dead" (v. 5). Whenever resurrection comes, the important thing to notice is that there is an interval between death and resurrection spent in one or more intermediate states (vv. 20-21).

The Book of Mormon undercut criticisms of the Bible by denying traditional positions on biblical inspiration, thereby making for itself a necessary place alongside the Bible. Following the Reformation, Protestant churches supported the claim that the Bible was sole authority in matters of doctrine by appealing to biblical inspiration. Deists wondered how such inspiration could explain historical inaccuracies, contradictions, and errors in the biblical text. Smith sidestepped deistic objections and joined in protest against the orthodox position. The Nephite writers of the American scripture held that their records contained the word of God but not that every word was God's word. They admitted the possibility of errors, but "if there be fault, it be the mistake of men" (Title Page; 1 Ne. 19:6).

The Book of Mormon thus proposed a different model of inspiration than those current at the time of its publication. No one in the first quarter of the nineteenth century would have expected the writers of God's word to select their materials as the Nephite writers of the Book of Mormon did theirs. They wrote "according to my memory" (Ether 5:1), "according to the best of my memory" (Jacob 7:26), "according to our knowledge" (Morm. 8:1), "as seemeth me good" (Morm. 10:1), what they thought was "sacred" (1 Ne. 19:16) or "considered to be precious" (Jacob 1:2), and in Mormon's case what his father had told him (Morm. 9:32). Book of Mormon authors altered records by abridging, omitting, or adding to their subjects. Jesus himself dictated a section of the records which had been omitted (3 Ne. 23). This open admission of an incomplete collection of records in the Book of Mormon struck hard at the idea of a closed canon.

Nephi and Moroni even called attention to their literary incompetencies. Nephi admitted that his ability to write was overshadowed by his ability as a public speaker, "for when a man speaketh by the power of the Holy Ghost the power of the Holy Ghost carrieth it unto the hearts of the children of men" (2 Ne. 33:1). Resigned to the fact that many harden themselves against the Holy Ghost and "cast many things away which are written and esteem them as things of naught" (v. 2), Nephi still believed that his words would "be made strong unto his readers and lead them to Christ" (v. 4).

Similarly Moroni wrote from the material available to him only a few words "because of my weakness in writing" (Ether 12:40). Imperfections might be found in his records, but he knew of none, but explained that "if there be faults they be the faults of a man" (Morm. 8:12, 17). Compared to the overwhelming effect of the writings of Jared's brother (no sample is supplied in the Book of Mormon), Moroni knew that his production was lackluster. What he had to write was so awe-inspiring "that we cannot write them; wherefore, when we write we behold our weakness, and stumble because of the placing of our words; and I fear lest the Gentiles shall mock at our words" (Ether 12:15).[18] In prayer Moroni asked the Lord to let the gentiles read his words with charity and to accept the truth of his message however inept the phrasing and expression. His attitude, and that of Smith, is summed up in these words: "Condemn me not because of mine imperfection, neither my father, because of his imperfection, neither them who have written before him; but rather give thanks unto God that he hath made manifest unto you our imperfections, that ye may learn to be more wise than we have been" (Morm. 9:31).

Mormon exposed another route by which imperfections might have crept into the Book of Mormon. Any fault, he wrote, could be attributed to their using a form of Hebrew altered by contact with the Egyptian language. Had he been able to use pure Hebrew, no such problem would exist (Morm. 9:32-33).[19]

Thus the Book of Mormon admits that human weakness can affect the composition of scripture. At the very moment Christians generally were trying to fortify an apologetic of verbal or plenary inspiration for scriptures, Smith abandoned this defense. Thomas Paine had criticized changeable language and vulnerable manuscripts, but Smith turned this weakness into a strength. By deserting the traditional argument, Smith foiled such deist criticism and was free to advocate a new basis for accepting the Bible as the word of God—and by implication the Book of Mormon as well.

Questions about the golden plates made Smith vulnerable, but he shifted attention from the plates to the translated manuscript. Martin Harris's loss of the first manuscript was the immediate cause of the shift. If Smith's enemies had stolen the manuscript, then comparison between the old translation and a new one might turn up differences. God revealed that he would still bring forth his record, even without the missing manuscript, but he gave Smith alternate plates to translate up to the point reached in the first attempt (D&C 3). The alternate plates contained essentially the same materials and formed what is now 1 and 2 Nephi.

Another impetus for shifting attention from the plates to the record came in Smith's interchange with Oliver Cowdery, his scribe. The third time Cowdery asked for assurance that Smith really had the plates, God referred him back to that material already transcribed and to his previous sense of assurance. If Cowdery was satisfied that his spiritual manifestations were genuine, then he was commanded to "rely upon the things which are written: For in them are all things written concerning the foundation of my church, my gospel, and my rock" (D&C 18:3-4). The message was clear: when a spiritual witness is not enough, rely on the Book of Mormon in its English translation.

Perhaps the most pressing reason for shifting attention to the written record was Smith's knowledge that every convert and skeptic would want to examine the plates. Pre-publication requests to see them were forestalled by having the plates revealed only to worthy men. After the three witnesses saw them the angel reclaimed the plates—thus eliminating the problem.[20] This situation was anticipated and dealt with in advance. Moroni explained that he was the one "who hideth up this record unto the Lord; the plates thereof are of no worth. . . . But the record thereof is of great worth" (Morm. 8:14). With the plates declared unavailable for public viewing, attention is directed to the record in hand, the Book of Mormon.

Smith adapted a standard Protestant position in his explanation of the Book of Mormon. With no access to original biblical manuscripts, Protestants developed textual criticism to arrive at an authentic biblical text. Out of necessity and conviction, they held that if careful copies were made of original biblical writings and if these copies were reliably translated, then one possessed the word of God.

Smith applied this same reasoning to the Book of Mormon. God does not want people to value the plates themselves, for, as was the case with medieval relics, they could be exploited "to get gain" (Morm. 8:14). It is rather the message of the plates which must be valued and heeded. Smith had provided a reliable translation with the aid of the glasses and the Holy Ghost, and therefore there was no need for concern about the absence of the plates.

Focusing on the translation, Smith established a new foundation for the Book of Mormon. The only inspiration claimed for the Book of Mormon is that it was given to Smith by inspiration; to others, it is confirmed "by the ministering of angels" (D&C 20:10). The testimony of the three witnesses stated that an angel showed them the plates and that the voice of God declared "that they have been translated by the gift and power of God" (compare ibid.). The men could not read the plates and did not know if the translation was true or not.[19] Rather their testimony dealt with Cowdery's handwritten transcription of Joseph Smith's dictation.

Personal revelation then is the basis for determining the reliability of any claim to revelation. Smith translated by inspiration, but he translated a book which had been edited, contained possible flaws, and possibly was incomplete. One can have the angel's assurance that the translation is faithful to the original on the plates; one can have a "witness," a "testimony," by following Moroni's advice to seekers of religious certitude (Moro. 10:3-5). Based on personal assurance or revelation, the Book of Mormon is placed beyond the power of deistic logic. The claim of the American scripture to be God's revelation rests entirely with the readers' desire to accept it as such.

The Book of Mormon may have been subject to certain imperfections. However, Smith made it clear that these were fundamentally different than problems associated with the Bible. In the Book of Mormon the Lord's doctrine was given in "plainness, even as plain as word can be" (2 Ne. 32:7). Repentance and glad tidings alike were preached "in plain terms, that we may understand, that we cannot err" (Alma 13:22), simple enough that even children could understand (Mosiah 2:40).

When a Nephite prophet hurled denunciations, it was done "according to the plainness of the word of God" (Jacob 2:11), for only bluntness can save people from destruction (Enos 23; Alma 5:43). Lucidity in preaching might engender hostility; people in the Book of Mormon like those in the Bible kill prophets (14:2; Jacob

4:14). But hostility in the Book of Mormon is always straightforward: they understand the message well.

As noted, in the Book of Mormon "plainness" was God's style when prophesying (2 Ne. 32:2-3). The prophets prophesied "to the understanding of man; for the Spirit speaketh the truth and lieth not. Wherefore, it speaketh of things as they really are, and of things as they really will be; wherefore, these things are manifested unto us plainly for the salvation of our souls" (Jacob 4:13). For example, Nephi's predictions were so plainly understood that "no man can err . . . man shall know of a surety, at the times when they shall come to pass" (2 Ne. 25:7, 20). Prophecy of this quality meant that people could not "misunderstand" the import of the prediction nor the indications of its fulfillment (v. 28).

Through such rhetorical devices the deists' complaint was nullified that predictive prophecy was equivocal. Prophecy was distinct as to its intent and obvious as to its fulfillment. The mysteries of faith in the Book of Mormon are matters of information previously unknown but susceptible to human intellect. Paul's estimate of God's judgments as unsearchable and his ways inscrutable (Rom. 11:13) is not characteristic of mysteries of faith in the Book of Mormon, which contains no obscurity or paradox.

The Stick of Judah, therefore, needs the Stick of Joseph for its understanding and defense. If one rejects the Book of Mormon, one cannot defend the Bible against deism, skepticism, and unbelief. God told Ezekiel to join the stick of Judah with the stick of Joseph and "make them one stick" (Ez. 37:19). That was Smith's task. He provided for believers two witnesses of Jesus Christ and evidence of God beyond the testimony of nature: the new stick of Joseph (the Book of Mormon) and the newly-defended stick of Judah (the Bible). The Book of Mormon depends on the Bible for its source material and the Bible depends on the Book of Mormon for its defense. Readers of the Book of Mormon, therefore, find themselves urged to accept as a sort of package God, the Bible, the Book of Mormon, and the Latter-day Saint prophet Joseph Smith who had access to continuing revelation.

NOTES

1. A popular contemporary introduction to biblical study, Thomas Hartwell Horne's *An Introduction to the Critical Study and Knowledge of the*

Holy Scriptures, 2 vols., 8th ed. (New York: Robert Carter & Brothers, 1856), 1:5-6, contained in its 1834 preface: "VOLUME I, contains a CRITICAL INQUIRY into the Genuineness, Authenticity, uncorrupted Preservation and Inspiration of the Holy Scriptures, . . . Particularly a *new branch of evidence* for their credibility, which is furnished by coins, medals, inscriptions, and ancient structures. This is followed by a refutation of the very numerous objections which have been urged against the Scriptures in recent deistical publications." Joseph Smith owned a four-volume edition of Horne at Kirtland, Ohio, in 1834. See Richard P. Howard, "Latter Day Saint Scriptures and the Doctrine of Propositional Revelation," *Courage* 1 (June 1971): 214. Smith's copy of Horne is in the archives of the Reorganized Church of Jesus Christ of Latter Day Saints in Independence, Missouri.

2. Between 1826 and 1828 the issue of whether or not to include the Apocrypha with the canonical books was debated. The *Wayne Sentinel,* 3 Mar. 1826, carried an item on the question, noting that "the General Committee of the Bible Society, in London, have determined henceforward, wholly to exclude the apocrypha from their edition of the Sacred Scriptures." Three months later the *Sentinel* printed an informative article explaining the origin and canonical status of the Apocrypha (2 June 1826). Two years later the notice appeared that "The American Bible Society have unanimously resolved, that no books continuing the apocrypha, shall hereafter be issued from their depository" (6 June 1828). The "lost" books, such as the Book of Jashar and other chronicles referred to in the Old Testament, were the subject of conjecture and conversation among Saints. Smith believed that the apostolic church had had some of them (Joseph Smith et al., *History of the Church of Jesus Christ of Latter-day Saints,* 7 vols. [Salt Lake City: Deseret Book Co., 1927], 1:132; hereafter HC).

3. 1 Ne. 15:18; 22:9; 2 Ne. 19:14; 3 Ne. 20:25, 27; Morm. 5:20; Ether 13:11.

4. Mosiah 7:19; 1 Ne. 17:40; Alma 5:24.

5. Alma 46:24; 1 Ne. 5:14; Ether 13:7.

6. Alma 10:3; 1 Ne. 5:14; 2 Ne. 3:4; 4:1.

7. Ether 12:11; 1 Ne. 4:15-16; 5:11; 2 Ne. 3:17; 25:30; 3 Ne. 15:4-8; 25:4.

8. B. H. Roberts, *New Witnesses for God,* 3 vols. (Salt Lake City: Deseret Book Co., 1926), 2:47-48, applied this corroboration of the Pentateuch against the inroads of higher criticism.

9. Paine had stressed his outrage at the Bible for making God command wars of destruction. Smith developed a rationale for such commands in the episode of Nephi getting the brass plates from his uncle Laban (1 Ne. 4:1-8). The spirit told Nephi: "Slay him, for the Lord hath delivered him into thy hands; Behold the Lord slayeth the wicked to bring forth his righteous purposes. It is better that one man should perish than that a nation should dwindle in unbelief" (vv. 11-12). Nephi thought that his posterity could keep

God's commandments in the land of promise only if they had the commandments which were engraved on Laban's brass plates. The parallel this provides to Israel entering the promised land to live in a covenant relationship with God is clear. Their wars of destruction wiped out the local population to enable the people of Israel to keep the law by eliminating possible sources of spiritual contamination. This was a widely-used explanation.

10. 1 Ne. 1:13; 10:3; 17:43; 20:14, 20; 2 Ne. 6:8-9; 25:10-11.

11. Hel. 8:20; 1 Ne. 5:13; 7:14; 3 Ne. 24:1; 25:5.

12. 1 Ne. 20-21; 2 Ne. 7-8; 12-24.

13. Mosiah 3:5-7; 1 Ne. 11:28-36; 12:9; 13:24, 26, 39-41; 3 Ne. 17:7-8; 28:21-22; Mosiah 3:7.

14. 2 Ne. 12:1-2 corrects Isa. 2:2-4; 2 Ne. 23:11—Isa. 3:17; 2 Ne. 17:19—Isa. 8:19; 2 Ne. 29:3—Isa. 9:2; Mosiah 5:7, 14:10-13, 15:10-13—Isa. 53:10; 3 Ne. 12:6—Matt. 5:6; 3 Ne. 13:24-25—Matt. 6:25; 3 Ne. 13:30—Matt. 6:30; 3 Ne. 13:32—Matt. 6:32; 3 Ne. 13:34—Matt. 6:34; 3 Ne. 15:16-24—John 10:16; 3 Ne. 28:3-9, 12-15, D&C 7:6 (see 7:1-8)—John 21:21-23; Alma 21:37—Genesis 3:24. This is a partial list.

15. As Mario DePillis ("The Quest for Religious Authority and the Rise of Mormonism," *Dialogue: A Journal of Mormon Thought* 1 [Spring 1966]: 79) pointed out, the famous quote from Alexander Campbell (*Delusions: An Analysis of the Book of Mormon* [Boston: n.p., 1832], 13) claiming that Smith had answered every current theological question is an overstatement. Ross Warner, "The Fulfillment of Book of Mormon Prophecies: A Study of Problems Relative to the Fulfillment of Selected Prophecies in the Book of Mormon, with Particular Reference to the Prophetic View from 1830 Onward," M.A. thesis, Brigham Young University, 1961, 52, lists the doctrines which are clarified in the Book of Mormon: the nature and personality of God, the fall of humanity, the Atonement, free will, the nature of the gospel, faith, repentance, baptism, the work of the Holy Ghost, the Lord's Supper, the Judgment, the Resurrection, and the reality of the devil. Warner cites proof texts for each. These doctrines may also be found in the index of modern editions of the Book of Mormon. Warner (45-49) also deals with Christ's fulfillment of Mosaic law.

16. Later Mormons took the Book of Mormon position that Jesus Christ was both the Son and the Father and explained that since Christ is also the father of the spirits in this world (a teaching not in the Book of Mormon), he is therefore both the Father and the Son. Still another explanation later derived from the teaching that each exalted man will be a god on his own planet: The father of Christ appointed Christ to be God to the people on earth. He is the only God we know and the Father of all spirits on earth; therefore, he is the Father but still the Son.

17. That evolution is traced by George B. Arbaugh, "Evolution of

Mormon Doctrine," *Church History* 9 (1940): 157-69. See also Smith's redefinition of "eternal damnation" and "endless torment" in D&C 19 (given Mar. 1830). The interpretation is Universalistic.

18. See chap. 2, n22.

19. Inevitably Smith's attitude that the Bible was full of errors came full circle. He had to concede the same possibility for the Book of Mormon, but it was translated by someone with the "gift of translation." How could Mormons explain a phenomenon in the Book of Mormon which Smith had criticized in the Bible? They adapted an argument from Protestant apologetics: the many editorial changes have not altered the meaning of even one passage. See Hugh Nibley, *Since Cumorah* (Salt Lake City: Deseret Book Co., 1967), 6.

But Nibley is wrong. A case in point is 1 Ne 11:18. After Smith dictated the manuscript of the Book of Mormon, Cowdery and others emended it for the press. This version is designed E MS (1829). The original manuscript, the E MS, and the 1830 edition all have "the virgin which thou seest, is the mother of God." After 1830 the E MS was revised. The post-1830 revision and the 1837 edition have what appears in the present version: "the virgin whom thou seest, is the mother of the Son of God." Similar changes were made to 1 Ne 11:21, 32, and 1 Ne. 13:40. Compare Richard P. Howard, *Restoration Scriptures: A Study of Their Textual Development* (Independence, MO: Herald Publishing House, 1969), 47-49, who notes that these changes correspond to Smith's developing ideas of God as found in the 1835 edition of the Doctrine and Covenants in Smith's "Lectures on Faith."

It has been argued that since Smith was dictating and not writing the Book of Mormon manuscript, mistakes are those of his scribes and not his own. That would be true for mistakes of spelling and punctuation. But theological alterations as extensive as these are not due to a scribe missing a word here and there.

20. Smith said, "When, according to arrangements, the messenger called for them, I delivered them up to him; and he has them in his charge until this day" (HC 1:19). A patriarchal blessing given to Newel K. Whitney, however, may indicate that the spectacles were still being used. The introduction to the blessing states that Joseph Smith, Jr., gave it "through the Urim and Thummim" on 7 October 1835 and that the blessing was written by Frederick G. Williams. It was "recorded by Oliver Cowdery, Jan. 22, 1836," in the patriarchal blessing book of Joseph Smith, Sr., LDS church archives. See *The Contributor* 6 (Jan. 1885): 129. We know that Cowdery copied some blessings on this date, since he put down in his Sketch Book for that date, "Copied blessings." *Brigham Young University Studies* 12 (Summer 1972): 419.

James Lancaster's suggestion that the designation "Urim and Thummim" was used for both the glasses and seerstone could account for this usage. See chap. 2.

21. John Whitmer, one of the Eight Witnesses, said just this in his exchange with Theodore Turley in 1839 (HC 3:308).

12.

An American Prophet

> Once in the world's history we were to have a Yankee prophet, and we have had him in Joe Smith. For good or for evil, he has left his track on the great pathway of life; or, to use the words of Horne, "knocked out for himself a window in the wall of the nineteenth century," whence his rude, bold, good humored face will peer out upon the generations to come.
>
> —John Greenleaf Whittier,[1] American poet and journalist

Joseph Smith once declared in a funeral sermon, "No man knows my history," but his achievement, his claims, and the movement he bequeathed posterity demand that we hear him as fairly as we can. Of all the titles and offices he assumed, that of prophet is best known. He assumed the role by criticizing his society for creating a climate in which unbelief and immorality could flourish, by calling respectable religionists to account for their failure to carry out what he saw as the requirements of their profession, by standing outside the accepted religious groupings while considering himself God's standard bearer.

All facets of his career proclaim him distinctly American in concern and aspiration, American in his theology, with its New England roots intertwined with political doctrines of the previous fifty years. Subversive international forces were seen at work behind the scenes when William Morgan disappeared in 1826. The resulting anti-Masonic furor was, in part, a reaction against foreign entangle-ments. Smith donned the prophet's mantle against this backdrop to warn America about apostasy from God. His jeremiads against unbelief point to apostasy as the precursor of unhappiness, degra-dation, and eventual personal and national disaster.[2] Loss of belief in personal and present-day revelation, disregard for gifts of the spirit, and a dearth of angelic ministrations strip a would-be Chris-tian nation of its pretensions, revealing how far America had fallen. Affiliation with Freemasons was unthinkable then because it smacked of French deism and atheism. The watchman of Israel was sounding the alarm.

Smith held that a nation can become implicated in infidelity only so much before God chastens it with wars and suffering. Ultimately God may let a wicked nation be destroyed as were the earlier American civilizations of the Nephites and Jaredites. Smith pointed to native Americans as living examples of God's displeasure. Their dark skins, lack of civilized arts, and fragmented traces of pure religion which had been corrupted should warn America to repent of its skepticism and immorality, its religiosity and philosophy, and to return to Jesus Christ in humble faith. In this Smith propounded a view of repentance which came from the post-Revolutionary War period. Perry Miller argued that during this period repentance was seen as a motivating force: "Out of the years between the Stamp Act and the Treaty of Paris emerged a formidable, exhaustive (in gen-eral, a repetitious) enunciation of the unique necessity for America to win her way by reiterated acts of repentance." What moved rank-and-file Americans to victory in the War for Independence was not the use of political terms but "the universal persuasion that they, by administering to themselves a spiritual purge, acquired the energies God had always, in the manner of the Old Testament, been willing to impart to His repentant children. Their first responsibility was not to shoot red coats but to cleanse themselves, only thereafter to take aim." Repentance was not "a failure of the will but a dynamo for generating action." It was "Protestant self-distrust with confi-dence in divine aid."[3] As Smith urged it in the Book of Mormon, repentance was a call to action.

Smith coupled that call with a warning to persevere in obedience to God's commandments.[4] Here too he could rely on the fusion of religious and patriotic motifs. "What kept them going," to apply Miller, "was an assurance that by exerting themselves they were fighting for a victory thus providentially predestined."[5] The rise of the Masonic lodge and rampant skepticism showed that America was on the verge of apostasy, but the nation could do something about it. By repenting America could receive God's approval once again.

The Book of Mormon chronicled an American exodus story. The story was repeated again and again to recall America to its former greatness. In prehistoric times God preserved for the Jaredites a wilderness, a land for "a righteous people," the "quarter where there never had man been" (Ether 2:4, 7). He led them into America with the promise that they would be the greatest nation on earth (1:42-43). God brought to America only those people he wanted here (2 Ne. 1:6). He withheld knowledge of the New World from many nations for the sake of the patriarch Joseph's descendants (3:2). God planted that broken-off branch "in a good spot of ground . . . choice unto me above all other parts of the land of my vineyard," specifically, in the United States (Jacob 5:43). He consecrated the best of lands for the Nephites and Lamanites (2 Ne. 10:19), a land which is "most precious," "holy," "delightsome," "choice," "choice above all other lands," the "land of promise," the "land of liberty," the "promised land."

America would be a Christian land because God specifically consecrated it thus (2 Ne. 1:7). The Nephites received it for their inheritance (3 Ne. 16:16). This land would be the New Jerusalem (20:22), and its inhabitants would be considered blessed among the nations of the world (24:12). America is God's reward for fidelity (Ether 1:38), and those who receive it will prosper (1 Ne. 2:20). Biblical Joseph's posterity would keep America forever (2 Ne. 3:2), "and there shall be none to molest them, nor to take away the land of their inheritance; and they shall dwell safely forever" (1:9).

Faithfulness to God's commandments ensures freedom from bondage to other nations. When gentiles would come into the land and receive the restored gospel, America would be a land of liberty and blessing. During their stay no kings should rule,[6] for God would protect gentiles against kings and outside tyranny. Those who fight against this nation, against Zion, would perish (2 Ne. 10:10-13), but by their willing obedience gentiles would be adopted as Nephites (1 Ne. 14:2). God would raise them up as a mighty nation on the "face of this land" to scatter the seed of Nephi—the Indians (22:7-8). Like Jaredites, Nephites, and Lamanites before them, gentiles would be guided by the hand of God to America. Inspired by God, Columbus would go "forth upon the mighty waters" to "the promised land" (13:12). Similarly colonial Americans would be led here to "prosper and obtain the land for their inheritance" (ibid.).

The Book of Mormon brings its reader to the present by drawing a parallel between ancient and modern times. The calamitous end of Nephite and Jaredite civilizations indicates that if the inhabitants of America realize God's promise for this land, they will have to fulfill the condition required of all who live here. Those who possess America "should possess it unto the Lord" (Ether 9:20) and be faithful to God (1 Ne. 7:13). As from the earliest times, that means serving the only true God, "the God of the land, who is Jesus Christ" (Ether 2:8, 12), by worshipping God (2 Ne. 10:19) and keeping his commandments (1 Ne. 2:2). Moroni sums up the consequences of ignoring God's special promises for the land: "this is a land which is choice above all other lands; wherefore he that doth possess it shall serve God or shall be swept off for it is the everlasting degree of God. And it is not until the fullness of iniquity among the children of the land, that they are swept off. And this cometh unto you, O ye Gentiles, that ye may know the decrees of God—that ye may repent, and not continue in your iniquities until the fullness come, that ye may not bring down the fullness of the wrath of God upon you as the inhabitants of the land have hitherto done. Behold, this is a choice land, and whatsoever nation shall possess it shall be free from bondage, and from captivity, and from all other nations under heaven, if they will but serve the God of the land, who is Jesus Christ, who hath been manifested by the things which we have written" (Ether 2:10-12).

The Book of Mormon guarantees that nineteenth-century readers would understand that the message was meant for them. Nephite prophets moralize for the specific benefit of future gentiles. Rebellion and iniquity would bring a curse on the land. Transgressors are brought down with sorrow (Enos 10), and people may be taken into captivity (2 Ne. 1:7). When those who possess the land are "ripened in iniquity," they would be "swept off" and "destroyed" by the "fullness of his wrath" (Ether 2:8-9; 9:20). Thus the book urges Americans to make or renew covenants made with God by previous generations and civilizations.

Smith's persecution at the hand of American religionists—his church's pilgrimage to Kirtland, Ohio, and then to Far West, Missouri, and then to Commerce (later Nauvoo), Illinois; his imprisonments; the church's suffering—all illustrated how close America was to judgment. The shabby treatment given his church by Missouri's judiciary did not lessen Smith's faith in the principles upon which the country had been founded. His attitude toward the U.S. Constitution was positive enough that Mormons still consider it an inspired document—proof of God's hand in founding the country. Ultimately Smith was to seek redress for losses sustained by his people in Missouri by running for the nation's highest office. Such was his faith in America.

To seekers and dissenters of his time, Smith had the answer to their quest—the true Church of Christ restored to earth.[7] The Book of Mormon clearly showed that Christ had once established his church in America with a full complement of offices and spiritual gifts. Following the death of its apostles, the ancient American church—like the Old World churches—lost its apostolic fervor, faith, and validity. The Protestant polemic which identified the apostasy with the rise of the Roman Catholic Church was applied to the ancient American scene to explain the loss of the American church. The apostasy of the church in both the eastern and western hemispheres demonstrated the need for a restoration.

According to Smith, churches in the burned-over district of New England were clearly apostate, bereft of spiritual gifts, denying the principle of on-going revelation, served by self-seeking ministers, doctrinally contentious, and without apostolic church organization. But his new scripture and his restored Aaronic and Melchizedek priesthoods bestowed by John the Baptist, Peter, James, and John the apostles, together with the full complement of church officers as in apostolic times, cemented Smith's claim to have effected the displacement of the false churches by the true church. Church polity and practice had already been introduced in the Book of Mormon and was further explicated for several years in the Book of Commandments and the Doctrine and Covenants.

Certain that Satan was the cause of doctrinal strife,[8] Smith cleared away the clutter of religious controversy and enabled the restored church to get on with preparations for the Millennium. Other religious organizations were thereby denied any authority to engage in ministry, argue doctrine, or challenge Smith's church. Nor could corruption of the clergy, decimation of the Bible, or doctrinal aberrations and historic scandals which weakened Christendom's witness to Jesus Christ be charged to the restored Church of Christ.

Smith was so sure about the importance of the work in which he was engaged that he thought the Millennium might dawn at the turn of the century and anticipated seeing Christ at his second coming.[9] He promised others that they too would see Christ.[10] Oliver Cowdery headed the 1830 mission to Missouri with the same enthusiastic expectation. He was reported by an Ohio newspaper to have predicted the world's end within a few years.[11] Sidney Rigdon had a ten-hour conversation with W. W. Phelps of Canandaigua about the new faith and "declared it was true, and he knew it by the power of the Holy Ghost, which was again given to man in preparation for the millennium."[12] Four months after Cowdery's visit the same newspaper reported Martin Harris's declaration "that all who believed the new bible would see Christ within fifteen years."[13] Thus the name of the church was changed from the Church of Christ to the Church of the Latter Day Saints.

This time-setting did not persist as the all-encompassing focus of Smith's millennial hope.[14] He soon centered instead on gathering a people from the nations to meet the Lord. This strategy was more consistent with the prevalent belief in western New York that the efforts of the faithful in evangelism, education, or missions could help usher in the Day of the Lord. "It might even be the case that the Mormons," wrote Klaus Hansen, "by assigning to man the primary responsibility for creating the millennium, interjected into the optimistic doctrine an insurance clause against a remote possibility that the Lord, perhaps, might fail to appear."[15]

Thus Smith sent missionaries to recruit converts to help build the city of God. Cowdery traveled to Missouri to found a city of refuge.[16] Rigdon followed in 1831 to consecrate the land to the west of Independence as "Zion." Here the Indians could gather as the tribes of Joseph were increasingly displaced by the U.S. government's removal policy. In 1836 at the dedication of the temple in Kirtland, Ohio, Smith and Cowdery saw the heavens open. Moses appeared to give them "the keys of the gathering of Israel from the four parts of the earth" (D&C 110:11-16). The time was near. In 1837 the English mission field was opened to yield 2,500 converts who set sail to join the prophet before his death.[17] Thousands more were to follow from Scandinavia in the 1850s.[18]

Through such efforts goals stated again and again in the Book of Mormon began to be fulfilled. Zion was being formed in the United States, the Indians had the restored gospel preached to them, and within a few years Orson Hyde consecrated the Holy City of Jerusalem for the gathering of the Jews.[19] All was being readied for Christ's coming.

Fifteen hundred years of church history had encrusted revelation with the weight of tradition and institutional inertia. In spite of Protestant efforts to let God speak through the Bible, some perceived him as more remote than ever. Deism rejected special revelation but accepted a remote god who could communicate through nature. Orthodoxy reacted by developing its science of textual criticism and relying on its doctrine of biblical inspiration to assure contact with God. Catholicism guaranteed the institution as the assurance. Pietism looked within the human heart.

Joseph Smith sided with Pietism in favoring his own inner assurance. But after he won the changes and freedom he wanted, Smith set in motion the very forces he once had decried in the churches of his day. The principle of personal revelation led to power struggles within the infant latter-day church until Smith received revelations allowing only him to get instruction, teaching, or revelation for the church (D&C 28:11; 43:3-6) He taught that no one could receive revelation for someone of higher authority.[20] Secure within the church, Smith was able to lead as Prophet, Seer, and Revelator.

Revelation continued in books from ancient patriarchs, written instructions for restoring the church, other revelations that were not officially recorded, and the inspiration to revise the Bible. Some of the written revelations were published in 1833 and revised and enlarged in 1835. These were to become the most influential of the Mormon scriptures. Approximately 65 percent of Smith's revelations came in the first four years of his public activity, 1828-33; from 1834-39, 18 percent; none in 1840; and 8 percent in 1841-44. Following Smith's death revelation for the church effectively ceased. George B. Arbaugh compared Mormon revelation after Smith to the dogma of papal infallibility: it lent a "certain spiritual potentiality."[21]

R. W. B. Lewis characterized post-revolutionary American optimism with the literary figure of the American Adam. He used Emerson's categories of the Party of Memory and the Party of Hope to analyze American intellectual thought from 1820-60. The model provides a helpful way to view Joseph Smith.[22] Huddled along the eastern edge of a vast continent, many looked back in Memory to the Old World and its traditions. Others faced west in Hope. With them Joseph Smith breathed the optimistic air flowing in from the Rockies. Fearful that the call from the west was a summons to barbarism, American Christendom launched the Second Great Awakening to stem the tide. Perry Miller has shown that the battle of the churches against deism was part of a larger strategy to save the west for civilization. And Joseph Smith was animated by the same spirit which was quickening the nation.

Lewis described the intellectual history of a nation as the exposure of dominant conflicts over ideas and the "story" which animates them. As the crucifixion and resurrection of Christ is the story behind Christianity, so the American story is about an "Adamic person" without a past, timeless. He had known God and nature but found himself suddenly alive in a certain place and time.[23] Joseph Smith entered this debate with his own story of seeing visions, finding and translating an American scripture—the story behind Mormonism.

The Party of Hope saw America with a present and a future but rejected the immediate past in order to search for ultimate origins. Smith too was searching for a source of guidance for the New World. Old World revelation was repudiated as the ultimate authority and subjected to the revelation and scripture of the New World. Mormon biographer John Evans concluded that Smith appeared unaware of the mass of Christian exegetical literature.[24] I would amend Evans's observation to say that Smith discarded traditional interpretations because he claimed a right to start anew. Even when he appropriated a current approach, such as the millennial hope of Protestants or the theory of Israelite origins for the Indians, he charted his own course.

Smith's handling of temptation and sin as a Fortunate Fall is an instance of his moving within the Party of Hope. Humanity needed to taste the bitter to know the sweet and prize the good.[25] Temptation and sin were necessary for people so that they could experience sexuality, joy, the goodness of life, and—most important of all—true freedom. The triumph of Arminianism in Smith's thought made of sin an enabling force, freeing men and women to discover and make of themselves gods. The Party of Memory, by contrast, taught a doctrine of the Fall and original sin which left humanity debilitated beyond power to extricate itself.

Smith taught that God willed human freedom even at the risk of losing it. When Satan offered himself as redeemer for all humanity (Moses 4:1), God saw the offer as an attempt to destroy human freedom and a criticism of God's will. So Adam was not really beguiled but rather chose to transgress in order to become a creator of new life through sexuality. By the proper use of sexual and procreative powers, Smith was eventually to reveal, the doctrine emerged that humans could even become gods.

Smith shunned mysticism to explicate the workings of matter in later revelations about polygamy, polytheism, and a kingdom of this world. It is fair to compare him to Emerson in his effort to harmonize matter with spirit, although Emerson realized his vision in poems and essays and Smith realized his in action.

If polygamy was the most sensational of Smith's revelations, the "gathering" was the most far-reaching. It offered a focus for religious fervor which revivalism had similarly stirred up but allowed to dissipate.[26] Appropriate for a prophet, Smith offered his converts a program: gather in America to prepare for the Millennium; build a city of refuge, a city of God. Mormon efforts were thwarted in Missouri, but on a swampy site along the Mississippi River, Smith and his converts built what was Illinois's foremost city and Smith's Mormon capital—Nauvoo. Hopeful thousands gathered to help the American prophet build the temple into which the Lord would suddenly come.

When it was clear that persecution was also in the Illinois air, Smith convened a Council of Fifty to lay plans for one final exodus.[27] After Smith's death, Apostle Lyman Wight attempted to carry out an early council plan to establish the Kingdom of God in Texas.[28] Apostle Brigham Young, Smith's ultimate successor in the eyes of the majority of Saints, led the church west into Mexican territory and carved out the State of Deseret. From 1850 to 1852 Smith's followers in Deseret lived in a theocracy which exercised— and was to exercise after its dissolution at the hands of the U.S. government—tremendous influence over the settlement of the American west.

Joseph Smith was, therefore, author not only of an American scripture but of an amazing life[29] and a dynamic movement within American history. His biography, to paraphrase Lewis, is the story begotten by the noble myth of an American Adam. He set out to defend God and in that defense died a martyr's death. Through the Book of Mormon, his revelations, and the church he restored, his converts declare that Joseph Smith is *still* "an ambassador for the religion of Jesus Christ" (D&C 135:7). By virtue of his martyrdom, they believe, he still defends God.

NOTES

1. "A Mormon Conventicle," *Howitt's Journal*, reprinted in *Littell's Living Age* (Oct.-Nov. 1847), from which it was reprinted in William Mulder and A. Russell Mortensen, eds., *Among the Mormons: Historic Accounts by Contemporary Observers* (New York: Alfred Knopf, 1958), 159.

2. 1 Ne. 4:13; 10:11; 12:22-23; 13:35; 15:35; 2 Ne. 1:10; 26:15, 17, 19; Mosiah 1:5; Alma 45:10, 12; 50:22; Hel. 6:34; 15:11, 15; 3 Ne. 21:5; 4 Ne. 1:34, 38; Moro. 9:20, 35; Ether 4:3.

3. "From the Covenant to the Revival," in *Nature's Nation* (Cambridge, MA: Harvard University Press, 1967), 94, 97, 102.

4. Perseverance: 1 Ne. 13:37; 2 Ne. 31:15-20; Omni 26; Mosiah 2:41; 4:6; 30; Alma 5:13; 3 Ne. 15:9. Obedience to commandments: 1 Ne. 2:20-22; 15:11; 2 Ne. 1:20; 9:27; Enos 10; Mosiah 1:11; 2:4; 13:22, 31, 33, 36, 41; Alma 7:23; 12:32; 28:1; Hel. 5:6; 3 Ne. 12:20.

5. Miller, "Covenant to Revival," 102.

6. Anti-monarchial sentiment: 2 Ne. 5:18; Mosiah 2:14-18; 6:7; 23:6-14; 29:13-18, 23, 30, 31; Alma 43:45; 46:10; 51:5, 8; 3 Ne. 6:30; Ether 6:22-26.

7. Restoration of the true church: Morm. 1:13-15; 3:2-3; 8:10-11, 26, 28, 32-33, 37-41; 9:7-26; 4 Ne. 1:19 (the ideal church), 20, 26-34, 38-42; 3 Ne. 11:28-29, 32; 16:6-7, 10-13.

8. D&C 10:63; 3 Ne. 11:28-29.

9. Joseph Smith et al., *History of the Church of Jesus Christ of Latter-day Saints*, 7 vols. (Salt Lake City: Deseret Book Co., 1927), 2:182; hereafter HC.

10. For example, Lyman E. Johnson, Orson Hyde, and Smith's brother, William. See *Latter-day Saints' Millennial Star* 15 (26 March 1853): 206-207.

11. *Palmyra Reflector*, 14 Feb. 1831, from a Painesville, Ohio, correspondent. A church in the town of Mendon, Monroe County, ten miles from Palmyra, was influenced by Mormonism in 1832; *Wayne Sentinel*, 18 Apr. 1832. The preacher said "that he shall never die, but be *translated*, after the manner of Enoch, and that in eighteen months Mormonism will be the prevailing religion; and that in five years the wicked are to be swept from the face of the earth."

12. Eber D. Howe, *Mormonism Unvailed* (Painesville, OH, 1834), 274.

13. *Painesville Telegraph*, 15 Mar. 1831.

14. Contrast this to the Adventist movement set in motion by William Miller and carried on by Ellen G. White.

15. *Quest for Empire: The Political Kingdom of God and the Council of Fifty in Mormon History* (East Lansing: Michigan State University Press, 1967), 18. Compare William Mulder, "Mormonism's 'Gathering': An American

Doctrine with a Difference," *Church History* 23 (1954): 248-64. The Millerites had failed to consider such an insurance clause and had to explain the Lord's failure to appear as due to their misunderstanding of certain key biblical passages.

16. *Painesville Telegraph*, 16 Nov. 1830.

17. Richard L. Evans, *A Century of "Mormonism" in Great Britain* (Salt Lake City: Deseret News Press, 1937), appendix, "British Mission Emigration by Years," 245.

18. This story is told by William Mulder's *Homeward to Zion: The Mormon Migration from Scandinavia* (Minneapolis: University of Minnesota Press, 1957).

19. See Orson Hyde, *A Voice from Jerusalem, or a Sketch of the Travels and Ministry of Elder Orson Hyde* (Boston, 1842).

20. HC 1:338.

21. George B. Arbaugh, *Revelation in Mormonism: Its Character and Changing Forms* (Chicago: University of Chicago Press, 1932), 182.

22. *The American Adam: Innocence, Tragedy, and Tradition in the Nineteenth Century* (Chicago: University of Chicago Press, 1955).

23. Ibid., 89.

24. John Henry Evans, *Joseph Smith: An American Prophet* (New York: Macmillan, 1933), 11.

25. D&C 29:39; Moses 5:10-13; 6:55.

26. See Mulder, "Mormonism's 'Gathering,'" 250, 260.

27. Hansen, 72-89.

28. Davis Bitton, "Mormons in Texas: The Ill-Fated Lyman Wight Colony, 1844-1858," *Arizona and the West* 11 (Spring 1969): 5-26.

29. Arbaugh, 28.

Epilogue

The strength of Joseph Smith's defense of God was personal revelation, but it would also prove to be one of its weaknesses. To explain why Oliver Cowdery and Hiram Page failed to sell the copyright to the Book of Mormon after a revelation told them they would succeed, Smith said that "some revelations are of God, some revelations are of man, and some revelations are of the devil."[1] This kind of reply offered no security to one who relied on revelation coming through Mormon priesthood channels, for Smith was as high as one could go.

In addition, that security was tied to the truth of Smith's story of the origins of the Book of Mormon and the testimony of the three witnesses. These stories were to guarantee the existence of the plates and the validity of the translation, to demonstrate that Smith was a man through whom God was working. All converts could obtain assurance of an angel that what the witnesses heard and saw was true and could themselves "know" that it was true. When pressed, however, the witnesses also admitted that their "seeing" the plates was more like something they imagined. If believers should ever doubt that such "seeing" was valid, then they had no assurance at all of the truth of Smith's defense of God.

Not only might believers doubt the witnesses "seeing" the plates, but what assurance remained if even the Book of Mormon witnesses doubted or no longer believed that they had seen an angel? Or worse, if one of them, David Whitmer, for example, claimed to know that Smith had fallen into error?[2]

Ultimately, all this comes down to the question of whether one can believe Joseph Smith, which returns us to Thomas Paine in the mid-1790s: believers believe the Old Testament or the Koran (and now the Book of Mormon) only if they believe Moses or Mohammed (and now Joseph Smith). In the end there was no gain over the way people came to accept Jesus Christ as Lord and Savior.

Knowledge then cannot replace faith. Faith is a gift, is itself revelation, is a sign that God is at work. Knowledge will fail and then faith must carry the believer. Smith himself said just that to Oliver Cowdery when Cowdery failed to translate the plates. Cowdery was told to "rely upon the things which are written." But if people cannot believe the Bible or its story of Christ on the basis of apostolic witness, then they can no more believe in Christ on the witness of the Book of Mormon and the witness of Mormonism's living apostles.

To defend God, Smith tried to preserve the Bible as special revelation through the Book of Mormon, but in the end he made it more difficult to accept the Bible, since one had to accept two books instead of one. In his battle with skeptics, Smith tried to refurbish the Bible in order to make it intellectually acceptable. He supplied portions which were lost, corrected contradictions[3] he discerned, and eliminated italicized words which were "the work of man."

However, his strategy was compromised when the Book of Mormon manuscript itself turned out to have omissions, corrections, emendations, and contradictions. If the Book of Mormon was to be a corrective for the Bible, what was one to do if it also needed correcting? Or if immediate revelation could supply the correction, what was one to do if the revelator later received contradictory revelations?

Smith wanted to settle all doctrinal contention and denominational strife. But within a few years after his death, there were several contending factions which claimed Smith as founder and the Book of Mormon as scripture. The very thing Smith criticized and tried to correct in Christendom had come to his own movement. Personal revelation could not solve the problem of Mormons contending over who had authority, succession, priesthood, and true doctrine. Each made the claim and could well produce a young man who would look at rival Mormon factions, the contending denominations of his day, and come to the conclusion that none was right.

NOTES

1. David Whitmer, *An Address to All Believers in Christ* (Richmond, MO, 1887), 54. Compare D&C 46:7. Smith said that one could tell the difference

when a former revelation is contradicted; see *History of the Church of Jesus Christ of Latter-day Saints,* 7 vols. (Salt Lake City: Deseret Book Co., 1927), 4:581.

2. Brigham Young et al., *Journal of Discourses,* 26 vols. (Liverpool: F. D. Richards et al., 1854-86), 7:164. No less a person than Brigham Young said of the witnesses of the Book of Mormon: "some of the witnesses of the Book of Mormon, who handled the plates and conversed with the angels of God, were afterwards led to doubt and to disbelieve that they had ever seen an angel." Ibid.

3. Ironically, Smith introduced contradictions between the monogamy of the Book of Mormon and the polygamy of the Doctrine and Covenants, the Unitarian monotheism of the Book of Mormon and the polytheism of the Doctrine and Covenants. The Book of Mormon account of Jesus' birth names Jerusalem as the birthsite rather than the New Testament's location of Bethlehem (Alma 7:9-10).

Appendix 1.

Did Joseph Smith Consult Ethan Smith?

The first non-Mormon scholar to accept the influence of *View of the Hebrews* on Joseph Smith was Fawn Brodie.[1] Catholic sociologist Thomas F. O'Dea followed suit,[2] as did others.[3] In fact, a line can be drawn between George Arbaugh's 1932 study of Mormonism and revelation and Brodie's 1945 biography of Joseph Smith. Arbaugh knew that *View of the Hebrews* was one of many books advancing a theory of Hebrew/native American origins but favored the Spaulding manuscript theory of Mormon beginnings.[4]

Mormon consideration of the influence of Ethan Smith predates Brodie. In the 1920s B. H. Roberts identified four books possibly available to Joseph Smith but felt that realistically Smith would only have had access to works by James Adair and Ethan Smith. Roberts pointed out that no direct evidence connected Ethan Smith with Joseph Smith. The prophet had not used the theory, Roberts thus concluded, because he was too young, was not a student, and it would have been too difficult to have assimilated the knowledge of American antiquities necessary to dictate the Book of Mormon.[5] Later, Roberts studied the possible connection further and drew up a list of parallels between the Book of Mormon and *View of the Hebrews*. He circulated his research among some in Utah but did not publish it.[6] After Roberts's death his son mimeographed the list and distributed it, and his studies were finally published in 1987.[7]

According to Roberts's later studies, some features of *View of the Hebrews* are paralleled in the Book of Mormon. (1) Indians buried a book they could no longer read. (2) A Mr. Merrick found some dark

yellow parchment leaves in "Indian Hill." (3) Native Americans had
inspired prophets and charismatic gifts, as well as (4) their own kind
of Urim and Thummim and breastplate. (5) Ethan Smith produced
evidence to show that ancient Mexican Indians were no strangers to
Egyptian hieroglyphics. (6) An overthrown civilization in America is
to be seen from its ruined monuments and forts and mounds. The
barbarous tribes—barbarous because they had lost the civilized
arts—greeting the Europeans were descendants of the lost civilization. (7) Chapter one of *View of the Hebrews* is a thirty-two-page
account of the historical destruction of Jerusalem. (8) There are
many references to Israel's scattering and being "gathered" in the
last days. (9) Isaiah is quoted for twenty chapters to demonstrate the
restoration of Israel. In Isaiah 18 a request is made to save Israel in
America. (10) The United States is asked to evangelize the native
Americans. (11) Ethan Smith cited Humboldt's *New Spain* to show
the characteristics of Central American civilization; the same are in
the Book of Mormon. (12) The legends of Quetzacoatl, the Mexican
messiah, are paralleled in the Book of Mormon by Christ's appearing
in the western hemisphere. Mormon responses to these parallels
have variously addressed one or more of the following questions:
Did Joseph Smith know enough about native American antiquities
to dictate the Book of Mormon? Did he know about the theory of
the Indian-Israelite identification? Did he actually use *View of the
Hebrews?*

One line of defense has been to assert that information about
native American antiquities was unavailable to Joseph Smith. As
noted, Roberts initially felt that only four works could have been
available to Smith. Evan Fry of the RLDS church subsequently
contended that books describing Mexican and American Indian
archaeology such as Humboldt's *New Spain* would not have been
available to a boy in western New York before 1839.[8] But Roberts
came to recognize that, at least in the case of Ethan Smith's book,
such works were widely available.[9]

Roy Weldon and Edward Butterworth cited and dismissed six
similarities between *View of the Hebrews* and the Book of Mormon
because Joseph Smith treated them differently than Ethan Smith.[10]
For example, Ethan Smith applied "the stick of Ephraim" of Ezekiel
37 to the ten lost tribes of Israel, but Joseph Smith applied it only to
the tribe of Manasseh. Weldon and Butterworth reason that one
usage should duplicate the other in order to establish borrowing.

They also cite contradictions between the two texts as well as suggest that Joseph Smith could have borrowed more, which by inference rule out borrowing. However, dependence cannot be dismissed because of what Joseph Smith did *not* use from the *View of the Hebrews*, or because he altered the features of resemblance between the two books, or because he contradicted some features of the earlier work.

The next line of defense was to recognize that information about early Indian life was indeed at hand but that since Joseph Smith was young and not a student, he could not have assimilated enough information to produce the Book of Mormon. However, the Book of Mormon is vague about details of ancient American geography and antiquities, enough so that no area can be specifically pinpointed on a map. M. Wells Jakeman and Ross Christensen, anthropologists at Brigham Young University in 1959 to 1960, denied that certainty was possible regarding the Book of Mormon's statements about America. Not enough was known about the period of time covered, about Indian origins, or about ancient America to say that the Book of Mormon had been proved scientifically or archaeologically.[11] Even Hill Cumorah as the death site of the last Nephite is uncertain.

Lucy Smith's picture of her son as a thoughtful young man filled with Indian lore indicates that he absorbed the constant flow of information about native Americans. One need only show that the ideas of the Book of Mormon were in reach of Joseph Smith.

Another line of defense has been to acknowledge that *View of the Hebrews* was available but that Joseph Smith did not need to consult it: the ideas were in the air.[12] Hugh Nibley advanced this position to free Joseph Smith from the charge that he used Ethan Smith's book, but in doing so Nibley undermined earlier Mormon defenses. In denying the force of Roberts's parallels but admitting that *View of the Hebrews* was available to Joseph Smith, Nibley has not destroyed the possibility of Joseph Smith's dependence on Ethan Smith.

Nibley is correct that such ideas were in the air. The Indian-Israelite identification with its many parallels between Hebrew and Indian culture and religion was offered by Mordecai M. Noah as the reason for his establishing a City of Refuge for world Jewry. The article about Professor Seyffarth discovering the Old and New Testaments in Egyptian and a Mexican manuscript in hieroglyphics and suggesting that these were interrelated cultures offered a theme which is echoed in the Book of Mormon. Newspapers speculated about the times and places of native American origins and their routes of emigration. All of this information was available in places other than *View of the Hebrews*. Given the wide availability of such sources, it is difficult denying their possible influence on Joseph Smith.

Mormon writers Spencer Palmer and William Knecht tackled the reliance of both Ethan Smith and Joseph Smith on Isaiah.[13] They concluded that "the book of Isaiah is a primary source for anyone dealing with the subject of the dispersion and gathering of Israel." If Joseph Smith had not used Isaiah in common with Ethan Smith, they say, it would have appeared that he was trying "to avoid suspicion."[14] This argument acknowledges that Joseph Smith knew the work of Ethan Smith but then says the same thing as Weldon and Butterworth: one usage must duplicate the other to demonstrate borrowing, an argument which discounts the workings of human creativity. One can show hundreds of musical influences working on Beethoven, but the great composer brought forth a new kind of music.

Certainly Joseph Smith knew the Bible, Ethan Smith's ideas, and Masonic lore well enough to have been influenced by them. Mormon attempts to downplay the Mormon prophet's sources reverse older Mormon apologetics. Orson Pratt defended the authenticity of the Book of Mormon on the basis that Joseph Smith did not know Isaiah 29 before the Harris-Anthon consultation.[15] If he did know of the passage, as it is now conceded, then the question of intention comes to the fore.

View of the Hebrews circulated widely in New York. It was also condensed in Josiah Priest's *The Wonders of Nature and Providence*, one of the more widely circulated books of the Manchester rental library in 1827. The Rev. Anson Sha, pastor of the Manchester Baptist Church, was one of the members of the rental library. During his pastorate, one member related, Joseph Smith occasionally attended his church service. The name of Ethan Smith or at least his views could easily have been presented in a sermon meant to kick the corpse of deism.

Francis Kirkham published the table of contents of the books by Adair, Boudinot, and Ethan Smith to show how they differ in purpose and content from the Book of Mormon. That seemed to disprove any connection, but this position is vulnerable on two counts. First, the raw materials can serve many purposes. Second, the books are not dissimilar in purpose, since both Boudinot and Ethan Smith wrote to demonstrate that the Indians have a Hebrew origin and thereby bolster the proof for biblical revelation.[17]

There are other parallels between the two works by Ethan and Joseph Smith besides those listed by Roberts. Additional important parallels include: the Pittsfield Parchment story (which may already have circulated in the Palmyra area as early as 1817 or 1818) with its two sets of witnesses, the visit to consult scholars about the translation to get it verified, and the belief that it proved the presence of Hebrew religion among the Indians. Many others could be mentioned. For example, both books use Ezekiel 37 (especially v. 16) and are millennially oriented.

Joseph Smith knew the theory of the Hebrew origin of native Americans and knew the Bible well enough to have used them as sources. The possibility is there and the probability is strong that he used *View of the Hebrews*. Still the case is circumstantial until evidence is found that ties *View of the Hebrews* to Joseph Smith *before* he produced the Book of Mormon. If no absolute connection between Ethan Smith and Joseph Smith is found, the data still indicate that the Israelite theory of native American origins was there as a source for Joseph Smith to use in defending God against the forces of deism and rationalism.

NOTES

1. Fawn Brodie, *No Man Knows My History: The Life of Joseph Smith*, 2nd ed. rev. (New York: A. A. Knopf, 1971), 46-48. Isaac Woodbridge Riley, *The Founder of Mormonism: A Psychological Study of Joseph Smith, Jr.* (New York: Dodd, Mead & Co., 1902), 171, referred to the Pittsfield Parchment story as part of the milieu from which Smith came. At the time her biography was first published, Brodie was a Mormon. Shortly afterwards, however, she was excommunicated from the church.

2. Thomas F. O'Dea, *The Mormons* (Chicago: University of Chicago Press, 1957).

3. Larry W. Jonas, *Mormon Claims Examined* (Grand Rapids: Baker Book Co., 1961); Wesley M. Jones, *A Critical Study of Book of Mormon Sources* (Detroit: Harlo Press, 1964).

4. George Bartholomew Arbaugh, *Revelation in Mormonism: Its Character and Changing Forms* (Chicago: University of Chicago Press, 1932).

5. Brigham Henry Roberts, *New Witnesses for God*, 3 vols. (Salt Lake City: Deseret Book Co., 1926), 3: 28-39. Later (49-50) Roberts cited the Pittsfield Parchment story as evidence for the Book of Mormon. In *American Antiquities* 2nd ed. rev. (Albany: Hoffman and White, 1835), 65-67, Josiah Priest used the story to prove the theory of a Hebrew origin for the Indians. In 1837 Parley P. Pratt, *Voice of Warning and Instruction to All People, or An Introduction to the Faith and Doctrine of the Church of Jesus Christ of Latter Day Saints* (Salt Lake City: The Deseret News Steam Printing Establishment, 1874), 103-107, used Priest's just cited work plus the Stockbridge tradition (81) which Ethan Smith had used to clinch the argument of the Pittsfield Parchment story to show that Americana supports the Book of Mormon story of Indian civilization in early America.

6. Brodie, *No Man*, 47n.

7. See Jerald and Sandra Tanner, "Ethan Smith Parallels," in *Mormonism–Shadow or Reality?* (Salt Lake City: Modern Microfilm Co., 1964), 418-31. Roberts's exhaustive, private studies of the Book of Mormon were finally published by the University of Illinois Press in 1987 as *Studies of the Book of Mormon*, edited by Brigham D. Madsen.

8. Evan A. Fry, *The Restoration Faith* (Independence, MO: Herald Publishing Co., 1962), 222.

Alexander de Humboldt and Aime-Bonpland, *Personal Narrative of Travels to the Equinoctial Regions of the New Continent, During the Years 1799-1804*, trans. Helen Maria Williams (Philadelphia: M. Carey, 1815) was available in the Manchester rental library as accession number 119.

Humboldt's *Political Essay on the Kingdom of New Spain* was first published in New York in English in 1811 in two volumes with no maps. It came out in four volumes with plates, maps, plans, and tables in London during 1811-12. A second London edition came out in three volumes in 1822. In 1813 *An Abridgement of Humboldt's Statistical Essay on New Spain* by a citizen of Maryland (Baltimore: Wayne and O'Reilly, 1813) appeared and was likely the work advertised in the *Palmyra Register*.

His *Researches, Concerning the Institutions & Monuments of the Ancient Inhabitants of America, with Descriptions & Views of Some of the Most Striking Stones in the Cordilleras*, trans. Helen Maria Williams (London: Longman, Hurst, Rees, Orme and Brown, J. Murray and H. Colburn, 1814) was also available in this country. This puts to rest the argument that such works were not available.

9. Roberts, *New Witnesses*, 2:28-39.

10. Roy E. Weldon and F. Edward Butterworth, *Criticism of the Book of Mormon Answered* (Independence, MO: Herald House, 1973), 14-16. Compare also Charles A. Davies, "'View of the Hebrews' and the Book of Mormon," *Saints' Herald*, 1 Aug. 1962, 537-39.

11. *Brigham Young University Archaeological Society Newsletter* 57 (25 Mar.

1959): 4; 64 (30 Jan. 1960): 3.

12. Hugh Nibley, "The Comparative Method," in "'Mixed Voices': A Study in Book of Mormon Criticism," *Improvement Era* 62 (Mar.-Aug., Oct.-Nov. 1959).

13. Spencer J. Palmer and William L. Knecht, "View of the Hebrews: Substitute for Inspiration?" *Brigham Young University Studies* 5 (Winter 1962): 105-13.

14. Ibid., 108.

15. Orson Pratt said of Smith in 1855: "Mr. Smith did not know anything about this prophecy at that time, for he was unacquainted with the contents of the Bible," "The Ancient Prophecies," 188. This position has been abandoned.

16. Accession number 108.

17. Francis W. Kirkham, *A New Witness for Christ: The Book of Mormon*, 2 vols. 3rd ed. rev. (Independence, MO: Zion's Printing and Publishing Co., 1951), 2:392. I made this point in "The Lost Tribes of Israel and the Book of Mormon," *Lutheran Quarterly* 22 (Aug. 1970): 319-29.

Appendix 2.

Textual Comparison of Isaiah 29

Joseph Smith Revision, Isaiah 29	*Book of Mormon, 2 Nephi 25*	*King James Version, Isaiah 29*
1 Woe to Ariel, to Ariel, the city where David dwelt! add ye year to year; let them kill sacrifices. 2 Yet I will distress Ariel, and there shall be heaviness and sorrow; for thus hath the Lord said unto me, It shall be unto Ariel; 3 That I the Lord will camp against her round about, and will lay siege against her with a mount, and I will raise forts against her. 4 And she shall be brought down, . . .	15 After my seed and the seed of my brethren shall have dwindled in unbelief, and shall have been smitten by the Gentiles; yea, after the Lord God shall have camped against them round about, and shall have laid siege against them with a mount, and raised forts against them; and after they shall have been brought down low in the dust, even that they are not, yet the words of the righteous shall be written, and the prayers of the faithful shall be heard, and all those who have dwindled in unbelief shall not be forgotten. 16 For those who shall be destroyed . . .	1 Woe to Ariel, to Ariel, the city where David dwelt! add ye year to year; let them kill sacrifices. 2 Yet I will distress Ariel, and there shall be heaviness and sorrow; for thus hath the Lord said unto me, It shall be unto Ariel; 3 And I will camp against thee round about, and will lay siege against thee with a mount, and I will raise forts against thee. 4 And thou shalt be brought down, . . .

191

and shall speak out of the ground, and their speech shall be low out of the dust, and their voice shall be as of one that hath a familiar spirit, . . .

shall speak unto them out of the ground, and their speech shall be low out of the dust, and their voice shall be as one that hath a familiar spirit,

17 For thus saith the Lord God: They shall write the things which shall be done among them, and they shall be written and sealed up in a book and those who have dwindled in unbelief shall not have them, for they seek to destroy the things of God.

and shalt speak out of the ground, and thy speech shall be low out of the dust, and thy voice shall be, as of one that hath a familiar spirit, . . .

[Verses 11-19 contain the same text as for 2 Nephi 27:6-14, except for differences in numbering, punctuation, and capitalization. The following text is from the Book of Mormon:]

11 (6) And it shall come to pass that the Lord God shall bring forth unto you the words of a book, and they shall be the words of them which have slumbered.

12 (7) And behold the book shall be sealed; and in the book shall be a revelation from God, from the beginning of the world to the ending thereof.

13 (8) Wherefore, because of the things which are sealed up, the things which are sealed shall not be delivered in the day of the wickedness and abominations of the people. Wherefore the book shall be kept from them.

14 (9) But the book shall be delivered unto a man, and he shall deliver the words of the book, which are the words of those who have slumbered in the dust, and he shall deliver these words unto another;

— (10) But the words which are sealed he shall not deliver, neither shall he deliver the book.

15 (—) For the book shall be sealed by the power of God, and the revelation which was sealed shall be kept in the book until the own due time of the Lord, that they may come forth; for behold they reveal all things from the foundation of the world unto the end thereof.

16 (11) And the day cometh that the words of the book which were sealed shall be read upon the house tops; and they shall be read by the power of Christ; and all things shall be revealed unto the children of men which ever

have been among the children of men, and which ever will be even unto the end of the earth.

17 (12) Wherefore, at that day when the book shall be delivered unto the man of whom I have spoken, the book shall be hid from the eyes of the world, that the eyes of none shall behold it save it be that three witnesses shall behold it, by the power of God, besides him to whom the book shall be delivered; and they shall testify to the truth of the book and the things therein.

18 (13) And there is none other which shall view it, save it be a few according to the will of God, to bear testimony of his word unto the children of men; for the Lord God hath said that the words of the faithful should speak as if it were from the dead.

9 (14) Wherefore, the Lord God will proceed to bring forth the words of the book; and in the mouth of as many witnesses as seemeth him good will he establish his word; and wo be unto him that rejecteth the word of God!

Joseph Smith Revision, Isaiah 29	*Book of Mormon 2 Nephi 27*	*King James Version Isaiah 29*
20 But, behold, it shall come to pass, that the Lord God shall say unto him to whom he shall deliver the book, Take these words which are not sealed and deliver them to another, that he may show them unto the learned, saying, Read this, I pray thee. 21 And the learned shall say, Bring hither the book and I will read them; and now because of the world, and to get gain will they say this, and the man shall say, I cannot bring the book for it is sealed. . .	15 But behold, it shall come to pass that the Lord God shall say unto him to whom he shall deliver the book: Take these words which are not sealed and deliver them to another, that he may show them unto the learned, saying: Read this, I pray thee. And the learned shall say, Bring hither the book, and I will read them. 16 And now, because of the glory of the world and to get gain will they say this, and not for the glory of God. 17 And the man shall say: I cannot bring the book for it is sealed;	11 And the vision of all is become unto you as the words of a book that is sealed which men deliver to one that is learned, saying, Read this, I pray thee: and he saith, I cannot, for it is sealed:

. . . Then shall the learned say, I cannot read it.

22 Wherefore it shall come to pass, that the Lord God will deliver again the book and the words thereof to him that is not learned and the man that is not learned shall say, I am not learned.

18 Then shall the learned say: I cannot read it.

19 Wherefore it shall come to pass, that the Lord God will deliver again the book and the words thereof to him that is not learned; and the man that is not learned shall say, I am not learned.

20 Then shall the Lord God say unto him: The learned shall not read them, for they have rejected them, and I am able to do mine own work; wherefore thou shalt read the words which I shall give unto thee.

12 And the book is delivered to him that is not learned, saying, Read this, I pray thee: and he saith, I am not learned.

Bibliography

BOOKS

Adair, James. *The History of the American Indians*. London: Edward and Charles Dilly, 1775.

Adams, Samuel Hopkins. *Canal Town*. Toronto: Random House, 1944.

American Antiquarian Society Transactions. Vol. 1. Worchester, MA, 1820.

Arbaugh, George Bartholomew. *Revelation in Mormonism: Its Character and Changing Forms*. Chicago: University of Chicago Press, 1932.

Austin, Emily M. *Mormonism; or Life Among the Mormons*. Madison, WI: M. J. Cantrell Book and Job Printer, 1882.

Backman, Milton V., Jr. *American Religions and the Rise of Mormonism*. Salt Lake City: Deseret Book Co., 1965.

Ballou, Hosea. *A Treatise on Atonement*. Randoph, VT: Serano Wright, 1805.

Barrett, Ivan J. *Joseph Smith and the Restoration: A History of the Church to 1846*. Provo, UT: Brigham Young University Press, 1973.

Barruel, Abbe. *The Anti-Christian and Antisocial Conspiracy*. Lancaster, PA: Joseph Ehrenfried, 1812.

Beaver, R. Pierce. *Church, State, and the American Indians*. St. Louis: Concordia Publishing House, 1966.

Becker, John E. *A History of Freemasonry in Waterloo, New York, 1817-1942*. Waterloo, NY: Seneca Lodge No. 113, F. & A.M., 1942.

Bernard, David. *Light on Masonry*. Utica: William Williams, 1829.

Berrett, William E. and Alma P. Burton, eds. *Readings in LDS History from Original Manuscripts*. 3 vols. Salt Lake City: Deseret Book Co., 1953.

Boudinot, Elias. *A Star in the West; or, A Humble Attempt to Discover the Long Lost Ten Tribes of Israel, Preparatory to the Return to Their Beloved City, Jerusalem*. Trenton, NJ: D. Fenton, S. Hutchinson, and J. Dunham, 1816.

Brodie, Fawn M. *No Man Knows My History: The Life of Joseph Smith*. 2d ed. rev. New York: A. A. Knopf, 1971.

Campbell, Alexander. *Delusions: An Analysis of the Book of Mormon . . . and a Refutation of Its Pretences to Divine Authority*. Boston, 1832.

Cassara, Ernest, ed. *Universalism in America: A Documentary History*. Boston: Beacon Press, 1971.

Cerza, Alphonse. *Anti-Masonry*. Fulton, MO: Ovid Bell Press, Inc., 1962.

Cheville, Roy A. *Scriptures from Ancient America: A Study of the Book of Mormon*. Independence, MO: Herald Publishing House, 1964.

Clark, John Alonzo. *Gleanings by the Way*. Philadelphia: W. J. & J. K. Simon, 1842.

Coil, Henry Wilson. *Masonic Encyclopedia*. New York: Macoy Publishing & Supply Co., 1961.

Collections of the New York Historical Society, for the Year 1821. New York: Bliss & White, 1821.

Copeland, Lewis, ed. *The World's Great Speeches*. New York: Garden City Publishing Co., 1942.

Cross, Whitney R. *The Burned-over District: The Social and Intellectual History of Enthusiastic Religion in Western New York, 1800-1850*. Ithaca: Cornell University Press, 1956.

Dwight, Timothy. *Travels; in New England and New York*. 4 vols. New Haven: S. Converse, Printer, 1821-22.

Evans, John Henry. *Joseph Smith: An American Prophet*. New York: Macmillan Co., 1933.

Evans, Richard L. *A Century of "Mormonism" in Great Britain*. Salt Lake City: Deseret News Press, 1937.

Ferguson, Thomas Stuart. *One Fold, One Shepherd*. San Francisco: Books of California, 1958.

Ferm, Vergilius. *Classics of Protestantism*. New York: Philosophical Library, 1959.

Fife, Austin and Alta. *Saints of Sage and Saddle: Folklore Among the Mormons*. Bloomington: Indiana University Press, 1956.

Finney, Charles Goodison. *Lectures on Revivals of Religion*. Rev. ed. Oberlin, OH: E. J. Goodrich, 1868.

Fry, Evan A. *The Restoration Faith*. Independence, MO: Herald Publishing House, 1962.

Glaser, Lynn. *Indians or Jews? An Introduction to a Reprint of Manasseh Ben Israel's The Hope of Israel*. Gilroy, CA: Roy V. Basell, 1973.

Goodwin, S. H. *Additional Studies in Mormonism and Masonry*. Salt Lake City: Grand Lodge of F. & A.M. of Utah, 1932.

Handy, Robert T. Lefferts, A. Loetscher, and Smith H. Shelton. *American Christianity: An Historical Interpretation with Representative Documents*. Vol. 1. New York: Charles Scribner's Sons, 1960.

Hannah, Walton. *Darkness Visible: A Revelation & Interpretation of Freemasonry*. London: Augustine Press, 1952.

Hansen, Klaus J. *Quest for Empire: The Political Kingdom of God and the Council of Fifty in Mormon History*. East Lansing: Michigan State University

Press, 1967.

Hardie, James. *The New Free-Mason's Monitor*. New York: George Long, 1818.

Horne, Thomas Hartwell. *An Introduction to the Critical Study and Knowledge of the Holy Scriptures*. New edition from the 8th London edition, corrected and enlarged. 2 vols. New York: Robert Carter & Brothers, 1856.

Hotchkin, James H. *A History of the Purchase and Settlement of Western New York, and of the Rise, Progress, and Present State of the Presbyterian Church in That Section*. New York: M. W. Dodd, 1848.

Howard, Richard P. *Restoration Scriptures: A Study of Their Textual Development*. Independence, MO: Herald Publishing House, 1969.

Howe, Eber D. *Mormonism Unvailed*. Painseville, OH: By the Author, 1834.

Hudson, Winthrop S. *Religion in America: An Historical Account of the Developments of American Religious Life*. New York: Charles Scribner's Sons, 1965.

Humboldt, Alexander de. *Personal Narrative of Travels to the Equinoctial Regions of the New Continent, During the Years 1799-1804*. Translated by Helen Maria Williams. Philadelphia: M. Carey, 1815.

———and Aime-Boupland. *Political Essay on the Kingdom of New Spain*. Translated by John Black. 2 vols. New York: I. Riley, 1811.

Hyde, Orson. *A Voice from Jerusalem, or a Sketch of the Travels and Ministry of Elder Orson Hyde*. Boston: Albert Morgan, 1842.

Johnson, Allen, ed. *Dictionary of American Biography*. 22 vols. New York: Charles Scribner's Sons, 1928-58.

Jonas, Larry W. *Mormon Claims Examined*. Grand Rapids, MI: Baker Book Co., 1961.

Jones, Wesley M. *A Critical Study of Book of Mormon Sources*. Detroit: Harlo Press, 1964.

Josephus, Flavius. "Antiquities of the Jews." In *The Life and Works of Flavius Josephus*. Book 1, chapter 2. Translated by William Whiston. Philadelphia: John C. Winston, Co., n.d.

Journal of Discourses. Edited by G. D. Watt et al. 26 vols. Liverpool: F. D. Richards, 1854-86.

Kidder, Daniel P. *Mormonism and the Mormons: A Historical View of the Rise and Progress of the Sect Self-Styled Latter-day Saints*. New York: G. Lane and P. P. Sanford, 1842.

Kirkham, Francis W. *A New Witness for Christ in America: The Book of Mormon*. 2 vols. 3rd ed. rev. Independence, MO: Zion's Printing and Publishing Co., 1951.

Koch, Gustav A. *Religion of the American Enlightenment*. New York: Thomas Y. Crowell Co., 1968.

Lee, John Doyle. *Mormonism Unveiled: or the Life and Confession of the*

Late Mormon Bishop John D. Lee. Omaha: F. H. Rogers, 1891.

Lewis, R. W. B. *The American Adam: Innocence, Tragedy, and Tradition in the Nineteenth Century*. Chicago: University of Chicago Press, 1955.

Mackey, Albert C. *The History of Freemasonry: Its Legends and Traditions; Its Chronological History*. 7 vols. New York: Masonic History Co., 1905.

Marks, David. *The Life of David Marks to the 26th Year of His Age*. Limerick, ME: Office of the Morning Star, 1831.

Marty, Martin E. *The Infidel: Freethought and American Religion*. Cleveland: World Publishing Co., 1961.

Mayer, Frederick E. *The Religious Bodies of America*. St. Louis: Concordia Publishing House, 1961.

McChesney, James. *An Antidote to Mormonism*. New York: By the Author, 1836.

Mead, Sidney E. *The Lively Experiment: The Shaping of Christianity in America*. New York: Harper & Row, 1965.

Metcalf, Anthony. *Ten Years Before the Mast*. Mildad, ID: By the Author, 1888.

Meyer, Eduard. *Ursprung and Geschichte der Mormonen mit Exkursen uebre die Anfange des Islams and des Christentums*. Halle: Max Niemeyer, 1912.

Millard, David. *The True Messiah*. Canandaigua, NY, 1823.

Miller, Perry. *Nature's Nation*. Cambridge: Harvard University Press, 1967.

Milliken, Charles F. *A History of Ontario County, New York and Its People*. 2 vols. New York: Lewis Historical Publishing Co., 1911.

Morais, Herbert M. *Deism in Eighteenth Century America*. New York: Russell & Russell, 1934.

Morgan, William. *Illustrations of Masonry*. Reprinted as *Morgan's Freemasonry Exposed and Explained*. New York: L. Fitzgerald, 1882.

Morris, Rob. *William Morgan: or Political Anti-Masonry its Rise, Growth and Decadence*. New York: Robert Macoy, 1883.

Mulder, William. *Homeward to Zion: The Mormon Migration from Scandinavia*. Minneapolis: University of Minnesota Press, 1957.

————and A. Russell Mortensen. *Among the Mormons: Historic Accounts by Contemporary Observers*. New York: A. A. Knopf, 1958.

Nibley, Hugh. *An Approach to the Book of Mormon*. Salt Lake City: Deseret New Press, 1964.

————. *Since Cumorah*. Salt Lake City: Deseret Book Co., 1967.

Nibley, Preston. *The Witnesses of the Book of Mormon*. Salt Lake City: Deseret Book Co., 1953.

O'Dea, Thomas F. *The Mormons*. Chicago: University of Chicago Press, 1957.

Odierne, James. *Opinions on Speculative Masonry*. Boston: Perkins & Marvin, 1830.

Paddock, Z. *Memoir of Rev. Benjamin G. Paddock, with Brief Notes of Early Ministerial Associates.* New York: Nelson & Phillips, 1875.

Paine, Thomas. *The Age of Reason: Being an Investigation of True and Fabulous Theology.* Edited by Moncure Daniel Conway. New York: G. P. Putnam's Sons, 1898.

Post, Albert. *Popular Freethought in America, 1825-1850.* New York: Columbia University Press, 1943.

Pratt, Orson. *A Series of Pamphlets.* Liverpool: R. James, 1848-51.

————. *Doctrines of the Gospel.* Salt Lake City: Juvenile Instructor Office, 1884. This is a reprint of *A Series of Pamphlets* with some material omitted.

Pratt, Parley Parker. *Key to Science of Theology.* Liverpool: By the Author, 1855.

————. *A Voice of Warning and Instruction to All People, or An Introduction to the Faith and Doctrine of the Church of Jesus Christ of Latter Day Saints.* Salt Lake City: Deseret News Steam Printing Establishment, 1874.

————. *Writings of Parley Parker Pratt.* Edited by Parker Pratt Robison. Salt Lake City: By the Editor, 1952.

Priest, Josiah. *The Wonders of Nature and Providence.* Albany: By the Author, 1825.

Proceedings of the United States Anti-Masonic Convention, Held at Philadelphia, September 11, 1830. New York: Skinner and Dewey, 1830.

Publications of the American Tract Society, The Vol. XIV. New York: American Tract Society, [1827].

Reynolds, George. *A Dictionary of the Book of Mormon.* Salt Lake City: Philip C. Reynolds, 1954.

Rich, Ben E. *Scrap Book of Mormon Literature.* 2 vols. Chicago: Henry C. Etten & Co., n.d.

Riley, Isaac Woodbridge. *The Founder of Mormonism: A Psychological Study of Joseph Smith, Jr.* New York: Dodd, Mead & Co., 1902.

Roberts, Brigham Henry. *A Comprehensive History of the Church of Jesus Christ of Latter-day Saints.* 6 vols. Salt Lake City: Church of Jesus Christ of Latter-day Saints, 1930.

————. *New Witnesses for God.* 3 vols. Salt Lake City: Deseret Book Co., 1926.

Sacher, Abram Leon. *A History of the Jews.* 4th ed. rev. New York: A. A. Knopf, 1953.

Silverberg, Robert. *Mound Builders of Ancient America: The Archaeology of a Myth.* Greenwich, CT: New York Graphic Society Ltd., 1968.

Smith, Ethan. *View of the Hebrews: or the Ten Tribes of Israel in America.* Poultney, VT: Smith & Shute, 1825.

Smith, Joseph, Jr. *A Book of Commandments, for the Government of the Church of Christ* Zion [Independence], MO: W. W. Phelps & Co., 1833.

————. *The Book of Mormon*. Palmyra, NY: E. B. Grandin, 1830.

————. *The Book of Mormon*. Kirtland, OH: Oliver Cowdery & Co., 1837.

————. *The Book of Mormon*. Nauvoo, IL: Joseph Smith, 1840.

————. *The Book of Mormon*. Salt Lake City: Church of Jesus Christ of Latter-day Saints, 1921.

————. *Doctrine & Covenants*. Kirtland, OH: F. G. Williams & Co., 1835.

————. *Doctrine & Covenants*. Salt Lake City: Church of Jesus Christ of Latter-day Saints, 1921.

———— *History of the Church of Jesus Christ of Latter-day Saints*. 7 vols. Salt Lake City: Deseret Book, Co., 1927.

————. *Inspired Version of the Holy Scriptures: Inspired Revision of the Authorized Version*. A New Corrected Edition. Independence, MO: Herald Publishing House, 1944.

————. *Pearl of Great Price*. Salt Lake City: Church of Jesus Christ of Latter-day Saints, 1921.

Smith, Lucy Mack. *Biographical Sketches of Joseph Smith, the Prophet, and His Progenitors for Many Generations*. Liverpool: S. W. Richards, 1853.

Sperry, Sidney B. *Book of Mormon Compendium*. Salt Lake City: Bookcraft, Inc., 1968.

————. *The Voice of Israel's Prophets*. Salt Lake City: Deseret Book Co., 1952.

Sprague, William. *Annals of the Congregational Pulpit*. Vol. 2. New York: Robert Carter & Brothers, 1869.

Stone, William L. *Letters on Masonry and Anti-Masonry, Addressed to The Hon. John Quincy Adams*. New York: O. Halstaad, 1832.

Sweet, William Warren. *The Story of Religions in America*. New York: Harper and Brothers, 1930.

Tanner, Jerald and Sandra. *Joseph Smith and Money Digging*. Salt Lake City: Modern Microfilm Co., 1970.

————. *Joseph Smith's 1826 Trial*. Salt Lake City: Modern Microfilm Co., 1971.

————. *Mormonism Like Watergate?* Salt Lake City: Modern Microfilm Co., 1974.

————. *Mormonism–Shadow or Reality?* Rev. ed. Salt Lake City: Modern Microfilm Co., 1972

Testimony of Christ's Second Appearing, Exemplified by the Principles and Practice of the True Church of Christ. 2d ed. Albany: United Society [Shakers], 1856.

Tucker, Pomeroy. *The Origin, Rise, and Progress of Mormonism*. New York: D. Appleton and Co., 1867.

Turner, O[rsamus]. *History of the Pioneer Settlement of Phelps and*

Gorham's Purchase. Rochester: Wm. Alling, 1851.

Ward, Henry Dana. *Free Masonry. Its Pretensions Exposed in Faithful Extracts of its Standard Authors*. New York, 1828.

Wauchope, Robert. *Lost Tribes & Sunken Continents: Myth and Method in the Study of American Indians*. Chicago: University of Chicago Press, 1962.

Webb, Robert C. [J. C. Homans]. *The Real Mormonism: A Candid Analysis of an Interesting but much Misunderstood Subject in History, Life and Thought*. New York: Sturgie & Walton Co., 1916.

Webb, Thomas S. *The Freemason's Monitor; or Illustrations of Masonry*. New York: Southwick and Crookar, 1802.

———. *The Freemason's Monitor*. Cincinnati: Applegate & Co., 1860.

Weldon, Roy E. and F. Edward Butterworth. *Criticism of the Book of Mormon Answered*. Independence: Herald House, 1973.

Whitmer, David. *An Address to All Believers in Christ*. Richmond, MO: By the Author, 1887.

Whitmer, John. *John Whitmer's History*. Salt Lake City: Modern Microfilm Co, n.d.

ARTICLES, SPEECHES, SERMONS, AND TRACTS

"The Aborigines," *Wayne Sentinel*, 24 July 1829.

Adamson, J. W. "The Treasure of the Widow's Son." *Mormon Miscellaneous* 1 (Oct. 1975).

Allen, James B. "The Significance of Joseph Smith's 'First Vision' in Mormon Thought." *Dialogue: A Journal of Mormon Thought* 3 (Winter 1966): 29-45.

Anderson, Richard L. "Martin Harris, the Honorable New York Farmer." *Improvement Era* 72 (1969): 18-21.

Arbaugh, George B. "Evolution of Mormon Doctrine." *Church History* 9 (1940): 157-69.

Arrington, Leonard J. "James Gordon Bennett's 1831 Report on 'The Mormonites.'" *Brigham Young University Studies* 10 (Spring 1970).

Backman, Milton V., Jr. "Awakenings in the Burned-over District: New Light on the Historical Setting of the First Vision." *Brigham Young University Studies* 9 (Spring 1969): 301-20.

Bitton, Davis. "Mormons in Texas: The Ill-Fated Lyman Wight Colony, 1844-1858." *Arizona and the West* 11 (Spring 1969): 5-26.

Briggs, R. C. "Interview with William Smith." *Deseret News*, 20 Jan. 1894.

Bronk, Mitchell. "The Baptist Church at Manchester." *The Chronicle: A Baptist Historical Quarterly* 11 (Jan. 1948): 17-30.

Bushman, Richard L. "The First Vision Story Revived." *Dialogue: A Journal of Mormon Thought* 4 (Spring 1969): 82-93.

————. *Joseph Smith and Skepticism*. Provo, UT: Brigham Young University Press, 1974.

Channing, William Allery. "Baltimore Sermon." In *Classics of Protestantism*. Edited by Vergilius Ferm, 244-77.

Chase, Abner. "Revival of Religion on Ontario District." *Methodist Magazine* 7 (1824): 435.

"The Converted Jew." *Western Farmer*, 29 Aug. 1821.

Crowley, Ariel. "The Anthon Transcript." *Improvement Era* 45 (Jan., Feb., Apr. 1942); 47 (Sept., Dec. 1944).

Davies, Charles A. "'View of the Hebrews' and the Book of Mormon." *Saints' Herald*, 1 Aug. 1962, 533-39.

Davis, David Brion. "The New England Origins of Mormonism." *New England Quarterly* 27 (June 1953): 148-63.

De Pillis, Mario. "The Quest for Religious Authority and the Rise of Mormonism." *Dialogue: A Journal of Mormon Thought* 1 (Spring 1966): 68-88.

————. "The Social Sources of Mormonism." *Church History* 37 (Mar. 1968): 50-79.

"Decyphering of Hieroglyphics." *Wayne Sentinel*, 1 June 1827.

DeVoto, Bernard. "The Centennial of Mormonism." *American Mercury* 19 (Jan. 1930): 1-13.

Durham, Reed C., Jr. "Is There No Help for the Widow's Son?" *Mormon Miscellaneous* 1 (Oct. 1975): 11-16.

"Elias Boudinot." In *Dictionary of American Biography* 2:477-78.

Fuller, Andrew. "Three Queries to the Rejecters of Christianity," *Publications of the American Tract Society* 14.

Gilbert, John H. "Joe Smith." *Post & Tribune (Detroit, Michigan)*, 3 Dec. 1877, 3.

Godfrey, Kenneth W. "A Note on the Nauvoo Library and Literary Institute." *Brigham Young University Studies* 14 (Spring 1974): 286-89.

"Golden Bible." *Rochester Daily Advertiser and Telegraph*, 31 Aug. 1829.

"Golden Bible." *Rochester Gem*, 5 Sept. 1829.

"The Great Polemical Disputation." *Wayne Sentinel*, 29 May 1829.

Hill, Marvin S. "Secular or Sectarian History? A Critique of *No Man Knows My History*," *Church History* 42 (Mar. 1974): 78-96.

Hogan, Mervin B. "The Founding Minutes of Nauvoo Lodge." *Further Light in Masonry*. Des Moines: Research Lodge No. 2, n.d.

Howard, Richard P. "Latter Day Saint Scripture and the Doctrine of Propositional Revelation." *Courage* 1 (June 1971): 209-25.

Hullinger, Robert N. "Joseph Smith, Defender of the Faith." *Concordia Theological Monthly* 42 (Feb. 1971): 72-87.

————. "The Lost Tribes of Israel and the Book of Mormon." *Lutheran Quarterly* 22 (Aug. 1970): 319-29.

Jarvis, Samuel Farmer. "Discourse on the Relations of the Indian Tribes of North America: Delivered Before the New York Historical Society, 20 December 1819," *Collections of the New York Historical Society for the Year 1821*, 183ff.

Jessee, Dean C. "The Early Accounts of Joseph Smith's First Vision." *Brigham Young University Studies* 9 (Spring 1969): 275-94.

―――. "Joseph Knight's Recollection of Early Mormon History." *Brigham Young University Studies* 17 (Aug. 1976): 29-39.

Kimball, Stanley B. "The Anthon Transcript: People, Primary Sources, and Problems." *Brigham Young University Studies* 10 (Spring 1970): 325-52.

Knecht, William L., and Spencer J. Palmer. "View of the Hebrews: Substitute for Inspiration?" *Brigham Young University Studies* 5 (Winter 1962): 105-13.

Lancaster, James E. "'By the Gift and Power of God': The Method of Translation of the Book of Mormon." *The Saints Herald*, 15 Nov. 1962, 798-806, 817.

Lane, George. "Revival of Religion on Ontario Circuit." *Methodist Magazine* 8 (1825): 158-61.

Lapham, Fayette. "The Mormons." *Historical Magazine* (New Series) 7 (May 1870): 305-9.

Leslie, Charles. *A Short and Easy Method with Deists, wherein the Certainty of the Christian Religion is Demonstrated by Infallible Proofs from Four Rules, in a Letter to a Friend*. New American Edition. Cambridge, 1805.

"Luther Bradish." In *Dictionary of American Biography* 2:567-68.

"Martin Harris, the Mormon." *Rochester Daily Democrat*, 23 June 1841.

Mitchill, Samuel Lapham. "The Original Inhabitants of America Shown to Be of the Same Family with Those of Asia." *American Antiquarian Society Transactions*, I (1820).

"Money Digger." *Palmyra Herald*, 24 July 1822.

"Mr. Owen and Mr. Campbell." *Wayne Sentinel*, 19, 16 June 1829.

Mulder, William. "Mormonism's 'Gathering': An American Doctrine with a Difference." *Church History* 23 (1954): 248-64.

Nibley, Hugh. "Censoring the Joseph Smith Story." *Improvement Era* 64 (July-Aug., Oct.-Nov. 1961).

―――. "The Comparative Method." In the series "Mixed Voices: A Study in Book of Mormon Criticism." *Improvement Era* 62 (Oct.-Nov. 1959).

―――. "A New Look at the Pearl of Great Price: Part I. Challenge and Response." *Improvement Era* 71 (Feb. 1968): 14-21.

―――. "The Stick of Judah." *Improvement Era* 56 (Jan.-June 1953).

"Noah, Mordecai Manuel." In *Dictionary of American Biography* 13:534-35.

Noah, Mordecai Manuel. "Proclamation to the Jews." *Wayne Sentinel*, 27 Sept. 1825.

―――. "Speech at the Consecration of the Cornerstone of the City of Ararat, Buffalo, N. Y., 15 September 1825." *Wayne Sentinel*, 4, 11 Oct. 1825.

Owen, Robert. "Declaration of Mental Independence." *Wayne Sentinel*, 25 Aug. 1826.

Phelps, William Wines. "Israel Will be Gathered." *The Evening and Morning Star*, June 1833.

Pratt, Orson. "The Ancient Prophecies." *Journal of Discourses* 2:284-98.

———. "Divine Authenticity of the Book of Mormon." *Doctrines of the Gospel*. 124-314.

———. "Divine Authority, or the Question, Was Joseph Smith Sent of God?" *Doctrines of the Gospel*, 7-40.

———. *An Interesting Account of Several Remarkable Visions and of the Late Discovery of Ancient American Records*. England, 1840; New York: By the Author, 1841.

———. "Review of God's Dealings with the Prophet Joseph." *Journal of Discourses* 15:178-91.

Prince, Walter F. "Psychological Tests for the Authorship of the Book of Mormon." *American Journal of Psychology* 27 (July 1917): 373-89.

Purple, W. D. "Account of Joseph Smith's 1826 Trial at Bainbridge, N.Y., Chenago Union, 2 May 1877." In *Among the Mormons*, 34-37.

Quinn, D. Michael. "The First Months of Mormonism: A Contemporary View by Rev. Diedrich Willers." *New York History* 54 (July 1973): 317-31.

Red Jacket, Chief. "Speech to a White Missionary, Western New York, 1805." In *The World's Great Speeches*, edited by Lewis Copeland, 266-68. New York: Garden City Publishing Co., 1942.

"Revival of the Jewish Government." *Wayne Sentinel*, 27 Sept. 1825.

Roberts, Brigham Henry. "Ethan Smith Parallels." *Rocky Mountain Mason*, Jan. 1956.

"Samuel Latham Mitchill," *Dictionary of American Biography* 13:69-71.

Schroeder, Theodore. "Authorship of the Book of Mormon." *American Journal of Psychology* 30 (Jan. 1919): 66-72.

Shipps, Jan. "The Prophet Puzzle: Suggestions Leading Toward a More Comprehensive Interpretation of Joseph Smith." *Journal of Mormon History* 1 (1974): 3-20.

Squier, E. G. "Report upon the Aboriginal Monuments of Western New York." In *Proceedings of the New York Historical Society*, 44-62. New York: William Van Norden, 1849.

Tiffany, Joel. "Mormonism No. II." *Tiffany's Monthly* 5 (Aug. 1859): 163-70.

Walters, Wesley P. "Joseph Smith Among the Egyptians." *The Journal of the Evangelical Theological Society* 16 (Winter 1973): 25-45.

———. "Joseph Smith's Bainbridge, N. Y. Court Trials." *Westminster Theological Journal* 36 (Winter 1974): 123-55.

————. "New Light on Mormon Origins from the Palmyra Revival." *Dialogue: A Journal of Mormon Thought* 4 (Spring 1969): 60-81.

————. "A Reply to Dr. Bushman." *Dialogue: A Journal of Mormon Thought* 4 (Spring 1969): 94-100.

————. "From Occult to Cult with Joseph Smith, Jr." *Journal of Pastoral Practice* 1 (1977).

Washington, George. "Farewell Address." In *The Worlds Great Speeches*, edited by Lewis Copeland, 248-59.

Whittier, John Greenleaf. "A Mormon Conventicle." In *Among the Mormons.*

Wild, Asa. "Remarkable VISION and REVELATION." *Wayne Sentinel*, 22 Oct. 1823.

PUBLISHED LETTERS

Anthon, Charles to Eber D. Howe, 17 Feb. 1834. Howe, *Mormonism Unvailed*, 270-72.

Anthon, Charles to T. W. Coit, 3 Apr. 1841. *The Church Record* (1841): 231-32.

Cowdery, Oliver to W. W. Phelps, Letters I-VIII, Sept. 1834-Sept. 1835. *Messenger and Advocate*, Oct. 1834-Oct. 1835.

Davis, Matthew L. to his Wife, 6 Feb. 1840. Ben E. Rich, *Scrap Book of Mormon Literature*, 2:404.

Harris, Martin to Mr. Emerson, Smithfield, UT, 23 Nov. 1870. *Saints Herald* 22 (1875): 630.

Larned, Sylvester to Mr. Merrick, Pittsfield, MA, 1815 (?). Ethan Smith, *View of the Hebrews*, 220.

Page, Hiram to William McLellin, 30 May 1847. *Ensign of Liberty, of The Church of Christ* 1 (Dec. 1847).

Phelps, William Wines to Eber D. Howe, 15 Jan. 1831. Howe, *Mormonism Unvailed*, 234.

Red Jacket, Chief to Captain Parish, 18 Jan. 1821. *Western Farmer*, 4 Apr. 1821.

Smith, Joseph, Jr., to W. W. Phelps, Nov. 1832. *History of the Church of Jesus Christ of Latter-day Saints*, 1:299.

Smith, Joseph, Jr., to Moses C. Nickerson, 19 Nov. 1833. *History of the Church of Jesus Christ of Latter-day Saints*, 1:441-42.

Smith, Joseph III, Letter to the Editor, "Last Testimony of Sister Emma." *Saints' Herald* 26 (1 Oct. 1879): 220.

Smith, Simon to President Joseph Smith III, 30 Dec. 1880. *Saints' Herald* 28 (1 Feb. 1881): 43.

Whitmer, David to Orson Pratt, 1878. *Millennial Star* 40 (1879): 772.

Willers, Rev. Diedrich to Rev. L. Mayer and Rev. D. Young, 18 June 1830. In Quinn, "The First Months of Mormonism," 317-31.

NEWSPAPERS AND PERIODICALS—MORMON

Brigham Young University Archaeological Society Newsletter, Provo, UT. 1959-60.

Brigham Young University Studies. Provo, UT. 1960-present.

The Contributor. Salt Lake City. Oct. 1879-Oct. 1896.

Deseret News. Salt Lake City. 1850-present.

Dialogue: A Journal of Mormon Thought. 1966-present.

The Ensign of Liberty, of the Church of Christ. Kirtland, OH. 1847-49.

The Evening and Morning Star. Independence, MO; Kirtland, OH. 1832-34.

Improvement Era. Salt Lake City. 1897-1970

Latter Day Saints' Messenger and Advocate. Kirtland, OH. 1834-37.

Millennial Star. Manchester and Liverpool. 1840-1970.

Saints' Herald. Lamoni, IA; Independence, MO. 1860-present.

Times and Seasons. Nauvoo, IL. 1839-46.

NEWSPAPERS AND PERIODICALS—OTHER

The Church Record. Flushing, NY. 1840-84.

Gospel Luminary. West Bloomfield, NY. 1825-33.

Kansas City Daily Journal. Kansas City, MO. 1881.

Methodist Magazine. New York City. 1818-40.

Ontario Phoenix. Canandaigua, NY. 1828-31.

Painesville Telegraph. Painesville, OH, 1822-present.

Palmyra Reflector. Palmyra, NY. 1829-31.

Palmyra Register. Palmyra, NY. 1817-21. Successively titled: *Western Farmer*. 1821-22. *Palmyra Herald*. 1822-23. *Wayne Sentinel*. 1823-60.

Rochester Daily Advertiser and Telegraph. Rochester, NY. 1826-56.

Rochester Daily Democrat. Rochester, NY. 1834-57.

Rochester Gem. Rochester, NY. 1829.

Rocky Mountain Mason. Salt Lake City. 1956.

UNPUBLISHED MATERIAL

Bidamon, Emma to Sister Pilgrim, 27 Mar. 1876, Nauvoo, IL. Reorganized LDS Archives, Independence, MO.

Burnett, Stephen to Br. Johnson, 15 Apr. 1838. Joseph Smith Letter

Book, 2. Joseph Smith Papers, LDS Archives, Salt Lake City.

Cheesman, Paul R. "An Analysis of the Accounts Relating to Joseph Smith's Early Vision." M.A. Thesis. Brigham Young University, 1965.

Durham, Reed C., Jr. "A History of Joseph Smith's Revision of the Bible." Ph.D. Dissertation. Brigham Young University, 1965.

Gilbert, John H. Memorandum dated 8 Sept. 1892. Palmyra, NY. Typescript, 4, LDS Archives, Salt Lake City.

Hullinger, Robert N. "An Apologist for Jesus Christ: The Purpose and Function of Joseph Smith's Theology." M.A. Thesis. Pacific Lutheran Theological Seminary, Berkeley, CA, 1969.

Membership Record Book, Manchester Rental Library, Manchester, NY. Canandaigua Historical Society, Canandaigua, NY.

Porter, Lawrence Cardon. "A Study of the Origins of the Church of Jesus Christ of Latter-day Saints in the States of New York and Pennsylvania, 1816-1831." Ph.D. Dissertation. Brigham Young University, 1971.

Shipps, Jan to Robert Hullinger, 10 June 1975.

Smith, Joseph, Jr. D MS (manuscript of the Book of Mormon dictated directly by Joseph Smith to his scribes, 1829). LDS Archives, Salt Lake City.

————. E MS (manuscript of the Book of Mormon which Oliver Cowdery prepared from the D MS for the printer, 1829). Reorganized LDS Archives, Independence, MO.

————. Manuscript History, Book A-1, Frontispiece. LDS Archives, Salt Lake City.

Smith, Lucy Mack. Second manuscript of *Biographical Sketches*, in the writing of Martha Jane Coray. LDS Archives, Salt Lake City.

Walters, Wesly P. to Robert Hullinger, 8 Jan. 1975.

Warner, Ross W. "The Fulfillment of Book of Mormon Prophecies: A Study of Problems Relative to the Fulfillment of Selected Prophecies in the Book of Mormon, with Particular Reference to the Prophet View from 1830 Onward." M.A. Thesis. Brigham Young University, 1961.

Willers, Rev. Diedrich to L. Mayer and D. Young, 18 June 1830. Diedrich Willers Collection, John M. Olin Library, Cornell University, Ithaca, NY.

Scriptural Index

Old Testament

Genesis
3:24—163

Exodus
6:3—110
13:11-16—62

Leviticus
8:7-8—108

Deuteronomy
6:4-90—62
11:13-21—62
12:5, 21—120
14:23-24—120
30—62

Joshua
10—154
10:12-14—156

1 Kings
8:16-20, 29—120

2 Kings
22—118

1 Chronicles
22:7-8, 10, 19—20
28:3—120

2 Chronicles
34:14—118
2:1—120
20:8-9—120
34—118

Ezra
7:6, 10, 14—118

Isaiah
2:1-4—147
2:14—74
2:2-4—163
3:17—163
5—92
7:11, 14—136
8:19—163
9:2—163
11:11-12—147
14—62
18—57, 62, 184
29—70, 74, 89, 128, 146, 151, 191-94
29:3-5—73, 92
29:3-5—92
29:4, 11-12—92
29:11-12—90, 11, 74, 80, 150
40—67
48-49—74, 151
49:18-23—62
50-51—74
52—74
53—74
53:10—163
54—74
60—62
65—62
66:20—62

Jeremiah
16:14-15—62

23:6, 8—62
30-31—55
30:3—62
Ezekiel
37—184, 187
37:1-17—66-70
37:16—118, 128
37:19—161
Hosea
2-3—62
Amos
8:11-12—55
Zephaniah
3:10—62
Zechariah
8:7—55
Malachi
4:2—150

New Testament
Matthew
5:6—163
6:25—163
6:30—163
6:32—163
6:34—163
16:15-18—134
16:18—135
John
10:16—163
21:21-23—163
Romans
11:13—161
Hebrews
3:4-4:9—120
4:12—120
7:1-4—120
7:3—120
13:33-36—105
Revelation
20—150
4:6-7—137

Apocrypha—2 Esdras
13—55
13:40-42—118
13:40-42—61

Latter-day Scriptures
Doctrine & Covenants
3—159
3:20—3
3:20—6
5:15—129
5:6, 10—4
5:6-15—2
6:14-17, 22-24—131
7:1-8—163
8:1-3—11
8:1-3—130
8:1-3—131
8:9-12—138
9:1, 7, 10, 11—138
9:8-9—130
10:44-63—156
10:46-63—4
10:63—176
11:16—4
14:10—3
14:8—131
17:2-3, 5, 9—131
18:3-4—131
18:3-4—159
18:13—4
20:10—160
20:11—2
20:11-12, 17—122
20:12, 17, 18-20—2
20:26-28—145
21:1—4
27:5—70
28:11—173
29:39—177
34:6-10—150
43:3-6—173

77:2—150
78:1—110
110:11-16—172
128—150
135:7—176
1 Nephi
1:1-3, 16-17—127
1:4—125
1:4—145
1:6-14—125
1:6-14—125
1:13—163
1:20—2
1:28-30, 41—155
2:1-2—125
2:2—170
2:20—139
2:20-22—176
3:2—125
3:3, 12, 24—127
3:12, 19-20, 24—118
3:12, 19-20, 24—118
3:20—127
3:29-31—126
3:30—143
4:1-8, 11-12—162
4:2—118
4:2—155
4:3—126
4:7-18—108
4:13—176
4:15, 38—127
4:15-16—162
4:24, 38—118
4:24, 38—118
5:4—125
5:10-22—118
5:11—162
5:12—118
5:13—163
5:21-22—127
6:4—4
7:13—170

7:14—163
8-15—123-25
8:2, 4, 36—125
9:1-5—137
10:1—12
10:1—17
10:3—163
10:7-10—155
10:9—125
10:11—176
10:12—147
10:12-24—147
10:13—145
10:19—124
11—126
11:7—126
11:13-20—155
11:18—147
11:25, 35-36—126
11:27—147
11:27—155
11:28-36—163
11:33—147
11:36—124
12:9—163
12:14—147
12:22-23—176
12:23—150
13—125-26
13:12—170
13:14-15—148
13:23—118
13:24, 25, 29—154
13:24, 26, 39-41—163
13:26, 29—154
13:27—154
13:34—148, 154
13:35—92, 176
13:37—176
13:39—3
13:39—6
13:40—150
13:41—68

14:2—169
14:5-7—149
14:6-7—148
14:20-27—155
14:29—126
15:11—176
15:13—148
15:14—148
15:15—148
15:18—162
15:35—176
16—126
16:10—108
16:38—124, 125
17:26-27—155
17:28-30—155
17:40—162
17:43—163
19:1-6—137
19:6—157
19:10—137
19:13—147
19:14—147, 150
19:16—157
19:17—150
19:22—118
20-21—74, 92, 163
20:14, 20—163
21:26—150
22:1-3, 6, 27—151
22:7—148
22:7-8—169
22:8—148
22:9—162
22:18—149
31:13-14—149

2 Nephi
1:6—169
1:7—169, 170
1:9—169
1:10—176
1:11—147

1:20—176
2:4—136
2:18-19—155
2:28-30—4
3—151
3:2—169
3:3—147
3:4—162
3:6-7, 15—4, 110, 148
3:7-11—6
3:11-12—69
3:17—155, 162
4:1—162
4:2—118
4:15—127
4:23—125
5:12—118
5:18—176
5:21-23—150
5:22—149
6:8-9—163
6:11—126
6:12—149
7-8—74, 163
9:9—115
9:27—176
10:3—126
10:8-9—147
10:10-13—169
10:19—169, 170
11:2-6—2
11:3—129
12-24—74, 163
12:1-2—163
12:1-4—147
15:13—147
15:15-187
17:11, 14—136
17:19—163
18:5-6—122
19:14—162
20:29—147

21:11-12—147
23:11—163
25—191-94
25:7—161
25:10-11—163
25:11—4
25:12—147
25:13—150
25:15-20—4
25:16—147, 150
25:19—126
25:20—161
25:28—161
25:30—162
26:9—150
26:14-22—148
26:15, 17, 19—176
26:15-18—92
26:22—115, 148
26:22-23, 24-30—115
26:29—120
27—74, 78, 80
27:1—148
27:9, 16—82
27:12—2, 130
27:15-18—88
28:17, 19—149
29:3—163
29: 3-8—69
29:3, 9—148
29:8—69
29:13—148
30:17—115
30:6—148
31:4-8—155
31:15-20—176
32:2-3—126
32:2-3—161
32:7—160
33:1, 2, 4—158
33:7, 11—147
33:9—147

33:13—74
35:23, 26—4

Jacob
1:2—157
1:17—120
2:2, 11—120
2:11—160
2:23-24—155
3:3—149
4—150
4:13—161
4:14—161
5:43—169
7:26—157

Enos
5, 10—125
10—170, 176
14:15—6
23—145, 160

Jarom
2—6

Omni
20-22—15
22—155
26—176

Words of Mormon
128
8—3

Mosiah
1:1-6, 16—128
1:3—127
1:3-4—118
1:5—176
1:11—176
1:18—120
2:4—176
2:14-18—176
2:40—160
2:41—176
3:2-27—126
3:5-7—163
3:7—163

3:8—147
3:11—147
4:6—176
5:7—163
6:7—176
7:19—162
7:27—155, 156
8:11-13—118
8:13, 19—15
8:13—110
8:17, 19—115
11:20-25—149
11:20-26—145
12:1-8—145
12:33-36—155
13:12-24—155
13:22, 31, 33, 36, 41—176
14—74
14:10-13—163
15:1—147
15:1-4—156
15:2—150
15:5—147
15:8—147
15:10-13—163
21:27-28—15
23:6-14—176
27:14—126
27:14-15—126
28:1-2—3
28:11-16—110
28:11-19—15
28:14—155
28:20—118
29:13-18, 23, 30, 31—176
29:19-20—149
29:28-32—115
30—176

Alma
3:6-9—150
5:13—176
5:14—147
5:24—162

5:38—50—150
5:43—160
5:51—149
7:10—155
7:23—176
8:14-15, 20—126
8:16, 29—149
8:25—150
9:16—147
10:2—15
10:3—162
10:7-8—126
10:9—126
10:20-23—149
10:27—115
11:20—115
11:39—150
12:7—120
12:21—155
12:27—120
12:32—176
13—109, 120
13:7, 9—120
13:14—120
13:14-19—155
13:22—126, 160
13:27, 30—149
14-15—126
14:2—160
21:5—126
21:37—163
23:6, 17-18—58
24:6-16—58
24:25—59
25:6—59
26:9—3
27:27—59
28:1—176
30:6—143
30:13-16—144
30:23-26—144
30:43-59—126
32:17-18, 21—126

32:23—126
37:3-12—118
37:4—127
37:8-9—3
37:21-32—115
37:23-24—115
37:23-36—115
37:27—29—115
37:30-31—115
39:17-19—146
40:4-21—157
40:11-15—126
42:2—155
43:45—176
45:10, 12—176
46:10—176
46:23—155
46:24—162
50:22—176
51:5, 8—176
63:1, 11-14—118, 138

Helaman
1:27, 29—115
3:23—115
5:6—176
6:21, 23—115
6:21—115
6:25-30, 38—115
6:27—155
6:28—155
6:34—176
6:39—115
8:11—155
8:19-22—125
8:20—163
9:24-41—126
12:13-15—156
13:7—126
14—147
14:2-6—136
14:14—137
14:29-31—150
15:11, 15—176

16:15-16—144
16:4, 13—141
3 Nephi
1:2—118, 138
1:15—136
3:3-18—128
6:6—9
6:10-30—115
6:21-30—115
6:30—176
7:19—155
8-9—92
11:1—120
11:28-29, 32—176
12-14—156
12:6—163
12:20—176
13:24-25—163
13:30, 32, 34—163
15:4-8—162
15:5-8—156
15:9—176
15:16-24—163
16:4—148
16:6-7, 10-13—176
16:9—147
16:10—120, 148
16:16—169
17:7-10—141
17:7-8—163
20:22—148, 169
20:25, 27—162
20:27—148
21:1-7—126
21:5—128, 176
21:19—120
21:22—148
21:22-23—148
22—74
24:1—163
24:12—169
25:4—162
25:5—163

26:15—141
28—157
28:3-9, 12-15, 21-22—163
30—74
30:2—120
4 Nephi
1:19, 20, 26-34, 38-42—176
1:34, 38—176
42—115
Mormon
1:13-15—176
1:18—105
3:2-3—176
3:20-22—3
3:21—3
5:9, 11, 14—3
5:9, 14-15—3
5:12—4
5:14—3
5:15—150
5:20—162
7:1-2—3
7:9—6
8—128
8:1—157
8:10-11, 26, 28, 32-33, 37-41—
    176
8:12, 17—158
8:14—159, 160
8:14-16—6
8:23, 26—92
8:26-34—148
8:27—115
9:7-11—122
9:7-26—176
9:31—158
9:32—157
9:32-33—158
9:32-34—78
10:1—157
Ether
1:3—155
1:38—169

1:42-43—169
2:4, 7—169
2:4—61
2:8, 12—170
2:8-9—170
2:10-12—170
2:11—3
2:13—127
3:14—157
3:18—125
3:21-22, 27—127
3:23, 28—15
4:1—127
4:3—176
4:5—15
5:1—157
5:2-4—2
5:3-4—130
6:22-26—176
8:18, 22, 24, 25—115
8:20—115
8:9-25—115
9:1, 5-6, 26—115
9:3—125
9:20—170
10:33—115
11:7, 15, 22—115
12:11—162
12:15, 40—158
13:7, 11—162
13:18—115
15:33—127
Moroni
1:4—6
7:16—175
7:27-38—122
7:37—126
8:8—156
8:11-12, 18—136
8:29—145
9:20, 35—176
10:3-5—134, 160
10:6—5

10:19, 24—122
10:27—74
Title Page
155, 157
Moses
147
4:1—175
5:10—149
5:10-13—177
5:29-32, 49-50—114

5:29-50—115
6—120
6:8—149
6:13—149
6:35-36—110
6:55—177
7:2, 41-46—149
7:3, 38-43, 69—110
8:3, 16—149

Index

A

Aaronic priesthood, 131, 109, 171
Abel, 155
Abinidai, 145
abominable church, 154
Abrac, magic and Masonry, 105,
    116
Abraham, 155
Adair, James, 54, 183, 186
Adam, 2, 54, 155; know Christ,
    145, 147
Adams, John Quincy, 78
Adventism, 176
Allen, Ethan, 21
America, 169-70
American Adam, 173-74
American Tract Society, 39, 40
angel(s), 88, 109, 116, 127, 128,
    130-31, 133, 138-39, 160
Ann Lee, 153
Anthon transcript, 81, 85-86, 94-
    95
Anthon, Charles, 10, 13, 74-92,
    146, 187
anthropology, and Indian origins,
    185
anti-Masonry, 29-20, 99-102, 168
Anti-Nephi-Lehi, 59
Apocrypha, 162
apostolic succession, 135
Ararat, City of, 54, 66
Arbaugh, George B., 121, 136,

163-64, 173, 183
archaeology, and Indian origins,
    185
Arminianism, 31, 174
Atonement, 163
Atwater, Caleb, 56
Austin, Emily M., 88

B

Babylonian captivity, 125
Ballou, Hosea, 26
baptism, 136, 163
Baptists, 28, 31, 41, 99, 101, 113,
    186
Bennett, James Arlington, 80
Bennett, James Gordon, 93
Benton, A. W., 140
Bernard, David, 91
Bible, 42
    and Catholicism, 154
    and Masonry, 99-100
    and Shakers, 154
    as Stick of Judah, 66-70
    confirmed by Book of Mor-
        mon, 2, 129, 154, 157
    deist case against, 19-20, 21-24,
        144, 153-54
    interpretation of, 136, 159
    Paine's case against, 128-29
    Protestant defense of, 162
    revising, 12
Book of Jashar, 154, 162

219

Book of Mormon, 60, 120, 143
  America and, 169-70
  angels, 126
  brass plates, 126
  doctrines clarified by, 156-57,
    163
  gentiles in, 3, 148
  God in, 156-57, 163
  imperfection of its authors, 158
  Indians in, 49, 147-48
  Isaiah, compared to Nephite
    editors, 137
  Jews in, 3, 147
  manuscript of,
    changes in, 164,
      importance of text rather
        than plates, 159-60,
      lost 116 pages, 10, 130, 159
  Masonry and, 110, 120
  Melchizedek priesthood and,
    109-110
  Messianic prophecies in, 146-47
  miracles and, 121-26, 135
  personal revelation in, 160
  predicts own appearance, 148
  prophecy in, 144
  purposes of, 1-3
  resurrection in, 157
  secret combinations in, 102-104
  selling for profit, 7, 149
  small plates in, 137
  status of Bible in 154-58
  temples in, 110, 120
  translation process, 9-12, 132,
    139
  witnesses for, 2, 130-33, 140
Booth, Ezra, 150
Boudinot, Elias, 57, 59, 66-67, 186
Bradish, Luther, 78, 83, 88, 93
brass plates, 118, 126
  and Masonry, 107
breastplate, 117, 184
  and Masonry, 106, 108

Brigham Young University, 185
Brodie, Fawn, 183
burned-over District, 28, 171
Butler, Charles, 80, 83
Butterworth, Edward, 184

C
Cain, 155
Campbell, Alexander, 134, 163
Campbellites (Disciples), 31, 37
Canada, selling of Book of Mor-
  mon copyright, 149
Canandaigua, New York, 36
canonicity, 157
Capron, Joseph, 116
Carroll, Lewis, 73
Carver, William, 29
Catholicism, 28, 120, 135, 154,
  171, 173
Channing, William Ellery, 136
charismatic gifts, 129
Chase, Abner, 41
Chase, Willard, 116, 117, 129
Chauncy, Charles, 20
children, baptism of, 136
Christ,
  rationalism and, 20
  place in trinity, 156-57
  as God of the Old Testament,
    122-23
  as son and father, 163
  background of Smith's pro-
    nouncements on, 38
  Book of Mormon defense of,
    2, 4, 5
  deist view of, 135-36
  Indians and, 3
  known in all ages, 145-46, 147
  prophecies of, 126, 146
  restoration of church, 171
  revelation as the rock, 134
  second coming, 172
  titles foreknown, 146

visit to America,144
Christensen, Ross, 185
Christian Connection (Christians), 31, 37-38, 136
Christianity, and Greek theology, 123
Church of Christ, mission in Book of Mormon, 4
Church of the Latter Day Saints, 172
Clark, John A., 1, 10, 11, 13, 78, 85, 86-87, 88, 89
Clinton, DeWitt, 100
Coit, T. W., 95
Columbus, 169-70
compass (Liahona), and Masonry, 106
Congregationalists, 20, 26, 29, 35, 59
conscience, as testimony of God, 24
Cooper, James Fenimore, 52
Council of Fifty, 175
Cowdery, Oliver, 11, 14, 16, 42, 75, 80, 82, 88, 90, 96-97, 108, 109, 117, 120, 130, 131, 132, 134, 137-38, 141, 149, 150, 159, 160, 164, 172
Cross, Whitney, 28, 30

D
David, biblical, 155
Davis, Matthew L., 9
De Pillis, Mario, 1, 31, 163
Deistical Society of New York, 24
deists, 21
  and Masonry, 99
  attacks against by tract societies, 39
  belief in natural religion, 19-20
  miracles and, 22-24
  objections to Bible, 21-24, 144, 157-58, 162

  prophecy and, 22-24, 144, 146
  revelation and, 22-23, 153, 173
  social factors restricting spread, 25
  views of God, 24, 134, 135
  views presented by Laman and Lemuel, 125
  wars of destruction and, 162-63
denominations, 137
Deseret, 175
devil, 163
Disciples, *see* Campbellites
Doctrine and Covenants, description of, 6-7
doctrine, same in all ages, 145
Druidical Society of Newburgh, 13
Dwight, Timothy, 24-25, 51-52
dying infidel stories, 29, 38

E
Egyptian hieroglyphics, 12, 73, 78, 80, 87, 90, 110-11, 158, 188, 189
eight witnesses, 133
Elijah, biblical, 155
Emerson, Ralph Waldo, 173, 175
Emmons, Nathaniel, 25
England, mission to, 172
Enoch, and Masonry, 119
Enos, 128, 145
Ephraim, 68, 71
eternal damnation, 164
evangelism, 28, 172, 174
Evans, John, 174
Eve, 155
Evening and the Morning Star, 136
evil spirits, 116
exhortations, at revivals, 40-41, 46
exorcism, 141

F
fall of Adam, 155, 163, 174, 175
Federalists, 21, 25

Finney, Charles, 27, 28, 30, 41-42
first vision, 137
foreknowledge, 144
Foster, John, 25
Franklin, Benjamin, 39
Free Enquirers of New York, 29
free will, 145, 163, 174
Freemasonry, *see* Masonry
French Revolution, 21
Fry, Evan, 184

G
Garden of Eden, 155
gathering, 175, 184
Genesis, authentic, 155
gentiles, 2, 3, 69, 148, 169
Gilbert, John H., 44, 78, 83, 89,
    133, 139
God,
    and angels, 126
    and charismatic gifts, 121-22
    and importance of written
        records, 126
    and signs, 126
    answer to deists, 20, 121, 123
    whether unchanging, 121-22,
        123, 136, 163
    Joseph Smith's changing ideas
        of, 164
    nature of, 2, 122-23, 134, 156-
        57, 163
golden plates, 1, 105-106, 107,
    129, 130-31, 139, 139-40, 159,
    160
Grandin, E. B., 11, 44, 82-83
Great Revival of 1799-1800, 27
Greeks, and Christianity, 123
Greeley, Horace, 65

H
Hale, Isaac, 116, 138
Hansen, Klaus, 172
Harmon, Reuben P., 133

Harris, Abigail, 117
Harris, George, 91
Harris, Henry, 80
Harris, Martin, 9, 11, 13, 14, 16,
    74-92, 108, 116, 117, 129, 130,
    131, 133, 146, 150, 172
Harris, Smith, 158
Hebrew(s), 78, 80, 158, 183-87
Hill Cumorah, 185
Hine, William R., 93, 105
Hobbes, Thomas, 25
Holy Ghost, 163
Horne, Thomas Hartwell, 161-62
Hotchkin, James, 26, 27
Howard, Richard P., 15, 164
Howe, E. D., 84, 138
Humboldt, Alexander, 184, 188
Hurlbut, Philastus, 138
Hyde, Orson, 173, 176

I
Independence, Missouri, as Zion,
    172
Indian Hill, 184
Indians, 49-60, 168, 169, 172, 174
    and a lost book, 56-57
    and Christ, 3
    and dark skin, 150
    and debate with deists, 58
    and Joseph Smith, 6
    Book of Mormon and, 1, 3, 7,
        60, 64, 147-48
    government removal policy, 65-
        66
    intermarriage, 150
    missions to, 53-54
    mound builders, 50-52, 61, 184
    nineteenth-century views, 51-
        54, 185
    origins, 2, 129, 183-87
    theological issues raised by dis-
        covery of, 54
    use of term Lamanite, 6

"Infidel" club, 33
Infidel International, 21, 24, 29, 102
infidel(s), 44-45, 168
Ingersoll, Peter, 116
Iroquois, 51-52
Isaac, biblical, 155
Isaiah, biblical, 58, 137, 155
Israel, Menasseh ben, 54

J
Jacobins, 21, 38, 99
Jakeman, M. Wells, 185
James, Edmund, 51
Jefferson, Thomas, 21, 25, 39, 52
Jeremiah, biblical, 155
Jerusalem, 125, 173, 184
Jews,
    and Ezekiel 37, 66-70
    and Indians, 66
    Book of Mormon and, 2, 3, 147
Jews, dedication of Jerusalem, 173
John the Apostle, 155
John the Baptist, 126, 131, 147, 155, 171
Johnson, Lyman, 176
Joseph, biblical, 4, 6, 68-69, 110, 137, 146, 169
Josephus, 117

K
Kidd, Captain, 105
Kidder, Daniel, 92
Kingdom of God, 175
Kirkham, Francis, 186
Kirtland temple, 172
Knecht, William, 186
Knight, Joseph, Sr., 84, 86, 93
Knight, Newel, 37
Koch, G. A., 27
Korihor, 126, 143-44

L
Laman, as deist, 125
Lamanite, *see* Indians
Lancaster, James, 164
Lane, George, 41, 42
Lapham, Fayette, 99, 117
Larned, Sylvester, 57, 63
last days, signs of, 144-45
latter days, name of church of Christ, 172
Lawrence, Samuel, 116
Lee, John D., 84
Lehi, 125
Lemuel, as deist, 125
Lewis, R. W. B., 173-74
Liahona, 108, 117
literal interpretation, 151
Locke, John, 25, 37, 44
Lord's Supper, 163
lost tribes, 4, 56-57, 67, 118, 184
    and Indians, 54-59, 62

M
McFarlane, M., 101
Mack, Jason, 36
Mack, Solomon, 36
M'Kune, Joshua, 117
magic, and money digging, 104-106
Malachi, biblical, 155
Manasseh, biblical, 68, 71
Manchester, New York, 35, 36
    Rental Library, 43-44
Marks, David, 7, 34, 38, 133
Marty, Martin, 44
martyrdom, 176
Mary, biblical, 125, 147, 155
Masonry, 29-30, 39, 91, 98, 99-120, 168, 169, 186
    Aaronic priesthood, 109
    breastplate, 108
    converts to early Mormonism, 111

Egyptian, 110-11
gold plates, 107
Liahona, 108
Melchizedek priesthood, 109
pillars, 106
plates of brass, 107
priesthood, 120
seerstones, 106
sword of Laban, 108
temples, 110, 120
Urim and Thummim, 108
Mayhew, Jonathan, 20
Meachem, Joseph, 30
Melchizedek priesthood, 109-10,
    119, 120, 171
Mendon, New York, 176
Merrick, Joseph, 56
Metcalf, Anthony, 84, 85, 89, 132
Methodists, 27, 28, 31, 40, 41, 42,
    101, 137, 138
Mexican territory, and Kingdom
    of God, 175
Meyer, Eduard, 73, 133
Millard, David, 37
Millennium, 1, 6, 27-28, 65-66, 67-
    70, 90, 137, 144-45, 171, 172,
    174, 175
Miller, Perry, 168, 169, 174
Millerites, 176
miracles, 22, 135, 141, 156
missionaries, Mormon
    to England, 172
    to Indians, 53-54
    to Scandanavia, 172
    use of Anthon story, 91-92
Mitchill, Samuel Latham, 76, 77,
    78, 80, 89
Mohicans, 51
money digging, 5, 103, 104-106,
    115, 138, 140
Morgan, Lucinda (Harris), 91,
    101-102
Morgan, William, 29, 39, 91, 100,

101-102, 105, 112, 114-15, 167
Mormon, abridgement of plates,
    128
Moroni, 2, 128, 129, 158
Morse, Jedediah, 24, 54
Mosaic law, 163
Moses, biblical, 1, 17, 149, 155
Mosiah, record of, 128
mound builders, 61, 62, 184. *See
    also* Indians
Murphy, John, 139
Murray, John, 20, 26
mysticism, 175

N
National Tract Society, 29
natural religion, 19-20, 24, 153
Neely, Albert, 103
Nephi, 2, 123-28, 158
New Jerusalem, in America, 169
New Testament,
    deist objections to, 23-24, 135
    events confirmed by Book of
        Mormon, 155-56
Nibley, Hugh, 89-90, 137, 164, 185
Nickerson, Freeman, 139
nihilism, 123
Noah, Mordecai M., 54-55, 66, 185

O
O'Dea, Thomas F., 183
Old Testament
    Christ as God of, 122-23
    deist objections to, 23
    events confirmed by Book of
        Mormon, 155
Oneida Institute, 28
Owen, Robert, 37

P
Page, Hiram, 133, 149
Paine, Thomas, 19, 20, 21-24, 25,
    29, 33, 35, 38, 39, 49, 55,

128-29, 134, 136, 145, 153, 158, 162
Palmer, Elihu, 21, 25
Palmer, Spencer, 186
Palmyra Academy, 132
Palmyra, New York, 36
papal infallibility, 135
Parsons, Tyler, 139
patriarchal blessing(s), 164
Paul, 161
peepstone, *see* seerstone
Peter, James, and John, 171
Phelps, W. W., 6, 49, 65, 72, 78, 80, 84, 93, 150, 172
pietists, 20-21, 32, 36, 173
pillars, and Masonry, 117
Pittsfield parchment, 57, 58-59, 63, 90, 187, 188
plates of Nephi, 127-28
polygamy, 155, 175
polytheism, 136, 157, 175
Pratt, Orson, 13, 83, 84, 97, 140, 186, 189
Pratt, Parley, 71, 83, 84, 97, 143
pre-Adamite theory of Indians, 54, 61
predestination, 20
Presbyterians, 26, 28, 30, 31, 36, 40, 41, 42, 45, 47, 99
Priest, Josiah, 186, 188
priesthood, Masonic, 120. *See also* Aaronic priesthood, Melchizedek priesthood
prophecy, 22, 143-50
prophet, 173

Q
Quetzacoatl, 184
Quincy, Josiah, 13

R
rationalism, 20, 25, 35, 123, 129, 187

Red Jacket, 49, 53
reformed Egyptian, *see* Egyptian hieroglyphics
repentance, 145, 168
restoration, of church of Christ, 171
resurrection, 23, 147, 157, 163
revelation, 9-12, 123
  and unchanging nature of God, 121-23
  and witnesses to Book of Mormon, 130-34
  deist definition of, 19, 22-23
  personal, 160, 173
  proved by prophecy, 143
  rock of Christ's church, 134, 135-36
  written, 173
revivalism, 27, 40-41, 42-43, 45, 46, 47
Revolutionary War, 168
Rigdon, Sidney, 13, 37, 135, 141, 153, 172
Roberts, B. H., 14, 183-84, 188

S
Sabelianism, 32
Samuel the Lamanite, 144
Satan, 171, 174
Scandanavia, mission to, 172
sealed book, 74, 118
Second Great Awakening, 21, 26-27, 174
Second Coming, 172
secret combinations, 102-104, 113, 115
sectarianism, 1, 30, 41-42, 46
seerstones, 9-12, 106, 140, 165
Seyffarth, Professor, 185
Sha, Anson, 186
Shakers, 30-31, 71, 153, 154
Sheldon, John, 110
Shipps, Jan, 1

signs, 126, 136-37, 141, 144
Smith, Alvin, 42, 47
Smith, Asael, 35
Smith, Emma, 10, 13, 15, 88, 90, 96, 105, 116, 117
Smith, Ethan, 55-59, 73, 90, 183-87, 188
Smith, Hyrum, 42, 104, 105, 116, 133
Smith, Jesse, 35
Smith, Joseph, Jr., 13-14, 32, 96
    Aaronic priesthood, restoration of, 109
    America, views of, 167-76
    and biblical Joseph, 4, 6, 69, 110
    and Book of Mormon, 1-2, 149, 160
    and golden plates, 105-106, 129-30
    and magic, 104, 116
    and Masonry, 99-120
    and Millennium, 145, 172
    and money digging, 5, 103, 105-106, 116, 138, 140
    and Moses, 149
    and pietism, 173
    and U. S. Constitution, 171
    Anthon-Harris incident, 74-92
    as man not learned, 6, 151
    Christ, teachings about, 38, 145-46
    education of, 13
    emphasis on records, 128-29
    God, views of, 136, 164
    his history of church, 97
    his mission, 4-5
    Indians, views of, 59, 168, 185
    Melchizedek priesthood, restoration, 110, 119, 120
    miracles, view of, 135
    religious influences on, 36-37
    revelation, view of 121-36
    revivals and, 40-43, 47
    role prophesied, 148-49
    translation process, 10
    unchanging gospel plan, view of, 150
Smith, Joseph, Sr., 11, 35, 36, 42, 78, 83, 96, 104, 116, 117, 133, 138
Smith, Lucy Mack, 13, 16, 36, 42, 46, 58, 86, 87, 96, 105, 106
Smith, Oliver, 105-106
Smith, Samuel, 42, 133
Smith, Simon, 85, 88
Smith, Sophronia, 42
Smith, William, 46, 176
Sodus Bay, 31
Solomon, biblical, 155
Solomon's temple, and Masonry, 106-107
Spaulding, Solomon, 13
spiritual interpretation, 151
Stafford, William, 138
Stevenson, Edward, 87-88
Stick of Ephraim, 184
Stick of Joseph, 65, 66-70, 118, 161
Stick of Judah, 65, 66-70, 118, 161
Stiles, Phineas, 139
Stockton, Benjamin, 40, 42
Stoddard, Goodwin, 40
Stoddard, Lucy, 41
Stowell, Josiah, 105, 140
Strong, Timonthy, 44
sword of Laban, 117
    and Masonry, 108

T
T. C. Strong Bookstore, 44
Tecumseh, 50
temples, and Masonry, 110, 120
ten tribes, *see* lost tribes
Texas, and Kingdom of God, 175
textual criticism, 159

theocracy, 175
three witnesses, 2, 108, 129-32,
    139-40, 147, 159, 160
Tower of Babel, 155
Townsend, Jesse, 133, 139
tract societies, 39-40, 45
translation
    and Oliver Cowdery, 138
    Book of Mormon process, 132,
    139
trinity, doctrine of, 123, 156-57
True, Oliver, 37
Tucker, Pomeroy, 44, 78, 83, 85,
    87, 89
Turley, Theodore, 133, 165
Turner, Orsamus, 13, 40-41
twelve apostles, biblical, 156

U
U.S. Constitution, 171
Unitarians, 20, 25-26, 28, 32, 36,
    38, 123, 136, 156, 157
Universalism, 20, 25, 26, 27, 28,
    29, 35, 36, 37, 38, 43, 47,
    136,164
Urim and Thummim, 15, 16, 86,
    90, 106, 108, 109, 129, 139,
    160, 164-65, 184

V
Van Rensselaer, Solomon, 110

View of the Hebrews, 55-59, 183-88
visions, 125, 133

W
Walters, Wesley P., 95
war, 162
Washington, George, 102
Weldon, Roy, 184
White, Ellen G., 176
Whitmer, David, 6, 9, 15, 80, 83,
    108, 110, 120, 130, 131, 132,
    138, 139, 149, 151
Whitmer, John, 120, 133, 165
Whitmer, Peter, 7, 13
Whitney, Newel K., 164
Whittier, John Greenleaf, 13, 164
Wight, Lyman, 120, 175
Willers, Diedrich, 11, 13, 132, 133
Williams, Frederick G., 164
Winchester, Elhanan, 26
writing sticks, 71-72
written records, importance for
    Book of Mormon, 126

Y
Young, Brigham, 150, 175

Z
Zedekiah, biblical, 155
Zion, 172, 175